PSYCHOLOGY OF EMOTIONS, MOTIVATIONS AND ACTIONS

NEUROTICISM

CHARACTERISTICS, IMPACT ON JOB PERFORMANCE AND HEALTH OUTCOMES

PSYCHOLOGY OF EMOTIONS, MOTIVATIONS AND ACTIONS

Additional books in this series can be found on Nova's website under the Series tab.

Additional e-books in this series can be found on Nova's website under the e-book tab.

PSYCHOLOGY OF EMOTIONS, MOTIVATIONS AND ACTIONS

NEUROTICISM

CHARACTERISTICS, IMPACT ON JOB PERFORMANCE AND HEALTH OUTCOMES

ANNAMARIA DI FABIO
EDITOR

nova publishers
New York

Library of Congress Cataloging-in-Publication Data

Names: Di Fabio, Annamaria, editor.
Title: Neuroticism : characteristics, impact on job performance and health outcomes / editor, Annamaria Di Fabio (Department of Education and Psychology, University of Florence, Italy).
Description: Hauppauge, New York : Nova Science Publisher's, Inc., [2016] | Series: Psychiatry- theory, applications and treatments | Includes index.
Identifiers: LCCN 2016019038 (print) | LCCN 2016029913 (ebook) | ISBN 9781634853231 (hardcover) | ISBN 9781634853354 (ebook) | ISBN 9781634853354 ()
Subjects: LCSH: Neuroticism. | Personality--Health aspects. | Performance--Health aspects.
Classification: LCC R726.5 .N47 2016 (print) | LCC R726.5 (ebook) | DDC 616.001/9--dc23
LC record available at https://lccn.loc.gov/2016019038

Published by Nova Science Publishers, Inc. † New York

CONTENTS

PREFACE

This book presents a review of current theoretical and research perspectives regarding neuroticism and its impact on job performance and health outcomes. The aim continues to stimulate the reflection on neuroticism, including both theoretical and intervention levels.

From the point of view of its structure, the volume is divided into two parts. The first part presents researches concerning neuroticism in organizational contexts. The second part is relative to innovative perspectives to widening the horizon in relation to neuroticism and its role in job performance and health outcomes.

Regarding the first part of the volume, the chapter by Annamaria Di Fabio opens the book by offering a review on neuroticism and its relations with both job performance and health outcomes. This review presents the evolution and the current state of research, also suggesting new perspectives for research and intervention.

The second chapter by Greta Mazzetti, Rita Chiesa, Michela Vignoli and Marco Depolo underlines that the effect of neuroticism on job performance is mediated by job satisfaction, and that the relation between job satisfaction and job performance is moderated by workaholism. The results showed that neuroticism decreased the level of job performance through the negative effect on job satisfaction. Furthermore, workers with a high level of job satisfaction exhibited better job performance in the case of low workaholism. These results open future perspectives of interventions in the organizational fields.

The third chapter by Marco Giannini and Yura Loscalzo is also relative to workaholism and its relations to neuroticism, considering health risks and prevention in organizations. The contribution is articulated in three parts. In the first part, many definitions of workaholism are proposed. In the second part, studies regarding the relations between neuroticism and workaholism are presented. In the third part, the negative consequences associated to workaholism for physical and psychological health, as well as for workplace and family wellbeing are shown. This contribution underlines the importance of promoting preventive interventions since they are scarcely disseminated.

The following chapter by Riccardo Sartori, Arianna Costantini and Andrea Ceschi describes a study carried out on trade agents that shows an indirect positive relationship between emotional stability (the opposite of neuroticism) and job performance passing through the effect of the length of service. These results underlined as emotional stability can be considered a valid predictor of job performance also in specific organizational contexts—such as trade contexts—considering the role of length of service.

The fifth contribution by Gabriele Giorgi, Javier Fiz Perez and Melissa Morone presents a research carried out in an Italian organization, that examines the role played by personality traits (particularly neuroticism) and motivation in organizational emotional intelligence. The results reveal that personality traits (particularly neuroticism) explain organizational emotional intelligence and work-related stress tolerance as factors behind the effect of work motivation. The role of neuroticism is highlighted, opening the reflection on how neuroticism could hinder self-awareness and self-management in relation to aspects of organizational emotional intelligence.

The contribution by Annamaria Di Fabio and Letizia Palazzeschi concludes this first part. The study aims to verify the association between both resilience and life satisfaction, and the "Big Five" personality traits among participants from three Italian organizational realities (physicians, nurses, and employees of an insurance company). The results of the present study showed that neuroticism consistently inversely explained a significantly large percentage of variance both in resilience and life satisfaction in all three groups, broadening knowledge regarding associations of both the constructs of resilience and life satisfaction with personality traits, and in particular with neuroticism in different organizational contexts.

The second part of the present book is relative to widen the horizon in relation to neuroticism and its impact on job performance and health outcomes.

The seventh contribution by Sowon Hahn and Yumin Chung is relative to associations of neuroticism with both attention and eye movements. This chapter presents theories and experimental findings related to the attentional control deficits associated with neuroticism. It also describes research regarding saccadic eye movements that reveal the relation between neuroticism and attentional mechanisms. The contribution particularly enhances the reflection on neuroticism, highlighting that neuroticism has a negative impact on performance.

The eighth chapter by Ahmed M. Abdel-Khalek analyses the relation between neuroticism and extraversion in Egyptian culture. This relation is controversial because Eysenck emphasized the independence of neuroticism and extraversion, whereas recent investigations revealed their negative correlation. The correlations between neuroticism and extraversion are analysed in different kinds of workers (for example, nurses, physicians, teachers, and clerks), showing a negative, but significant association. These results contribute to the study of the relations between neuroticism and extraversion in different organizational contexts.

The following chapter by Annamaria Di Fabio and Alessio Gori analyses the contribution of neuroticism, self-esteem and a new construct for the 21st century named intrapreneurial self-capital, for explaining flourishing as adaptive outcome. The study was carried out with white collar workers. Results showed that the model with neuroticism and self-esteem as independent variables and flourishing as dependent variable indicated a good mediation role of self-esteem. Furthermore, the model—with the intrapreneurial self-capital as a mediator—showed that this variable has a strong and direct effect on flourishing. Thus, the results of the present study extends the reflection on the role of mediating variables such as self-esteem and intrapreneurial self-capital as important individual resources to be considered in the relations between neuroticism and flourishing in workers.

The tenth contribution by Annamaria Di Fabio and Ornella Bucci presents a study on the association between career outcomes and the "Big Five" personalities simultaneously analyzed, confronting different groups of participants (high school students and university students) in the same study to compare results. The results of this research showed that neuroticism consistently explained a large percentage of variance in all career outcome variables, contributing to the in-depth exploration of career decision-making, self-efficacy, career decision, employability and its associations with neuroticism in young people. In a preventive perspective on the basis of these results, it is possible to individualize young people at risk with high neuroticism and intervene early with training on career outcomes to promote them.

The last chapter by Radek Trnka and Inna Čábelková closes the volume by stressing the importance of a cross-cultural perspective. The chapter presents explanations and interpretations for differences between cultures in neuroticism. This review also delineates the relations between neuroticism and cultural dimensions to provide an overview of current cross-cultural investigation regarding neuroticism, also offering the basis for further research in the study of neuroticism across cultures.

The hope is that this book can really help to enhance the study of neuroticism, its characteristics, and impact on job performance and health outcomes. The goal of the volume is to be a useful aid to the valorization and protection of human resources to favour both performance and well-being of workers, promoting organizational productivity, business success, well-being and healthy environments in organizations.

Annamaria Di Fabio

This book has been independently peer-reviewed by international academics who are experts in the field. The reviews included the entire text that appears in the published book and peer reviews were positive.

NEUROTICISM AND ORGANIZATIONAL CONTEXTS: RESEARCH AND PERSPECTIVES

In: Neuroticism
Editor: Annamaria Di Fabio

ISBN: 978-1-63485-323-1

Chapter 1

NEUROTICISM, JOB PERFORMANCE AND HEALTH OUTCOMES: A REVIEW

Annamaria Di Fabio,
Department of Education and Psychology (Psychology Section),
University of Florence, Italy

ABSTRACT

This review aims to outline the literature regarding relationships between personality traits – particularly neuroticism – and job performance on the one hand, and health outcomes on the other. The first part of the review is focused on the relation between personality traits and job performance, presenting studies produced between the mid-1950s and the present. The second part of the review focuses on the relation between personality traits and health outcomes, presenting studies in three distinct areas of research following the bio-psycho-social model: objective well-being, as absence of physical disease or psychopathology; hedonic well-being; and eudaimonic well-being. This review offers a framework of reference, presenting the evolution and current state of research on the relationships between personality traits (particularly neuroticism) and job performance and health outcomes, suggesting new perspectives for research and intervention.

INTRODUCTION

The relationship between personality and job performance has been studied since the middle of the last century, particularly in relation to personnel selection (Barrick and Mount, 1991; Ghiselli and Barthol, 1953; Guion and Gottier, 1965; Schmitt, Gooding, Noe, and Kirsch, 1984; Tett, Jackson, and Rothstein, 1991).

The relation between personality and health outcomes, likewise, has been the subject of extensive study (Blatný, 2015; Costa and McCrae, 1980; Pavot and Diener, 2011). Regarding health outcomes, it is important to consider the bio-psycho-social model, an approach developed by Engel (1977) on the basis of the multidimensional conception of health described in 1947 by the World Health Organization (WHO). Beginning from the WHO definition, this approach underlines the importance of considering physical, mental, social and spiritual components in the definition of health, taking into consideration objective and subjective aspects of well-being in the overall functioning of individuals. In relation to health outcomes, the bio-psycho-social model opens the question of the definition of the well-being of a person, going beyond purely biological aspects. Within this framework it is possible to specifically distinguish three areas of studies on the relations between personality traits and health outcomes: one area focused on well-being in terms of objective well-being as absence of physical disease or psychopathology (Friedman and Kern, 2014; Ozer and Benet-Martinez, 2006; Smith, 2006; Trull and Sher 1994); one focused on well-being in terms of hedonic well-being (Diener et al.,1985; Kahneman et al.,1999; Watson et al.,1988); and one focused on well-being in terms of eudaimonic well-being (Ryan and Deci, 2001; Ryff and Singer, 2008; Waterman et al., 2010). Over the following pages we present an outline of the literature on the relationships between personality traits, particularly neuroticism, and job performance on the one hand, and health outcomes on the other. This review aims to provide a framework for understanding the evolution and current state of research regarding the ways in which personality traits – in particular, neuroticism – relate to job performance and health outcomes.

Personality and Job Performance

Studies of the relations between personality traits and job performance can be divided into specific periods. The first period includes the traditional research conducted between the beginning of the twentieth century and the mid-1960s (Ghiselli and Barthol, 1953; Guion and Gottier, 1965). The second period includes the meta-analyses carried out in the 1980s and 1990s of studies produced between the mid-1960s and the end of the 1990s using meta-analytic procedures (Barrick and Mount, 1991; Schmitt et al., 1984; Tett et al., 1991). The third period includes studies on the relations between personality traits and job performance using a new approach for the twenty-first century (Barrick, Stewart, and Piotrowski, 2002; Cox et al., 2003; Hogan and Holland, 2003; Raja and Johns, 2010; Rothmann and Coetze 2003; Salgado, 2003; Smillie, Yeo, Furnham, and Jackson, 2006). The final period would be the last five years, with the recent perspectives on the relations between personality traits (particularly according to the Five Factor Model) and job performance (Abdullah, Rashid, and Omar, 2013; Ali, 2011; Bhatti, Battour, Ismail, and Sundram, 2014; Le et al., 2011; Uppal et al., 2014; Yang and Hwang, 2014).

First Period of Studies on Personality and Job Performance

The first studies on the relations between personality traits and job performance were carried out between the mid-1950s and the 1980s. Two reviews in particular represent key works regarding the relationships that emerged between neuroticism and job performance, summarising the results of the empirical studies conducted in the first half of the twentieth century. The first review was that of Ghiselli and Barthol (1953), conducted on 113 studies between 1919 and 1953. The authors reported the sample-weighted mean validities of personality measures used in employee selection for a number of different job categories. Results showed that mean validities ranged from .14 for supervisory positions to .36 for sales positions. The overall mean validity for the job categories considered was .22. Notwithstanding these quite positive results, the authors affirmed that “there have been enough studies reporting negative results to emphasize caution in their use” (p. 19). Furthermore, the average sample size of studies reviewed by Ghiselli and Barthol (1953) was 102, which is quite small, meaning that they could not be generalizable.

The review subsequently carried out by Guion and Gottier (1965) represents a work that has had a negative influence on research into the relation between personality traits and job performance. The study was a critique of the use of personality inventories in personnel selection. Guion and Gottier (1965) analyzed twelve volumes of the *Journal of Applied Psychology and Personnel Psychology* from 1952 to 1963. Only studies relating to selection were considered, whereas studies relating to placement were excluded. Selected articles from this period were summarized for presentation in a tabular summary. Analyzed articles included different measures of personality (for example, Bernreuter Personality Inventory, California Psychological Inventory, Edwards Personal Preference Schedule, Guilford Martin Personality Inventory, and others) in relation to different measures of performance (for example, ratings, efficiency ratio, percentage of sales, salary grade, and so on), examined in the most varied targets (for example, executives, supervisors, salesmen, engineers, policemen, etc.). The results are particularly daunting. None of the personality measures included in the study showed predictive validity in personnel selection, and in conclusion the authors are critical of the use of personality measures in selection procedures. Reactions to the negative results of this review are consistent and overstated. The consequence was a considerable reduction, over the following years, in studies of the relation between personality and job performance in the field of personnel selection specifically (Tett et al., 1991). The conclusions of the study by Guion and Gottier (1965) were submitted to reassessment in the following years, particularly with the introduction of meta-analysis techniques (Tett et al., 1991). Whereas Guion and Gottier (1965) simply analyzed the relative frequency of statistically significant findings, the meta-analytical procedure enabled the integration of results from different studies based on effect size and the computation of a weighted average of that common measure (Tett et al., 1991).

Personality and Job Performance: The Traditional Meta-Analyses

The 1980s saw the advent of meta-analytical procedures in the study of relations between personality and job performance (Barrick and Mount, 1991; Schmitt et al., 1984; Tett et al., 1991). The meta-analysis by Schmitt et al. (1984) examined all criterion-related validity studies in *Personnel Psychology* and the *Journal of Applied Psychology* between the years of 1964 and 1982. A total of 99 articles were included: 65 published in the *Journal of Applied Psychology* and 34 in *Personnel Psychology*. The analyzed articles included many performance predictors, including personality measures, but also, for example, assessment center, biodata, general cognitive ability, special aptitude scales and so on. The analyzed articles also included variable performance rating as a criterion (and others, such as turnover, grades, status change, etc.). Participants in the analyzed studies were drawn from different occupational groups (professionals, managers, clericals, sales, skilled labor, unskilled labor). In particular, the results of this meta-analysis by Schmitt et al. (1984) regarding the specific relations between personality measures and performance ratings as the criterion variable (studied in 32 of the 99 articles included) showed a sample-weighted mean correlation of .21. This value is better than the value for special aptitude (.16), slightly inferior to the value for general cognitive ability (.22), but smaller than the value for assessment center evaluation (.43).

The first meta-analysis specifically conducted on the relations between the Big Five personality dimensions and job performance was that by Barrick and Mount (1991). This meta-analysis included published and unpublished criterion-related validity studies of personality for selection purposes between 1952 and 1988. In all, 117 studies were included in the analysis. This meta-analysis thus investigated the relation of the Big Five personality dimensions (Extraversion, Emotional Stability, Agreeableness, Conscientiousness, and Openness to Experience) to three job performance criteria (job proficiency, training proficiency, and personnel data) for five occupational groups (professionals, police, managers, sales, and skilled/semi-skilled). Results showed that Conscientiousness showed consistent relations with all job performance criteria for all occupational groups. For the remaining personality dimensions, the estimated true score correlations varied according to occupational group and criterion type. Extraversion was a valid predictor of two occupations involving social interactions: managers and sales (across criterion types). Also, both Openness to Experience and Extraversion were valid predictors of the training proficiency criterion (across occupations). Other personality dimensions were also found to be valid predictors for some occupations and for some criterion types, but the magnitude of the estimated true score correlations was small ($p < .10$). Overall, the results illustrate the benefits of using the Five Factor Model of personality in job performance.

Another meta-analysis, carried out in 1991 by Tell et al., examined the relations between Five Factor Model dimensions of personality and job performance. This meta-analysis included psychological abstracts dated from 1968 to the present, which were searched electronically *(Knowledge Index,* 1991) using the union of "personality" and "job performance" as the main selection criterion. Four hundred and ninety four studies were analyzed, including 97 independent samples (total N = 13,521). The results of this meta-analysis showed that the corrected estimate of the overall relation between personality and job performance obtained in this study was .24. Results of the content-based meta-analysis indicated that mean validities reached meaningful levels: -.15 for Neuroticism, .18 for Openness to Experience, .22 for Agreeableness. This meta-analysis was the first in the literature that underlined the role of Neuroticism in job performance. This role of Neuroticism in job performance will be confirmed in following studies.

A subsequent meta-analysis by Barrick et al. (2001) identified 15 meta-analytic studies (11 published articles and four conference presentations) on the relations between Five Factor Model dimensions and job performance conducted between the mid-1980s and the end of the 1990s. Results showed that conscientiousness is a valid predictor across performance measures in all occupations studied. Emotional stability (the opposite of neuroticism) was also found to be a generalizable predictor when overall work performance was the criterion, but its relationship to specific performance criteria and occupations was less consistent than that of Conscientiousness. The other three Big Five traits (Extraversion, Openness and Agreeableness) did not predict overall work performance, but rather predicted success in specific occupations or related to specific criteria. For example, extraversion is positively related to performance in jobs with an important interpersonal component, especially those involving mentoring, leading, and persuading, such as management and sales positions; openness is positively related to jobs that involve considerable interpersonal interaction, particularly when the interaction involves helping, cooperating, and nurturing others; agreeableness is related to jobs characterized by a service orientation and teamwork (Barrick et al., 2001).

In a subsequent meta-analysis by Judge, Heller and Mount (2002), the association of Neuroticism (followed by Conscientiousness and Extraversion) in particular emerged in relation to job performance. This meta-analysis included studies on the relationship between the Big Five traits and job satisfaction retrieved searched in the PsycINFO database (1887-2000), considering studies (articles, book chapters, dissertations, and unpublished reports) on personality and job satisfaction. For the search, keywords such as personality, Big Five, Agreeableness, Conscientiousness, Extraversion, Openness to Experience, and Neuroticism were used. This search led to the identification of 1,277 abstracts (including doctoral dissertations).

Thus, Judge et al.'s (2002) meta-analysis linked traits from the Five Factor Model of personality to overall job satisfaction. Three hundred and thirty four correlations from 163 independent samples were classified according to the Five Factor Model. The estimated true score correlations with job satisfaction were .29 for Neuroticism, .26 for Conscientiousness, .25 for Extraversion, .17 for Agreeableness, .02 for Openness to Experience. As a set, the Big Five traits had a multiple correlation of .41 with job satisfaction, indicating support for the validity of the job satisfaction when personality traits are organized according to the Five Factor Model.

Thus, overall, the meta-analytic studies carried out underscore that two personality traits of the Five Factors Model (Conscientiousness and Emotional stability) in particular are associated with overall job performance (Anderson and Viswesvaran, 1998; Barrick and Mount, 1991; Judge et al., 2002; Salgado, 1997; Tett et al., 1991). Specifically regarding neuroticism (the opposite of emotional stability and the trait on which the present review is focused), it is possible to assert that individuals who are anxious, hostile, personally insecure, and depressed (high neuroticism) reach a low overall level of performance in all kinds of jobs (Barrick, Mount, and Judge, 2001). Furthermore, relations emerged between neuroticism and specific dimensions of job performance, for example success in teamwork (Barrick et al., 2001; Hough, 1992; Mount, Barrick, and Stewart, 1998). Individuals who are calm, secure, and not hostile (low neuroticism) are able to have more effective interactions with co-workers, obtaining a better performance when working in a team (Barrick et al., 2001; Hough, 1992; Mount et al., 1998). Low neuroticism also improves performance in jobs involving customer services and sales, as well as managerial jobs (Hurtz and Donovan, 2000). So, at the outset of the twenty-first century, the research on the relationship between neuroticism and job performance showed that individuals who are not anxious or worrisome (low neuroticism) are more likely to reach a good level of performance at work (Barrick et al., 2001; Hurtz and Donovan, 2000). These findings also led to a general consensus among researchers and practitioners that personality traits could be a useful predictor of job performance (Hurtz and Donovan, 2000), even if specific relations emerged between certain personality traits and performance in only a few jobs.

Personality and Job Performance: A Review of Studies in the Twenty-First Century

In the twenty-first century, research into the relations between personality traits and job performance includes studies which confirm previous results, as well as research with a new, specific focus. This section looks at these studies in chronological order.

A first new focus on the relations between personality and job performance concerned the study of possible mediators. In 2002, Barrick et al. conducted a study that verified a model of job performance which analysed the mediating effects of cognitive-motivational work orientations on the relations between personality traits according to the Big Five model and performance in a sales job. The results showed that proximal motivational variables influenced mechanisms through which distal personality traits affect job performance. Specifically, striving for status and accomplishment mediated the effects of extraversion and conscientiousness on ratings of sales performance. In this particular case, neuroticism was not linked to these motivational measures, probably because it is not associated to motivational goals and motivational aspects specifically in a sales job (Barrick et al., 2002).

Another variable taken into consideration in the study of the relations between personality traits, particularly neuroticism, and job performance is workload. In a study by Cox et al. (2003), workload levels were manipulated to examine individuals' differential responses to the stress of sudden shifts in workload. One hundred ninety four undergraduate students from the University of Oklahoma were randomly assigned to either a High-to-Low or Low-to-High testing condition. Participants performed an auditory vigilance task, while reaction time and correct responses were assessed. The results showed that higher levels of neuroticism were associated with decreased reaction time in both conditions. In addition, individuals higher in neuroticism evidenced fewer correct responses in the Low-to-High workload condition. These results can be interpreted as consistent with personality research which indicates that neuroticism is associated with maladaptive appraisal styles (Cox et al., 2003; Wells and Matthews, 1994). In fact, some individuals could be anxious when faced with relatively minor challenges (Cox et al., 2003; Wells and Matthews, 1994). Thus, individuals with a high score in neuroticism could consider the change in workload more negatively than those with a low score, with a decrease in attention and concentration which could have a negative impact on performance (Cox et al., 2003).

In 2003, a number of studies were carried out on relations between personality traits according to the Five Factor Model and job performance (Hogan and Holland, 2003; Rothmann and Coetzer, 2003; Salgado, 2003), confirming the results of the meta-analysis conducted in the twentieth century.

Hogan and Holland (2003) conducted a meta-analysis on 43 independent samples (N = 5,242) from published articles, chapters, technical reports, and dissertations between 1980 and 2000 to confirm the findings of the meta-analyses conducted between the mid-1960s and the end of the 1990s. The results showed that the stronger Big Five predictors of subjective performance criteria (overall job-performance ratings) resulted emotional stability (the opposite of neuroticism) and conscientiousness. Individuals who appear calm and self-confident (low neuroticism) or scrupulous and persevering (conscientiousness) are evaluated more positively by their supervisors.

The same year saw the publication of a study by Rothmann and Coetze (2003) regarding the relation between job performance and personality dimensions according to the Big Five model, conducted on 159 employees of a pharmaceutical company. The results showed that emotional stability (the opposite of neuroticism), extraversion, openness to experience and conscientiousness were related to task performance and creativity. Neuroticism and openness to experience showed the highest correlations. In particular, a low level of neuroticism in terms of general tendency to experience negative emotions, such as fear, sadness, and anger, is more related to creative tasks (Rothmann and Coetze, 2003).

A study by Nikolau (2003), carried out on employees from 22 small and medium-sized firms in Athens, Greece, concluded that personality traits according to Five Factor Model are related to overall job performance evaluated by supervisors, but not with performance-related variables, such as citizenship behaviours and generic work competencies, highlighting a direct role of personality traits on job performance and no indirect contribution by other variables that could influence performance.

Again in 2003, Salgado carried out a study that compared the criterion validity of the Big Five personality dimensions when assessed using Five Factor Model (FFM)-based inventories and non-FFM-based inventories, conducting a meta-analysis. The study included 92 papers (70 from the USA and 22 from Europe), reporting 139 independent samples. The group of samples in which FFM inventories were used consisted of 74 (81%) American samples and 17 (18%) European samples. The group of samples in which non-FFM inventories were used consisted of 26 (54%) American samples and 22 (46%) European samples. This meta-analysis showed differences between the two types of inventories in relation to performance for Emotional Stability (the opposite of neuroticism) and Conscientiousness. For Neuroticism specifically, the validity is stronger when measured with FFM-based inventories than the non-FFM-based inventories.

A subsequent study (Skyrme, Wilkinson, Abraham, and Morrison, 2005) analyzed the contribution of Big Five personality traits in predicting objective measures of employee productivity and subjective measure of training performance in a call center. Emotional Stability (the opposite of Neuroticism), Conscientiousness, and Agreeableness in particular were related to the productivity of call center workers. Moreover, Emotional Stability (the opposite of neuroticism), Conscientiousness, and Agreeableness are related with subjective training performance.

In 2006, Smillie et al. carried out a study specifically on Neuroticism to evaluate a model indicating that the performance of highly neurotic individuals, in comparison with emotionally stable ones, is more strongly influenced by factors relating to the allocation of attentional resources. In a first study, the authors used an air traffic control simulation to examine the interaction between effort intensity and neuroticism in the prediction of task performance. The results showed that, as effort intensity increased, performance for highly neurotic individuals increased more than for those with low neuroticism. In a second longitudinal study, the relation between neuroticism and telesales performance was analyzed. Changes in office busyness were related with higher performance improvements for highly neurotic individuals compared with less neurotic individuals. Overall, these studies indicate that highly neurotic individuals perform better than less neurotic individuals in a busy work environment or if they are expending a high level of effort.

In 2007 Judge and Erez investigated the constellation of two Big Five traits – Emotional Stability (the opposite of Neuroticism) and Extraversion – in predicting job performance. The study was carried out with employees and their supervisors at a regional health and fitness center. Results showed that the constellation of two Big Five traits (Emotional Stability and

Extraversion) predicted performance, even when controlling for the main effects of Emotional Stability and Extraversion. These results suggested that the combination of Emotional Stability and Extraversion may be more important in predicting job performance than either individual trait alone.

A subsequent study (Raja and Johns, 2010) analysed the relation between personality traits according to the Big Five and three dimensions of job performance (in-role performance, creativity, and citizenship behavior) under differing levels of job scope. Data were collected through onsite administration of a survey in 11 different organizations. The business/operations of the organizations included engineering services, manufacturing (e.g., paint, consumer goods, and petrochemical products), financial/banking services, and operations of governmental departments. In all, 435 workers participated in the study (response rate of 72.5 percent). The results indicated that higher job scope would facilitate performance for those who were dispositionally inclined toward a particular dimension of performance and damage the performance of those who were dispositionally disinclined. The results emphasized the role of interactions between Big Five personality traits and job scope in predicting various aspects of performance.

Zimmerman, Triana and Barrick (2010) sought to verify the predictive validity of observer ratings of personality and job-related competencies in a selection setting. Their study is based on ratings from multiple raters of both the predictors and the criteria in a sample of business students. The results showed that observer ratings of Emotional Stability (the opposite of Neuroticism), Conscientiousness, leadership, and interpersonal skills predicted work performance, team performance, and academic performance. In relation to work performance and team performance, a composite of the four predictors had incremental predictive validity over general mental ability, even after controlling for the familiarity between the rater and the ratee.

Overall, the results of the studies conducted in the first ten years of the twenty-first century confirmed the relation between personality traits (particularly neuroticism) and job performance.

Personality and Job Performance: Recent Perspectives

Over the last five years, studies on the relations between personality traits (according to the Five Factor Model) and job performance continue, introducing new perspectives and also confirming previous results. As with the preceding section, this section looks at these recent studies in chronological order.

This period in question opens with the study by Ali (2011), exploring the relationship between personality traits and performance among school principals. The main objective of this research was to analyze the relationship between principals' personality traits, such as introversion, extroversion, and neuroticism, between a number of different performance dimensions. A descriptive correlation research method was employed, with a sample size of 50 principals and 176 teachers in elementary schools, middle schools, and high schools, selected from the total population of principals and teachers in the 2008-2009 academic year through the stratified sampling method. The Eysenck Personality Questionnaire was used to assess principal's personality traits. The Weiss K performance evolution questionnaire was used to assess principals' performance. Results showed that the 40% of the variance in professional and educational dimensions was explainable by Neuroticism, and the 35% of the variance in leadership, human relationships, and organizational dimensions was attributable to Extroversion.

Another study conducted in the same year by Le et al. (2011) assumes that the relation between personality traits and job performance is curvilinear, and not linear as in the previous studies. A curvilinear relation is a relation between two variables where, as one variable increases, so does the other, but only up to a certain point, after which, as one variable continues to increase, the other decreases, or vice versa. In the first case, this relation can be represented graphically as an inverted-U whereas in the second case this relation can be represented graphically as a U-shaped curve. Results of the research by Le et al., (2011) are based on two different samples (602 employees of a large public organization and 956 employees from 25 organizations spanning different industries – healthcare, manufacturing, construction, testing, construction services and educational institutions). They showed a curvilinear relationship between personality traits, in particular conscientiousness and emotional stability (the opposite of neuroticism), and job performance dimensions, including task performance, organizational citizenship behavior, and counterproductive work behaviors. Furthermore, job complexity moderated the curvilinear personality-performance relationships such that the inflection points after which the relationships disappear were lower for low-complexity jobs than they were for high-complexity jobs. These results indicated that high levels of the two personality traits examined are more beneficial for performance in high-complexity jobs than low-complexity jobs.

Another study (Abdullah et al., 2013), carried out on 384 employees in the Pakistani banking sector, investigated relations between personality traits and job performance. This study showed that Extraversion, Conscientiousness, Agreeableness, and Openness to Experience were positively associated to job performance, while neuroticism was negatively associated to job performance, confirming the results of the previous studies in the literature.

A subsequent study (Bhatti et al., 2014) examined the relation between personality traits and job performance in expatriates, considering the mediating role of adjustment to a foreign country. Data were collected from 201 expatriates working in Malaysia and analyzed using structural equation modelling. The results showed that Extroversion, Openness to Experience, Agreeableness, Conscientiousness, and Emotional Stability are positively related to expatriate adjustment, which further influenced expatriate performance as rated by peers. In other words, expatriates' adjustment mediates the relationship between Big Five personality traits and expatriates' job performance (task, relationship building, and overall performance). The results of this study enable us to understand the importance of personality traits for successful completion of international assignment, suggesting that human resource professionals should take these personality traits into consideration before selecting an individual for international assignment.

Again in 2014, Uppal et al. carried out a study specifically looking at the relationship between neuroticism and job performance, introducing the mediating role of job characteristics (motivational, social, and contextual) detected through the Work Design Questionnaire (Morgeson and Humphrey, 2006). Conducting a longitudinal study over two time periods, using a sample (T1: n = 802; T2: n = 760) of employees in 13 job profiles from 22 private banks, this study supported the moderating effects of various job characteristics on the relations between neuroticism and job performance. The results highlighted a previously unidentified mechanism for explaining the complex relation between neuroticism and job performance (Yang and Hwang, 2014).

In 2014, the relation between personality traits and job performance was analyzed in the Taiwanese context (Yang and Hwang, 2014). The study was carried out on 392 participants from 31 companies in the financial, securities, and insurance industries in Taiwan. The results of this study indicated that all Big Five traits are significantly associated to job performance with Agreeableness presenting the higher association, followed by Extraversion. A possible reason for this is that 70% of participants were salespeople. Agreeableness is the personality trait essential to salespeople, the centrality of service quality and attitude in this role making a high level of agreeableness a prerequisite.

One recent study (Judge and Zapata, 2015) examined an interactionist model that analyses the relation between Big Five personality traits and job performance taking into consideration the characteristics of the job. A three-part search process was conducted in order to identify all possible studies examining the relations between the Big Five traits and job performance: first, authors manually searched through the reference sections of previously published articles which had meta-analyzed the relations between the Big Five personality traits and job performance; then, to identify articles that were not included in the preceding meta-analysis, the authors searched the PsycINFO database for studies that measured both personality and job performance; finally, the authors conducted a reverse citation search of previous meta-analyses. The results showed that all Big Five traits were more predictive of performance for jobs in which the process by which the work was done took the form of unstructured situations (for example, where the employee had full discretion in decision-making). Many of the traits also predicted performance in job contexts that activated specific traits (for example, extraversion better predicted performance in jobs requiring social skills). Overall, the results of the study supported an interactionist model, in which the situation exerts both general and specific effects on the degree to which personality is associated to job performance.

PERSONALITY AND HEALTH OUTCOMES

The relation between personality and health outcomes was extensively studied in the literature (Blatný, 2015; Costa and McCrae, 1980; Pavot and Diener, 2011). Firstly, it is important to consider the bio-psycho-social model developed by Engel (1977) on the basis of the multidimensional conception of health described in 1947 by the World Health Organization. This conception of health takes into account physical components (functions, organ structures), as well as mental (intellectual and psychological state), social (family life, work, economics, citizenship) and spiritual components (values), to identify among these the variables related to subjective and objective conditions of well-being (health in its positive conception) and malaise (disease, problem, discomfort) to be taken into account in consideration of individuals' health. The bio-psycho-social model thus places the patient at the center of a large system influenced by many variables. In order to understand and treat the disease, it is necessary to deal not only with the problems of functions and organs, but also to pay attention to the psychological, social, family, and individual aspects, interacting with each other and capable of influencing the evolution of the disease. The bio-psycho-social model is opposed to the bio-medical model (Engel, 1977), whereby the disease is caused by biological variables that need to be identified and corrected with treatment. In relation to health outcomes, the bio-psycho-social model opens the question of the definition of the well-being of the individual. In the literature it is possible to distinguish three separate domains: objective well-being (OWB), hedonic well-being or subjective well-being (SWB), and eudaimonic well-being or psychological well-being (PWB). The construct of objective well-being is considered as absence of physical disease or psychopathology (Andrews and Withey, 1976; Campbell, 1976; Diener, 1984). The construct of hedonic well-being can be expressed as "a broad category of phenomena that includes people's emotional responses, domain satisfactions, and global judgments of life satisfaction [...] a general area of scientific interest rather than a single specific construct" (Diener, Suh, Lucas, and Smith, 1999, p. 277). Eudaimonic well-being regards obtaining good results, growing and developing as a person and becoming adept at building significant relationships with others (Hird, 2003). It is thus possible to distinguish three areas of research in the field of relations between personality and health outcomes: one focused on well-being in terms of objective well-being as absence of psychopathology or physical disease (Friedman and Kern, 2014; Ozer and Benet-Martinez, 2006; Smith, 2006; Trull and Sher 1994); one focused on well-being in terms of hedonic well-being (Diener et al., 1985; Kahneman et al., 1999; Watson et al., 1988); and one focused on well-being in terms of eudaimonic well-being (Ryan and Deci, 2001; Ryff and Singer, 2008; Waterman et al., 2010).

Personality and Objective Well-Being

This first area of research on the relations between personality traits and health outcomes focused on well-being in terms of objective well-being as absence of physical disease or psychopathology.

Over the years, a growing body of research has analyzed the associations between personality traits and physical health (Friedman and Kern, 2014; Smith, 2006). Regarding physical health three outcomes were particularly extensively studied in the literature: general self-reported health (as indicator of current health status), body mass index, and substance use.

Self-reported health is a widely used indicator of current health status, an important predictor of many health outcomes, and it can be defined as the individual's rating of his/her own general health (Idler and Benyamini, 1997). Conscientiousness generally showed the strongest and most consistent relation with self-reported health (Atherton, Robins, Rentfrow, and Lamb, 2014; Hampson, Goldberg, Vogt, and Dubanoski, 2006; Takahashi, Edmonds, Jackson, and Roberts, 2013), but also, Neuroticism showed an inverse association with self-reported health (Atherton et al., 2014).

The study by Hampson et al. (2006) investigated longitudinally the associations between personality traits and self-reported health. Teachers assessed 963 elementary schoolchildren on Big Five personality traits. Self-reported health was assessed in the same children 40 years later in midlife. The results showed that childhood personality was significantly associated with self-reported health. For men and women, childhood Conscientiousness was associated with better self-rated health in adulthood.

A more recent longitudinal study by Takahashi et al. (2013) examined how Conscientiousness was linked to self-perceived physical health. Participants were 898 individuals ranging in age from 19 to 94. Personality and self-perceived health questionnaires were administered to participants in two waves, with an interval of approximately three years. The results of this study showed that Conscientiousness was significantly and positively related to self-perceived physical health over time.

A subsequent study by Atherton et al. (2014), using a large sample (N = 460,172) of adults who ranged in age from 18 to 90 years, examined the associations between Big Five personality traits and self-reported health. The results showed that individuals who are less responsible (low Conscientiousness) and less emotionally stable (high Neuroticism) reported poorer health.

Recent longitudinal research has also shown that increases in Conscientiousness, Openness, Extraversion, and Agreeableness are associated with improvements in self-reported health over time, whereas increases in Neuroticism are associated with poorer self-reported health over time (Letzring, Edmonds, and Hampson, 2014; Magee, Heaven, and Miller, 2013).

A study by Magee et al. (2013) examined whether personality change over a four-year period was associated with self-reported physical health. Participants were 11,105 Australian adults ranging in age from 20 to 79 years. Results showed that increases in Conscientiousness and Extraversion were associated with improved self-reported physical health, whereas an increase in Neuroticism was linked to poorer self-reported physical health.

In a study by Letzring et al. published the following year, longitudinal data from the Hawaii Personality and Health Cohort were used to examine associations between changes in Big Five personality traits and self-reported physical health. Seven hundred and thirty-three participants completed measures of the Big Five personality traits and self-reported physical health twice, approximately three years apart. Personality trait changes were associated with self-reported health change. Additionally, increases in Agreeableness, Conscientiousness, and Openness, and decreases in Neuroticism predicted increases in self-reported physical health, even when controlling for gender and education. These results have implications for understanding how changes in personality traits over time are related to self-reported physical health, and could be used to aid the development of effective health promotion strategies targeted at specific personality traits (Letzring et al., 2014; Magee et al., 2013).

A recent study (Luo and Roberts, 2015) analyzed longitudinally the relation between Conscientiousness and self-reported physical health, introducing the possible mediating effect of stress. This study was carried out on a representative sample of United States citizens (N = 2136 for wave 1 and N = 1170 for wave 2), who completed the questionnaires twice over a three-year period. The results showed that stress partially mediated the relation between Conscientiousness and self-reported physical health. This study opens new perspectives for research, introducing the role of possible mediators in the relations between personality traits and self-reported physical health.

The second health outcome considered, Body Mass Index (BMI), is a health marker known to be a causal predictor for many obesity-related disease outcomes (National Institutes of Health, 1998). Individuals who are more neurotic and extraverted, and less conscientious, tend to have higher BMI scores, based on both cross-sectional and longitudinal research (Sutin, Ferrucci, Zonderman, and Terracciano, 2011). In this study, Sutin et al. (2011) used data from a large-scale (N = 1,988 United States individuals) longitudinal study that spanned more than 50 years to examine how personality traits are associated with fluctuations in BMI. The results of this study, regarding concurrent data, showed that participants higher in Neuroticism and Extraversion and lower in Conscientiousness had higher BMI. Longitudinally, high Neuroticism and low Conscientiousness predicted a greater increase in BMI over time. More recently, Atherton et al. (2014), using a large sample of adults (N = 460,172), found that low Conscientiousness was associated with a higher BMI: individuals who are less responsible tend to be more overweight. Personality traits seem to contribute to unhealthy weight and difficulties with weight management. Such associations may elucidate the role of personality traits in disease progression, and may help to design more effective interventions (Sutin et al., 2011).

Furthermore, Brummett et al. (2006) found gender differences in the relations between personality traits and BMI: Neuroticism was related to BMI only in females, whereas Extraversion was related to BMI only in males. A more recent study (Sutin and Terracciano, 2015) regards the association between personality traits and adiposity in a young adult sample. The aim of this study was to verify whether personality was associated with the subjective experience of body weight and discrepancies between perceived and actual weight. Participants (N = 15,669) from wave 4 of the National Longitudinal Study of Adolescent Health completed a Five-Factor Model personality measure and reported their weight, height, and perception of weight category (e.g., overweight); trained staff measured participants' height, weight, and waist circumference. The results showed that Conscientiousness was associated with healthier weight. Neuroticism among women and Extraversion among men were associated with higher adiposity. Neuroticism was also associated with misperceived heavier weight, whereas Extraversion was associated with misperceived tallness and leanness. In summary, the results of the present study showed that personality traits were associated with objective and subjective adiposity in young adulthood.

The third health outcome considered, substance use, is a risky health behavior that has deleterious consequences for health later in life (Atherton et al., 2014). Individuals who are more neurotic, extraverted, and open, and less conscientious and agreeable, tend to engage in more substance abuse, based on both cross-sectional and longitudinal research (Turiano, Whiteman, Hampson, Roberts, and Mroczek, 2012). Turiano et al. (2012) in particular studied the associations between personality traits and substance abuse longitudinally in adult individuals. Participants in their study included approximately 4000 adults (aged 25-74) who participated in two waves of the Midlife in the US (MIDUS) study. Results of this study showed that higher levels of Neuroticism, Extraversion, Openness, and lower levels of Conscientiousness and Agreeableness predicted long-term substance use. Increases in Neuroticism and Openness predicted increased substance use while increases in Conscientiousness and Agreeableness predicted decreased substance use. More recently, Atherton et al. (2014), using a large sample of adults (N = 460,172), found that low Conscientiousness was associated with a higher level of substance use. Individuals who are less responsible and less controlled were found to be more heavily engaged in substance use. Furthermore, substance use and personality trait changes are reciprocally related over time (Littlefield, Sher, and Wood, 2009).

It is possible to delineate a specific focus on Neuroticism regarding substance abuse. In fact, Neuroticism presented clear associations with substance abuse, with neurotic individuals in particular being more likely to smoke cigarettes, and smoke a greater quantity thereof (Malouff et al., 2006; Mroczek, Spiro, and Turiano, 2009; Munafò, Zetteler, and Clark, 2007;

Rausch, Nichinson, Lamke, and Matloff, 1990). Neurotic individuals were also more likely to abuse alcohol (Grekin, Sher, and Wood, 2006; Larkins and Sher, 2006; Malouff et al., 2007; Terracciano et al., 2008). Results from the Hawaii Personality and Health cohort showed longitudinal evidence that children rated lower in emotional stability (high neuroticism) predicted greater alcohol use 40 years later in middle age (Hampson et al., 2006). Neuroticism showed also positive relations with marijuana, cocaine, and heroin use (Hopwood et al., 2007; Kashdan et al., 2005).

Another field of research in the area of physical health concerns the relations between personality traits and cardiovascular disease risk. Among health-related correlates of personality, recent research has considered premorbid indicators of disease risk, specifically metabolic syndrome (Mommersteeg and Pouwer, 2012). This syndrome includes insulin resistance, dyslipidemia, central adiposity, and elevated blood pressure. It could increase the risk for type 2 diabetes, and particularly incidence of cardiovascular disease (Agarwal, Shlipak, Kramer, Jain, and Herrington, 2012; Dearborn et al., 2014; Feng et al., 2013). Regarding the Five-Factor model of personality, the metabolic syndrome was associated with high Neuroticism and low Agreeableness, Conscientiousness, Extraversion, and Openness to Experience (Ross, Martin, Chen, and Miller, 2011; Sutin, Costa, et al., 2010; van Reedt Dortland, Giltay, Van Veen, Zitman, and Penninx, 2012). In some other studies the results concerning relations between the Five Factor Model traits and metabolic syndrome appeared more contradictory. In the study by Mommersteeg and Pouwer (2012), associations between Five Factor traits and the metabolic syndrome tend to be modest, and often do not reach statistical significance. Furthermore, other studies have not confirmed associations of the metabolic syndrome with Neuroticism (Ross et al., 2011; van Reedt Dortland et al., 2012), Conscientiousness (van Reedt Dortland et al., 2012), and/or Agreeableness (Ross et al., 2011). In relation to Extraversion, both increased and decreased risk for metabolic syndrome have emerged (Sutin, Costa, et al., 2010; van Reedt Dortland et al., 2012). These non-significant associations could be attributable to some variables that act as mediators in the relation between personality traits and the metabolic syndrome, such as substance use, diet, and physical activity (Mommersteeg and Pouwer, 2012). It is therefore crucial to pay attention to the possible mediators in the relation between personality traits and metabolic syndrome in order to predict cardiovascular disease risk (Mommersteeg and Pouwer, 2012; Dermody et al., 2015).

In this regard, a recent study (Dermody et al., 2015) examined dispositional correlates of cardio-metabolic risk within a hierarchical model of personality that proposes higher-order traits of Stability (shared variance of Agreeableness, Conscientiousness, inverse Neuroticism) and Plasticity (Extraversion, Openness), and verified a hypothesized mediation via biological and behavioral factors. The participants were 856 community volunteers aged 30-54. The results showed that lower Emotional Stability was associated with higher cardio-metabolic risk (indicators: insulin resistance, dyslipidemia, blood pressure, adiposity). This association was mediated by inflammation, autonomic function, and physical activity. The results of this study suggested the importance of considering possible mediator variables also in the relation between personality traits and physical health in terms of prevention of cardiovascular disease risk.

Regarding psychopathology, research has traditionally shown strong relations between personality traits and psychological disorders. In particular, higher Openness and lower Conscientiousness have been strongly associated with substance abuse disorders (Trull and

Sher 1994). Furthermore, higher Neuroticism was associated with anxiety, and higher Neuroticism and low Extraversion with depression (Trull and Sher 1994). It emerged that the five factors had substantial associations with personality disorders; Neuroticism showed strongest relations with personality disorders, whereas Openness to experience had only a modest relations (Trull and Durrett, 2005).

Thus, in the literature, personality traits have been found to be associated both with internalizing disorders (for example, mood and anxiety disorders) and externalizing disorders (for example, substance use disorder, antisocial personality disorder) (Kendler et al., 2003a; Krueger, 1999; Krueger et al., 2001; Markon, 2010; Miller et al., 2008; Miller et al., 2012; Slade and Watson, 2006; Watson, 2005).

Neuroticism, as the tendency to experience negative emotions, has been found to show high association with internalizing disorders (Watson, 2009; Watson, Gamez, and Simms, 2005), but also to present moderate relations with externalizing disorders (Krueger et al., 1996; Miller et al., 2006; Miller et al., 2012; Singh and Waldman, 2010). Low Extraversion showed with internalizing disorders, particularly depression and social anxiety (Naragon-Gainey et al., 2009; Watson and Naragon-Gainey, 2010). Low Agreeableness and low Conscientiousness presented associations only with externalizing disorders (Krueger et al., 2002; Krueger et al., 2007; Miller et al., 2012). It is also possible to affirm that certain traits could predict certain disorders (Krueger et al., 2002; Kendler et al., 2003b; Lahey, 2009). High levels of Neuroticism and low levels of Extraversion contributed to create a risk for depression. Low Agreeableness and low Conscientiousness and to a lesser extent Neuroticism by contrast contributed to the development of externalizing disorders (Krueger et al., 2002; Kendler et al., 2003b; Lahey, 2009).

Only very few studies have analyzed both the direct and indirect effects of personality on psychopathology longitudinally. Horwood and Fergusson (1986) found that neuroticism predicted depression both directly and via adverse life events. In a subsequent longitudinal study, Sadeh, Miller, Wolf, and Harkness (2015) showed that adverse life events mediated the relation between neuroticism, disinhibition, and Post Traumatic Stress Disorders (PTSD). A recent longitudinal study (Koffel et al., 2016), conducted on 522 US National Guard soldiers deployed to Iraq, showed that personality traits have both direct and indirect effects on the development of psychological symptoms, with indirect effects mediated by stressful or traumatic events. These results suggested the importance of examining the possible role of mediating variables in the relations between personality traits and psychopathology.

Personality and Hedonic Well-Being

Hedonic well-being refers to pleasure attainment and pain avoidance (Kahneman et al., 1999). It consists of an affective component, characterized by the prevalence of positive emotions rather than negative emotions (Watson et al., 1988), and a cognitive component of evaluation in terms of life satisfaction (Diener et al., 1985). The relations between personality traits and hedonic well-being have been a staple of the literature in this field (Costa and McCrae, 1980). The pioneering work by Costa and McCrae (1980), which included results from several different studies, including longitudinal data, concluded that Extraversion was significantly associated with positive affect but not negative affect, whereas Neuroticism was significantly associated with negative affect but not positive affect. This first series of studies showed that Extraversion and Neuroticism had an independent influence on hedonic well-being in terms of both positive and negative affects. Many other studies (Argyle and Lu, 1990; Diener, Larsen, and Emmons, 1984; Diener, Sandvik, Pavot, and Fujita, 1992; Emmons and Diener, 1985; Hayes and Joseph, 2003; Pavot, Diener, and Fujita, 1990) have showed positive associations of Extraversion with positive affect and inverse associations of Neuroticism with negative affect. These results indicated that individuals with a higher level of extraversion had a prevalence of positive emotions, whereas individuals with a higher level of neuroticism had a prevalence of negative emotions.

The study by Costa and McCrae (1980) focused only on the affective components of hedonic well-being, positive affect and negative affect, but further studies analyzing the association between personality traits and the cognitive component of hedonic well-being, life satisfaction, showed similar results. In fact, Neuroticism and Extraversion showed the highest associations with life satisfaction (Gannon and Ranzijn, 2005; Schimmack, Diener, and Oishi, 2002; Schimmack, Oishi, Furr, and Funder, 2004).

Schimmack et al. (2002) carried out a longitudinal study on students at the University of Illinois, showing that Neuroticism (inversely) and Extraversion (positively) predicted life satisfaction. A subsequent longitudinal study (Schimmack et al., 2004), also conducted on students of the university of Illinois, confirmed the previous results, and showed in particular that the depression facet of Neuroticism and the positive emotions/cheerfulness facet of Extraversion were the strongest and most consistent predictors of life satisfaction.

A later study (Gannon and Ranzijn, 2005), conducted on participants aged between 18 and 79, confirmed the negative association of Neuroticism with life satisfaction and the positive association of Extraversion with life satisfaction.

With the consolidation of the Five Factor Model of personality (McCrae and Costa, 1999), research was extended beyond Neuroticism and Extraversion to include the other personality traits: Conscientiousness, Agreeableness, and Openness to Experience. As did Neuroticism and Extraversion, Conscientiousness, Agreeableness, Openness to Experience also showed associations with hedonic well-being (Blatný, Jelínek, Blížkovská, and Klimusová, 2004; Hayes and Joseph, 2003).

Hayes and Joseph's 2003 study analyzed the relation between personality traits and both the affective component (happiness) and cognitive component (life satisfaction) of hedonic well-being. The results showed that Neuroticism (inversely) and Extraversion (positively) were associated with happiness, detected through the Oxford Happiness Inventory (Argyle, Martin, and Crossland, 1989), whereas Neuroticism (inversely) and Conscientiousness (positively) were associated to life satisfaction (Diener et al., 1985). In a subsequent study (Blatný et al., 2004) it emerged that Emotional Stability (the opposite of Neuroticism), Extraversion, and Conscientiousness were associated with life satisfaction, confirming in particular the inverse relation of Neuroticism with life satisfaction.

Two works of reference regarding the relation between personality traits and hedonic well-being are two meta-analyses, one by DeNeve and Cooper (1998), the other carried out ten year later by Steel, Schmidt and Schultz (2008). DeNeve and Cooper (1998) analyzed 146 studies (from 1970 to 1995) on the relations between personality traits and hedonic well-being. The results of the meta-analysis showed inverse relations between hedonic well-being and Neuroticism (-.22) and positive relations between hedonic well-being and Extraversion (.17), Conscientiousness (.21), Agreeableness (.17), and Openness to Experience (.11).

Overall, personality traits explained only a small percentage (4%) of variance in relation to hedonic well-being.

The subsequent meta-analysis by Steel et al. (2008), conducted ten years after the first one and benefiting from a much larger number of relevant studies, showed stronger relations between personality traits and hedonic well-being. The authors used a multivariate approach and techniques of categorization designed to reduce the effects of grouping dissimilar studies together. Using these techniques, the authors found that overall personality traits explained the 39% of variance in relation to hedonic well-being.

An important longitudinal study is that of Gale, Booth, Mõttus, Kuh, and Deary (2013). In this study, structural equation modelling was applied to data from 4583 individuals from the MRC National Survey of Health and Development in the United Kingdom. Results showed that Neuroticism and Extraversion detected between the ages of 16 and 26 predicted hedonic well-being in terms of life satisfaction in participants 40 years later, when the individuals concerned were in their 60s.

A recent study by Olesen, Thomsen, and O'Toole (2015) introduced the mediating role of autonomy orientation in the relation between personality traits (Neuroticism and Extraversion) and hedonic well-being (in terms of positive affect, negative affect, and life satisfaction). Structural equation modeling (SEM) was applied on data from a large sample (N = 1181). Results showed that a higher autonomy orientation mediated the relation between personality traits (Neuroticism and Extraversion) and hedonic well-being. Based on these results, the authors argued that individual differences should be considered in personality-based explanations of hedonic well-being.

Another study (Soto, 2015) examined longitudinal relations of the Big Five personality traits and hedonic well-being in terms of positive affect, negative affect and life satisfaction, this one conducted on a nationally representative sample of 16,367 Australian participants. Correlations showed that higher levels of subjective well-being were associated with higher levels of Extraversion, Agreeableness, and Conscientiousness, and with lower levels of Neuroticism. Moreover, this study underlined both prospective personality traits' effects on hedonic well-being and prospective hedonic well-being's effects on personality traits. In particular, prospective personality traits' effects indicated that individuals who were initially extraverted, agreeable, conscientious, and emotionally stable subsequently increased in well-being. Prospective hedonic well-being effects indicated that individuals with high initial levels of hedonic well-being subsequently became more agreeable, conscientious, emotionally stable, and introverted. These results could open a new, challenging perspective for research, calling into question the common hypothesis that relations of personality traits with hedonic well-being are entirely, or almost entirely, due to the influence of personality traits on well-being. These results seem to support the alternative assumption that personality traits and aspects of well-being reciprocally influence each other over time.

Personality and Eudaimonic Well-Being

Relations between personality traits have also emerged regarding eudaimonic well-being. This form of well-being is relative to self-realization, where well-being is seen as the full functioning of the person (Ryan and Deci, 2001), and it is focused on life meaning, authenticity, and purposefulness (Waterman et al., 2010). In an early study, Schmutte and

Ryff (1997) examined the associations between the Big Five personality traits and eudaimonic well-being according to the Ryff (1989a) model in two samples of midlife adults (N = 215 and N = 139). Eudaimonic well-being showed an inverse relation with Neuroticism and a positive relation with Extraversion (Schmutte and Ryff, 1997), indicating that individuals with low neuroticism and low extraversion had a higher level of eudaimonic well-being in terms of life meaning and self-realization. The relation between personality traits and eudaimonic well-being were further analyzed in studies by Burns and Machin (2010) and Garcia (2011). Burns and Machin (2010) considered only three factors of eudaimonic well-being according to the Ryff (1989a) model: Autonomy, Positive relations with others, and the EGPS factor, comprising Environmental mastery (E), Personal Growth (G), Purpose in Life (P), and Self-acceptance (S). The results showed that all of the three factors correlate with all of the Big Five traits, except for positive relations with others, which was not associated with openness to experience, whereas the highest positive relations were found with Extraversion and Conscientiousness, and the highest negative relations found with Neuroticism. A subsequent study by Garcia (2011), using a unidimensional measure of eudaimonic well-being (Ryff's Short Measurement of Psychological Well-Being; Clarke, Marshall, Ryff, and Wheaton, 2001), underlined stronger positive associations of eudaimonic well-being with Extraversion and Conscientiousness, and a stronger inverse association with Neuroticism.

In the next study (Kokko, Tolvanen, and Pulkkinen, 2013), associations of personality traits with eudaimonic well-being were analyzed across ages 33-50 (the detections were carried out when participants were 33, 42 and 50 years old) as part of an ongoing Finnish longitudinal study (initial N = 369). Results indicated that the inverse relation between eudamoinic well-being and Neuroticism and the positive relation between eudaimonic well-being and Extraversion remained high across different ages. Furthermore, the initial level of Neuroticism was inversely associated with eudaimonic well-being at 42 and 50 years, and the initial level of extraversion was inversely associated with eudaimonic well-being at 42 and 50. So the inverse relation of Neuroticism and the positive relation of Extraversion to eudaimonic well-being emerged over time.

A recent study by Villieux, Sovet, Jung, and Guilbert (2016) carried out in the French context with 403 French sophomore students, investigated the relations between Big-Five personality traits and psychological flourishing as a measure of eudaimonic well-being. The results showed that Conscientiousness had the highest positive correlation with psychological flourishing. Extraversion and Agreeableness were also positively related, whereas Neuroticism was negatively related. A low positive correlation was also observed between flourishing and Openness. Another study by Di Fabio and Palazzeschi (2015) was carried out in the Italian context with 168 Italian high school students, considering the relations of personality traits with both hedonic well-being (life satisfaction and positive affect) and eudaimonic well-being (meaning in life and authenticity), examined simultaneously in the same study.

The results showed positive relations of Extraversion with both hedonic and eudaimonic well-being and inverse relations of Neuroticism with both hedonic and eudaimonic well-being. New perspectives for research could be opened in particular on the relations between personality traits and eudaimonic well-being, introducing also promising new variables, such as flourishing (Diener et al., 2010), subjective experience of eudaimonia (Waterman et al., 2010), and existential fulfillment (Längle, Orgler, and Kundi, 2003).

CONCLUSION

This review has attempted to offer a framework presenting the evolution and current state of research regarding the relationships between personality traits (particularly neuroticism) and job performance and health outcomes.

The relations between personality traits and job performance have been a subject of scientific interest since the last century (Barrick and Mount, 1991; Ghiselli et al., 1965; Schmitt et al., 1984; Tett et al., 1991), and it is fair to say that these relations are now recognized as empirically established (Ali, 2011; Barrick et al., 2001; Hogan and Holland, 2003; Judge et al., 2002; Judge and Zapata, 2014).

With regard to Neuroticism, inverse relations with performance have been found in a range of different studies (Ali, 2011; Barrick et al., 2001; Hogan and Holland, 2003; Judge et al., 2002; Uppal et al., 2014), allowing us to underline that low neuroticism can offer an important contribution in job performance.

The relationship between personality and health outcomes has also been a subject of intensive investigation (Blatný, 2015; Costa and McCrae, 1980; Pavot and Diener, 2011). Three areas have been studied: one focused on well-being in terms of objective well-being as absence of physical disease or psychopathology (Friedman and Kern, 2014; Ozer and Benet-Martinez, 2006; Smith, 2006; Trull and Sher 1994); one focused on well-being in terms of hedonic well-being (Diener et al.,1985; Kahneman et al.,1999; Watson et al.,1988); and one focused on well-being in terms of eudaimonic well-being (Ryan and Deci, 2001; Ryff and Singer, 2008; Waterman et al., 2010).

Regarding the first area, in the literature personality traits showed relations with objective well-being as absence of physical disease or psychopathology (Friedman and Kern, 2014; Ozer and Benet-Martinez, 2006; Smith, 2006; Trull and Sher 1994). In relation to physical health, relations of Neuroticism with different outcomes emerged. Specifically, Neuroticism showed an inverse association with self-reported health (Atherton et al., 2014; Letzring et al., 2014; Magee et al., 2013). Furthermore, individuals who are more neurotic tend to have higher BMI scores (Brummett et al., 2006; Sutin et al., 2011; Sutin and Terracciano, 2015). Individuals who are more neurotic tend also to engage in more substance abuse, based on both cross-sectional and longitudinal research (Turiano et al., 2012). Finally, Neuroticism was associated with a higher incidence of cardiovascular disease (Agarwal et al., 2012; Dearborn et al., 2014; Feng et al., 2013). As regards psychopathology, Neuroticism has been found to be associated with anxiety, depression (Trull and Sher 1994), and personality disorders (Trull and Durrett, 2005). Furthermore Neuroticism, as the tendency to experience negative emotions, showed a high association with internalizing disorders, such as mood and anxiety disorders (Watson, 2009; Watson et al., 2005), but also to a lesser extent with externalizing disorders (for example, substance use disorders and antisocial personality disorder) (Krueger et al., 1996; Miller et al., 2006; Miller et al., 2012; Singh and Waldman, 2010). Neuroticism has been found to predict depression both directly and via adverse life events (Horwood and Fergusson, 1986; Sadeh et al., 2015).

Regarding the second area of the literature, relationships between personality traits and hedonic well-being emerged (Costa and McCrae, 1980; Emmons and Diener, 1985; Schimmack et al., 2004; Steel et al., 2008). In the third area, relations emerged between personality traits and eudaimonic well-being (Burns and Machin, 2010; Di Fabio and

Palazzeschi, 2015; Garcia, 2011; Schmutte and Ryff, 1997; Villieux et al., 2016). For both hedonic and eudaimonic well-being, positive associations of Extraversion and inverse associations of Neuroticism emerged. In particular, Neuroticism showed inverse relations with positive affects and life satisfaction (hedonic well-being), and with eudaimonic well-being according to the Ryff (1989a) model, as well as with other variables that represent eudaimonic well-being, such as, for example, flourishing (Diener et al., 2010), meaning in life (Morgan and Farsides, 2009), authenticity (Wood et al., 2008), subjective experience of eudaimonia (Waterman et al., 2010), and existential fulfillment (Längl et al., 2003). While the literature affirms the relations of personality traits (in particular Neuroticism) with both job performance and health outcomes, more recent studies have suggested the importance of considering variables that could mediate these relations. The importance of such mediating variables has been underlined in relation both to job performance (Bhatti et al., 2014; Uppal et al., 2014) and health outcomes well-being (Koffel et al., 2016; Luo and Roberts, 2015; Mommersteeg and Pouwer, 2012; Olesen et al., 2015). It could be interesting to study the role of mediating variables which can be enhanced through specific training, such as emotional intelligence (Di Fabio and Blustein, 2010; Di Fabio and Kenny, 2012a, 2012b), or promising new variables such as Intrapreneurial Self-Capital (Di Fabio, 2014), a core of individual intrapreneurial resources that allow people to deal with frequent changes and transitions by creating innovative solutions when confronted with constraints imposed by the environment so as to turn these constraints into resources.

In fact, in a preventive perspective (Di Fabio and Kenny, 2015, 2016; Di Fabio, Kenny, and Claudius, in press; Hage et al., 2007; Kenny and Hage, 2009) on the basis of the relations between personality traits, in particular neuroticism, and both job performance and health outcomes, it is possible to identify at-risk individuals with high neuroticism and intervene early with training of the enhancing mediating variables in order to promote both job performance and health outcomes.

REFERENCES

Abdullah, I., Rashid, Y. and Omar, R. (2013). Effect of personality on job performance of employees: Empirical evidence from banking sector of Pakistan. *Middle-East Journal of Scientific Research*, *17*(12), 1735-1741.

Agarwal, S., Shlipak, M. G., Kramer, H., Jain, A. and Herrington, D. M. (2012). The association of chronic kidney disease and metabolic syndrome with incident cardiovascular events: multiethnic study of atherosclerosis. *Cardiology Research and Practice*, *2012*, 1-8.

Anderson, G. and Viswesvaran, C. (1998). An update of the validity of personality scales in personnel selection: A meta-analysis of studies published after 1992. Paper presented at the *13th Annual Conference of the Society of Industrial and Organizational Psychology, Dallas*.

Andrews, F. M. and Withey, S. B. (1976). *Social indicators of well-being*. New York: Plenum Press.

Atherton, O. E., Robins, R. W., Rentfrow, P. J. and Lamb, M. E. (2014). Personality correlates of risky health outcomes: Findings from a large Internet study. *Journal of Research in Personality*, *50*, 56-60.

Ali, S. S. (2011). Relationship between personality traits and performance among school principals. *Higher Education Studies*, *1*(1), 38-45.

Argyle, M. and Lu, L. (1990). The happiness of extraverts. *Personality and individual differences*, *11*(10), 1011-1017.

Argyle, M., Martin, M. and Crossland, J. (1989). Happiness as a function of personality and social encounters. *Recent advances in social psychology: An international perspective*, 189-203.

Barrick, M. R. and Mount, M. K. (1991). The Big Five personality dimensions and job performance: A meta-analysis. *Personnel Psychology*, *44*, 1-26.

Barrick, M. R., Mount, M. K. and Judge, T. A. (2001). Personality and performance at the beginning of the new millennium: What do we know and where do we go next?. *International Journal of Selection and assessment*, *9*(1-2), 9-30.

Barrick, M. R., Stewart, G. L. and Piotrowski, M. (2002). Personality and job performance: Test of the mediating effects of motivation among sales representatives. *Journal of Applied Psychology*, *87*(1), 43-51.

Bhatti, A. M., Battour, M. M., Ismail, R. A. and Sundram, P. V. (2014). Effects of personality traits (big five) on expatriates adjustment and job performance. *Equality, Diversity and Inclusion: An International Journal*, *33*(1), 73-96.

Blatný, M. (Ed.). (2015). *Personality and well-being across the life-span*. London, UK: Palgrave Macmillan.

Blatný, M., Jelínek, M., Blížkovská, J., Klimusová, H. (2004). Personality correlates of self-esteem and life satisfaction. *Studia Psychologica, 46*(2), 97-104.

Brummett, B. H., Babyak, M. A., Williams, R. B., Barefoot, J. C., Costa, P. T. and Siegler, I. C. (2006). NEO personality domains and gender predict levels and trends in body mass index over 14 years during midlife. *Journal of research in personality*, *40*(3), 222-236.

Burns, R. A. and Machin, M. A. (2010). Identifying gender differences in the independent effects of personality and psychological well-being on two broad affect components of subjective well-being. *Personality and Individual Differences*, *48*(1), 22-27.

Campbell, A. (1976). Subjective measures of well-being. *American Psychologist, 31*, 117-124.

Clarke, P. J., Marshall, V. W., Ryff, C. D. and Wheaton, B. (2001). Measuring psychological well-being in the Canadian study of health and aging. *International Psychogeriatrics*, *13*(S1), 79-90.

Costa, P. T. and McCrae, R. R. (1980). Influence of extraversion and neuroticism on subjective well-being: Happy and unhappy people. *Journal of personality and social psychology*, *38*(4), 668-678.

Cox, K. (2003). *Individual workload perception scale user's manual.* Kansas City, MO: Children's Mercy Hospitals and Clinics.

Dearborn, J. L., Knopman, D., Sharrett, A. R., Schneider, A., Jack, J. C., Coker, L. H., et al., (2014). The metabolic syndrome and cognitive decline in the Atherosclerosis Risk in Communities Study (ARIC). *Dementia and Geriatric Cognitive Disorders*, *38*, 337-346.

DeNeve, K. and Cooper, H. (1998). The happy personality: A meta-analysis of 137 personality traits and subjective well-being. *Psychological Bulletin*, *124*(2), 197-229.

Dermody, S. S., Wright, A. G., Cheong, J., Miller, K. G., Muldoon, M. F., Flory, J. D., ... and Manuck, S. B. (2015). Personality correlates of midlife cardiometabolic risk: The explanatory role of higher-order factors of the Five-Factor Model. *Journal of Personality*. DOI: 10.1111/jopy.12216.

Diener, E. (1984). Subjective well-being. *Psychological Bulletin, 95*(3), 542-575.

Diener, E. D., Emmons, R. A., Larsen, R. J. and Griffin, S. (1985). The satisfaction with life scale. *Journal of personality assessment*, *49*(1), 71-75.

Diener, E., Larsen, R. J. and Emmons, R. A. (1984). Person×Situation interactions: Choice of situations and congruence response models. *Journal of personality and social psychology*, *47*(3), 580-592.

Diener, E., Sandvik, E. D., Pavot, W. and Fujita, F. (1992). Extraversion and subjective well-being in a US national probability sample. *Journal of research in personality*, *26*(3), 205-215.

Diener, E., Suh, E. M., Lucas, R. E., Smith, H. L. (1999). Subjective well-being: Three decades of progress. *Psychological Bulletin*, *125*(2), 276-302.

Diener, E., Wirtz, D., Tov, W., Kim-Prieto, C., Choi, D. W., Oishi, S. and Biswas-Diener, R. (2010). New well-being measures: Short scales to assess flourishing and positive and negative feelings. *Social Indicators Research*, *97*(2), 143-156.

Di Fabio, A. (2014). Intrapreneurial Self-Capital: A new construct for the 21st century. *Journal of Employment Counseling*, *51*, 98-111.

Di Fabio, A. and Blustein, D. L. (2010). Emotional intelligence and decisional conflict styles: Some empirical evidence among Italian high school students. *Journal of Career Assessment*, *18*(1), 71-81.

Di Fabio, A. and Kenny, M. E. (2012a). Emotional intelligence and perceived social support among Italian high school students. *Journal of Career Development*, *39*, 461-475.

Di Fabio, A. and Kenny, M. E. (2012b). The contribution of emotional intelligence to decisional styles among Italian high school students. *Journal of Career Assessment*, *20*, 404-414.

Di Fabio, A. and Kenny, M. E. (2015). The contributions of emotional intelligence and social support for adaptive career progress among Italian youth. *Journal of Career Development*, *42*, 48-49.

Di Fabio, A. and Kenny, E. M. (2016). From decent work to decent lives: Positive Self and Relational Management (PS&RM) in the 21st century. In A. Di Fabio and D. L. Blustein (Eds.), "From meaning of working to meaningful lives: The challenges of expanding decent work". Research topic in *Frontiers in Psychology. Section Organizational Psychology.*

Di Fabio, A., Kenny, M. E. and Claudius, M. (in press). Preventing distress and promoting psychological well-being in uncertain times through career management intervention. In M. Israelashvili and J. L. Romano (Eds.), *Cambridge handbook of international prevention science.* Cambridge: Cambridge University Press.

Di Fabio, A. and Palazzeschi, L. (2015). Hedonic and eudaimonic well-being: The role of resilience beyond fluid intelligence and personality traits. *Frontiers in Psychology*, *6*, 1367.

Emmons, R. A. and Diener, E. (1985). Personality correlates of subjective well-being. *Personality and Social Psychology Bulletin*, *11*(1), 89-97.

Engel, G. L. (1977). The need for a new medical model: A challenge for biomedicine. *Science*, *196*(4286), 129-136.

Feng, L., Chong, M. S., Lim, W. S., Lee, T. S., Collinson, S. L., Yap, P., et al., (2013). Metabolic syndrome and amnestic mild cognitive impairment: Singapore Longitudinal Ageing Study-2 findings. *Journal of Alzheimer's Disease*, *34*, 649-657.

Friedman, H. S. and Kern, M. L. (2014). Personality, well-being, and health. *Psychology*, *65*(1), 719-742.

Gale, C. R., Booth, T., Mõttus, R., Kuh, D. and Deary, I. J. (2013). Neuroticism and Extraversion in youth predict mental wellbeing and life satisfaction 40 years later. *Journal of research in personality*, *47*(6), 687-697.

Gannon, N. and Ranzijn, R. (2005). Does emotional intelligence predict unique variance in life satisfaction beyond IQ and personality? *Personality and Individual Differences*, *38*(6), 1353-1364.

Garcia, D. (2011). Two models of personality and well-being among adolescents. *Personality and Individual Differences*, *50*(8), 1208-1212.

Ghiselli, E. E. and Barthol, R. P. (1953). The validity of personality inventories in the selection of employees. *Journal of Applied Psychology*, *37*(1), 18-20.

Grekin, E. R., Sher, K. J. and Wood, P. K. (2006). Personality and substance dependence symptoms: Modeling substance-specific traits. *Psychology of Addictive Behaviors*, *20*(4), 415-424.

Guion, R. M. and Gottier, R. F. (1965). Validity of personality measures in personnel selection. *Personnel psychology*, *18*(2), 135-164.

Hage, S. M., Romano, J. L., Conyne, R. K., Kenny, M., Matthews, C., Schwartz, J. P. and Waldo, M. (2007). Best practice guidelines on prevention practice, research, training, and social advocacy for psychologists. *The Counseling Psychologist*, *35*(4), 493-566.

Hampson, S. E., Goldberg, L. R., Vogt, T. M. and Dubanoski, J. P. (2006). Forty years on: Teachers' assessments of children's personality traits predict self-reported health behaviors and outcomes at midlife. *Health psychology*, *25*(1), 57.

Hayes, N. and Joseph, S. (2003). Big 5 correlates of three measures of subjective well-being. *Personality and Individual differences*, *34*(4), 723-727.

Hird, S. (2003). *What is wellbeing? A brief review of current literature and concepts*. Retrieved from http://www.phis.org.uk/doc.pl?file=pdf/What%20is%20wellbeing % 202.doc.

Hogan, J. and Holland, B. (2003). Using theory to evaluate personality and job-performance relations: A socioanalytic perspective. *Journal of Applied Psychology*, *88*(1), 100-112.

Hopwood, C. J., Morey, L. C., Skodol, A. E., Stout, R. L., Yen, S., Ansell, E. B. and McGlashan, T. H. (2007). Five-factor model personality traits associated with alcohol-related diagnoses in a clinical sample. *Journal of Studies on Alcohol and Drugs*, *68*(3), 455-460.

Horwood, L. J. and Fergusson, D. M. (1986). Neuroticism, depression and life events: A structural equation model. *Social Psychiatry*, *21*(2), 63-71.

Hough, L. M. (1992). The 'Big Five' personality variables—construct confusion: Description versus prediction. *Human performance*, *5*(1-2), 139-155.

Hurtz, G. M. and Donovan, J. J. (2000). Personality and job performance: The Big Five revisited. *Journal of Applied Psychology*, *85*(6), 869-879.

Idler, E. L. and Benyamini, Y. (1997). Self-rated health and mortality: a review of twenty-seven community studies. *Journal of health and social behavior*, 21-37.

Judge, T. A. and Erez, A. (2007). Interaction and intersection: The constellation of emotional stability and extraversion in predicting performance. *Personnel Psychology*, *60*(3), 573-596.

Judge, T. A., Heller, D. and Mount, M. K. (2002). Five-factor model of personality and job satisfaction: A meta-analysis. *Journal of applied psychology*, *87*(3), 530-541.

Judge, T. and Zapata, C. (2014). The person-situation debate revisited: Effect of situation strength and trait activation on the validity of the big five personality traits in predicting job performance. *Academy of Management Journal*, 1149-1179.

Kahneman, D., Diener, E. and Schwarz, N. (Eds.). (1999). *Well-being: Foundations of hedonic psychology*. New York, NY: Russell Sage Foundation.

Kashdan, T. B., Vetter, C. J. and Collins, R. L. (2005). Substance use in young adults: Associations with personality and gender. *Addictive behaviors*, *30*(2), 259-269.

Kendler, K. S., Gardner, C. O. and Prescott, C. A. (2003a). Personality and the experience of environmental adversity. *Psychological medicine*, *33*(07), 1193-1202.

Kendler, K. S., Prescott, C. A., Myers, J. and Neale, M. C. (2003b). The structure of genetic and environmental risk factors for common psychiatric and substance use disorders in men and women. *Archives of general psychiatry*, *60*(9), 929-937.

Kenny, M. E. and Hage, S. M. (2009). The next frontier: Prevention as an instrument of social justice. *The Journal of Primary Prevention*, *30*, 1-10.

Koffel, E., Kramer, M. D., Arbisi, P. A., Erbes, C. R., Kaler, M. and Polusny, M. A. (2016). Personality traits and combat exposure as predictors of psychopathology over time. *Psychological medicine*, *46*(01), 209-220.

Kokko, K., Tolvanen, A. and Pulkkinen, L. (2013). Associations between personality traits and psychological well-being across time in middle adulthood. *Journal of Research in Personality*, *47*(6), 748-756.

Krueger, R. F. (1999). Personality traits in late adolescence predict mental disorders in early adulthood: A perspective-epidemiological study. *Journal of Personality*, *67*(1), 39-65.

Krueger, R. F., Caspi, A., Moffitt, T. E., Silva, P. A. and McGee, R. (1996). Personality traits are differentially linked to mental disorders: A multitrait-multidiagnosis study of an adolescent birth cohort. *Journal of abnormal psychology*, *105*(3), 299-312.

Krueger, R. F., Hicks, B. M., Patrick, C. J., Carlson, S. R., Iacono, W. G. and McGue, M. (2002). Etiologic connections among substance dependence, antisocial behavior and personality: Modeling the externalizing spectrum. *Journal of abnormal psychology*, *111*(3), 411-424.

Krueger, R. F., Markon, K. E., Patrick, C. J., Benning, S. D. and Kramer, M. D. (2007). Linking antisocial behavior, substance use, and personality: an integrative quantitative model of the adult externalizing spectrum. *Journal of abnormal psychology*, *116*(4), 645-666.

Krueger, R. F., McGue, M. and Iacono, W. G. (2001). The higher-order structure of common DSM mental disorders: Internalization, externalization, and their connections to personality. *Personality and Individual Differences*, *30*(7), 1245-1259.

Lahey, B. B. (2009). Public health significance of neuroticism. *American Psychologist*, *64*(4), 241-256.

Längle, A., Orgler, C. and Kundi, M. (2003). The Existence Scale: A new approach to assess the ability to find personal meaning in life and to reach existential fulfillment. *European Psychotherapy*, *4*(1), 135-151.

Larkins, J. M. and Sher, K. J. (2006). Family history of alcoholism and the stability of personality in young adulthood. *Psychology of Addictive Behaviors*, *20*(4), 471-477.

Le, H., Oh, I. S., Robbins, S. B., Ilies, R., Holland, E. and Westrick, P. (2011). Too much of a good thing: Curvilinear relationships between personality traits and job performance. *Journal of Applied Psychology*, *96*(1), 113-133.

Letzring, T. D., Edmonds, G. W. and Hampson, S. E. (2014). Personality change at mid-life is associated with changes in self-rated health: Evidence from the Hawaii Personality and Health Cohort. *Personality and individual differences*, *58*, 60-64.

Littlefield, A. K., Sher, K. J. and Wood, P. K. (2009). Is "maturing out" of problematic alcohol involvement related to personality change? *Journal of abnormal psychology*, *118*(2), 360-374.

Luo, J. and Roberts, B. W. (2015). Concurrent and longitudinal relations among conscientiousness, stress, and self-perceived physical health. *Journal of Research in Personality*, *59*, 93-103.

Magee, C. A., Heaven, P. C. and Miller, L. M. (2013). Personality Change Predicts Self-Reported Mental and Physical Health. *Journal of personality*, *81*(3), 324-334.

Malouff, J. M., Thorsteinsson, E. B. and Schutte, N. S. (2006). The five-factor model of personality and smoking: A meta-analysis. *Journal of Drug Education*, *36*(1), 47-58.

Markon, K. E. (2010). Modeling psychopathology structure: A symptom-level analysis of Axis I and II disorders. *Psychological Medicine*, *40*, 273-288.

McCrae, R. R. and Costa Jr, P. T. (1999). A five-factor theory of personality. *Handbook of personality: Theory and research*, *2*, 139-153.

Miller, J. D., Lynam, D. R., Rolland, J. P., De Fruyt, F., Reynolds, S. K., Pham-Scottez, A., Bgby, R. M. (2008). Scoring the DSM-IV personality disorders using the Five-Factor Model: Development and validation of normative scores for North American, French and Dutch-Flemish samples. *Journal of Personality Disorders*, *25*(5), 433-450.

Miller, J. D., Pilkonis, P. A. and Mulvey, E. P. (2006). Treatment utilization and satisfaction: Examining the contributions of axis II psychopathology and the five-factor model of personality. *Journal of personality disorders*, *20*(4), 369-387.

Miller, J. D., Zeichner, A. and Wilson, L. F. (2012). Personality correlates of aggression evidence from measures of the Five-Factor Model, UPPS model of impulsivity, and BIS/BAS. *Journal of Interpersonal Violence*, *27*(14), 2903-2919.

Mommersteeg, P. M., Herr, R., Zijlstra, W. P., Schneider, S. and Pouwer, F. (2012). Higher levels of psychological distress are associated with a higher risk of incident diabetes during 18 year follow-up: Results from the British household panel survey. *BMC public health*, *12*(1), 1109.

Mommersteeg, P. and Pouwer, F. (2012). Personality as a risk factor for the metabolic syndrome: A systematic review. *Journal of Psychosomatic Research*, *73*, 326-333.

Morgan, J. and Farsides, T. (2009). Measuring meaning in life. *Journal of happiness Studies*, *10*(2), 197-214.

Morgeson, F. P. and Humphrey, S. E. (2006). The Work Design Questionnaire (WDQ): Developing and validating a comprehensive measure for assessing job design and the nature of work. *Journal of applied psychology*, *91*(6), 1321-1339.

Mount, M. K., Barrick, M. R. and Stewart, G. L. (1998). Five-factor model of personality and performance in jobs involving interpersonal interactions. *Human performance*, *11*(2-3), 145-165.

Mroczek, D. K., Spiro, A. and Turiano, N. A. (2009). Do health behaviors explain the effect of neuroticism on mortality? Longitudinal findings from the VA Normative Aging Study. *Journal of Research in Personality*, *43*(4), 653-659.

Munafo, M. R., Zetteler, J. I. and Clark, T. G. (2007). Personality and smoking status: A meta-analysis. *Nicotine and Tobacco Research*, *9*(3), 405-413.

Naragon-Gainey, K., Watson, D. and Markon, K. E. (2009). Differential relations of depression and social anxiety symptoms to the facets of extraversion/positive emotionality. *Journal of abnormal psychology*, *118*(2), 299-310.

National Institutes of Health (1998). *NHLBI Obesity education initiative expert panel on the identification, evaluation, and treatment of obesity in adults (US). Clinical guidelines on the identification, evaluation, and treatment of overweight and obesity in adults: The evidence report.* Bethesda (MD): National Heart, Lung, and Blood Institute. Retrieved from: http://www.ncbi.nlm.nih.gov/books/NBK2003/

Nikolaou, I. (2003). Fitting the person to the organisation: Examining the personality-job performance relationship from a new perspective. *Journal of Managerial Psychology*, *18*(7), 639-648.

Olesen, M. H., Thomsen, D. K. and O'Toole, M. S. (2015). Subjective well-being: Above neuroticism and extraversion, autonomy motivation matters. *Personality and Individual Differences*, *77*, 45-49.

Ozer, D. J. and Benet-Martinez, V. (2006). Personality and the prediction of consequential outcomes. *Annual Review of Psychology*, *57*, 401-421.

Pavot, W., Diener, E. and Fujita, F. (1990). Extraversion and happiness. *Personality and individual differences*, *11*(12), 1299-1306.

Pavot, W. and Diener, E. (2011). Personality and Happiness. *The Wiley-Blackwell handbook of individual differences*, 699-717.

Raja, U. and Johns, G. (2010). The joint effects of personality and job scope on in-role performance, citizenship behaviors, and creativity. *Human relations*, 1-25.

Rausch, J. L., Nichinson, R., Lamke, C. and Matloff, J. (1990). Influence of negative affect on smoking cessation treatment outcome: A pilot study. *British journal of addiction*, *85*(7), 929-933.

Ross, K., Martin, T., Chen, E. and Miller, G. E. (2011). Social encounters in daily life and two-year changes in metabolic risk factors in young women. *Development and Psychopathology*, *23*, 897-906.

Rothmann, S. and Coetzer, E. P. (2003). The big five personality dimensions and job performance. *SA Journal of Industrial Psychology*, *29*(1), 68-74.

Ryan, R. M. and Deci, E. L. (2001). On happiness and human potentials: A review of research on hedonic and eudaimonic well-being. *Annual review of psychology*, *52*(1), 141-166.

Ryff, C. D. (1989a). Happiness is everything, or is it? Explorations on the meaning of psychological well-being. *Journal of personality and social psychology*, *57*(6), 1069.

Ryff, C. D. and Singer, B. H. (2008). Know thyself and become what you are: A eudaimonic approach to psychological well-being. *Journal of happiness studies*, *9*(1), 13-39.

Sadeh, N., Miller, M. W., Wolf, E. J. and Harkness, K. L. (2015). Negative emotionality and disconstraint influence PTSD symptom course via exposure to new major adverse life events. *Journal of anxiety disorders*, *31*, 20-27.

Salgado, J. F. (2003). Predicting job performance using FFM and non-FFM personality measures. *Journal of Occupational and Organizational Psychology*, *76*(3), 323-346.

Schimmack, U., Diener, E. and Oishi, S. (2002). Life-satisfaction is a momentary judgment and a stable personality characteristic: The use of chronically accessible and stable sources. *Journal of personality*, *70*(3), 345-384.

Schimmack, U., Oishi, S., Furr, R. M. and Funder, D. C. (2004). Personality and life satisfaction: A facet-level analysis. *Personality and social psychology bulletin*, *30*(8), 1062-1075.

Schmitt, N., Gooding, R. Z., Noe, R. A. and Kirsch, M. (1984). Meta-analysis of validity studies published between 1964 and 1982 and the investigation of study characteristics. *Personnel Psychology*, *37*, 407-422.

Schmutte, P. S. and Ryff, C. D. (1997). Personality and well-being: Reexamining methods and meanings. *Journal of Personality and Social Psychology*, *73*(3), 549-559.

Singh, A. L. and Waldman, I. D. (2010). The etiology of associations between negative emotionality and childhood externalizing disorders. *Journal of Abnormal Psychology*, *119*(2), 376-388.

Skyrme, P., Wilkinson, L., Abraham, J. D. and Morrison, J. D. (2005). Using personality to predict outbound call center job performance. *Applied HRM Research*, *10*(2), 89-98.

Slade, T. I. M. and Watson, D. (2006). The structure of common DSM-IV and ICD-10 mental disorders in the Australian general population. *Psychological medicine*, *36*(11), 1593-1600.

Smillie, L. D., Yeo, G. B., Furnham, A. F. and Jackson, C. J. (2006). Benefits of all work and no play: The relationship between neuroticism and performance as a function of resource allocation. *Journal of Applied Psychology*, *91*(1), 139-155.

Smith, T. W. (2006). Personality as risk and resilience in physical health. *Current directions in psychological science*, *15*(5), 227-231.

Soto, C. J. (2015). Is Happiness Good for Your Personality? Concurrent and Prospective Relations of the Big Five With Subjective Well-Being. *Journal of personality*, *83*(1), 45-55.

Steel, P., Schmidt, J. and Shultz, J. (2008). Refining the relationship between personality and subjective well-being. *Psychological bulletin*, *134*(1), 138-161.

Sutin, A. R., Costa Jr, P. T., Uda, M., Ferrucci, L., Schlessinger, D. and Terracciano, A. (2010). Personality and metabolic syndrome. *Age*, *32*(4), 513-519.

Sutin, A. R., Ferrucci, L., Zonderman, A. B. and Terracciano, A. (2011). Personality and obesity across the adult life span. *Journal of personality and social psychology*, *101*(3), 579-592.

Sutin, A. R. and Terracciano, A. (2015). Five-Factor Model Personality Traits and the objective and subjective experience of body weight. *Journal of personality*, *84*(1), 102-112.

Takahashi, Y., Edmonds, G. W., Jackson, J. J. and Roberts, B. W. (2013). Longitudinal correlated changes in conscientiousness, preventative health-related behaviors, and self-perceived physical health. *Journal of personality*, *81*(4), 417-427.

Terracciano, A., Löckenhoff, C. E., Crum, R. M., Bienvenu, O. J. and Costa, P. T. (2008). Five-Factor Model personality profiles of drug users. *Bmc Psychiatry*, *8*(1), 22.

Tett, R. P., Jackson, D. N. and Rothstein, M. (1991). Personality measures as predictors of job performance: A meta-analytic review. *Personnel psychology*, *44*(4), 703-742.

Trull, T. J. and Sher, K. J. (1994). Relationship between the five-factor model of personality and Axis I disorders in a nonclinical sample. *Journal of abnormal psychology*, *103*(2), 350-360.

Trull, T. J. and Durrett, C. A. (2005). Categorical and dimensional models of personality disorder. *Annual Review in Clinical Psychology*, *1*, 355-380.

Turiano, N. A., Whiteman, S. D., Hampson, S. E., Roberts, B. W. and Mroczek, D. K. (2012). Personality and substance use in midlife: Conscientiousness as a moderator and the effects of trait change. *Journal of research in personality*, *46*(3), 295-305.

Uppal, N., Mishra, S. K. and Vohra, N. (2014). Prior related work experience and job performance: Role of personality. *International Journal of Selection and Assessment*, *22*(1), 39-51.

van Reedt Dortland, A. K., Giltay, E. J., Van Veen, T., Zitman, F. G. and Penninx, B. W. (2012). Personality traits and childhood trauma as correlates of metabolic risk factors: The Netherlands Study of Depression and Anxiety (NESDA). *Progress in Neuro-Psychopharmacology and Biological Psychiatry*, *36*(1), 85-91.

Villieux, A., Sovet, L., Jung, S. C. and Guilbert, L. (2016). Psychological flourishing: Validation of the French version of the Flourishing Scale and exploration of its relationships with personality traits. *Personality and Individual Differences*, *88*, 1-5.

Waterman, A. S., Schwartz, S. J., Zamboanga, B. L., Ravert, R. D., Williams, M. K., Bede Agocha, V., Kim, S. Y., and Brent Donnellan, M. (2010). The Questionnaire for Eudaimonic Well-Being: Psychometric properties, demographic comparisons, and evidence of validity. *The Journal of Positive Psychology*, *5*(1), 41-61.

Watson, D. (2005). Rethinking the mood and anxiety disorders: A quantitative hierarchical model for DSM-V. *Journal of abnormal psychology*, *114*(4), 522-536.

Watson, D. (2009). Differentiating the mood and anxiety disorders: A quadripartite model. *Annual Review of Clinical Psychology*, *5*, 221-247.

Watson, D., Clark, L. A. and Tellegen, A. (1988). Development and validation of brief measures of positive and negative affect: The PANAS scales. *Journal of personality and social psychology*, *54*(6), 1063-1070.

Watson, D., Gamez, W. and Simms, L. J. (2005). Basic dimensions of temperament and their relation to anxiety and depression: A symptom-based perspective. *Journal of Research in Personality*, *39*(1), 46-66.

Watson, D. and Naragon-Gainey, K. (2010). On the specificity of positive emotional dysfunction in psychopathology: Evidence from the mood and anxiety disorders and schizophrenia/schizotypy. *Clinical psychology review*, *30*(7), 839-848.

Wells, A. and Matthews, G. (1994). *Attentions and emotion: A clinical perspective*. Hove, UK: Erlbaum.

Wood, A. M., Linley, P. A., Maltby, J., Baliousis, M. and Joseph, S. (2008). The authentic personality: A theoretical and empirical conceptualization and the development of the Authenticity Scale. *Journal of Counseling Psychology*, *55*(3), 385.

Yang, C. L. and Hwang, M. (2014). Personality traits and simultaneous reciprocal influences between job performance and job satisfaction. *Chinese Management Studies*, *8*(1), 6-26.

Zimmerman, R. D., Triana, M. D. C. and Barrick, M. R. (2010). Predictive criterion-related validity of observer ratings of personality and job-related competencies using multiple raters and multiple performance criteria. *Human Performance*, *23*(4), 361-378.

In: Neuroticism
Editor: Annamaria Di Fabio

ISBN: 978-1-63485-323-1

Chapter 2

The Bad Performance of Neurotic Employees: A Matter of Job Satisfaction and Workaholism

Greta Mazzetti[1,*], Rita Chiesa[2], Michela Vignoli[1] and Marco Depolo[2]

[1]Department of Education Studies, University of Bologna, Bologna, Italy
[2]Department of Psychology, University of Bologna, Bologna, Italy

Abstract

The present chapter investigates the role of neuroticism as antecedent of job performance. While the direct effect of neuroticism on job performance is well established, little attention was dedicated to the indirect effects. In the current research it was hypothesized that the effect of neuroticism on job performance would be mediated by job satisfaction and that the relationship between job satisfaction and job performance would be moderated by workaholism. The findings confirmed that neuroticism decreased the level of job performance through the negative effect on job satisfaction. Even more interesting is the role played by workaholism. Indeed, employees with high level of job satisfaction exhibited a better job performance in case of low workaholism, while employees characterized by low level of job satisfaction and high workaholism reported the lowest levels of job performance. These results provide new directions for organizational interventions aimed to prevent the impact of neuroticism on job performance through the enhancement of job satisfaction. Moreover, they indicate the relevance of intervention strategies to prevent and treat workaholism.

* Corresponding author: Greta Mazzetti, e-mail: greta.mazzetti3@unibo.it.

INTRODUCTION

The Association between Neuroticism and Job Performance

During the last three decades the relevance of personality variables to industrial, work and organizational (IWO) psychology has been extensively acknowledged and inspired a vast amount of research on their impact on different employment outcomes (Hough and Ones, 2001). Personality variables are now broadly recognized as noteworthy predictors of individual attitudes and behaviour as well as team and organizational functioning.

In particular, one of the most intensive investigations of personality variables in organizational settings entails the domain of job performance. Indeed, although research failed to find systematic and cross-occupational strong correlations between measures of personality and job performance ratings, there has been a growing consensus regarding the value of some personality variables for predicting this specific job outcome (Berry, Kim, Wang, Thompson, and Mobley, 2013; Chiaburu, Oh, Berry, Li, and Gardner, 2011). Using the Five Factor Model of personality, Barrick, Mount and Judge (2001) found that conscientiousness is a valid predictor across performance measures in different occupational groups, while emotional stability predicts performance measures in more specific areas (e.g., teamwork).

Based on the existing literature, the present chapter is designed to explore the role of neuroticism as antecedent of job performance.

Neuroticism is defined as a dimension of temperament characterized by great stress reactivity resulting in recurrent experiences of negative emotions such as anxiety, fear, irritability, anger, and sadness (Barlow, Ellard, Sauer-Zavala, Bullis, and Carl, 2014). This negative affectivity combines with a pervasive perception of the surrounding environment as a dangerous and threatening place and persistent beliefs of one's own failure in coping with challenging events (Barlow, Sauer-Zavala, Carl, Bullis, and Ellard, 2014). Some authors identified *volatility* and *withdrawal* as lower order traits underlying neuroticism (DeYoung and Gray, 2009). Volatility entails to high levels of impulsivity and hostility, whereas withdrawal entails a permanent state of anxiety, depressive outlook, and self-consciousness.

Neuroticism is strongly related to harmful consequences in individuals' mental health, including comorbidity (Krueger and Markon, 2006; Shipley, Weiss, Der, Taylor and Deary, 2007; Weinstock and Whisman, 2006). Moreover, neuroticism is associated with different physical problems such as cardiovascular disease, asthma, and irritable bowel syndrome (Smith and MacKenzie, 2006; Suls and Bunde, 2005). With regards to the work domain, the permanent focus on negative affect entailed by neuroticism may divert employees from tasks accomplishment and consequently it results in greater levels of time-related work strain (Wayne, Musisca, and Fleeson, 2004). Consequently, employees characterized by high levels of neuroticism experience greater amounts of stress regardless of actual workload (Conard and Matthews, 2008). In addition, neuroticism is linked to emotional exhaustion (Wright and Staw, 1999), workplace deviance (Berry, Ones, and Sackett, 2007), counterproductive work behaviours (Berry, Carpenter, and Barratt, 2012), and different facets of performance motivation (Judge and Ilies, 2002). Concerning the association between neuroticism and job performance, emotional stability (i.e., as the opposite of neuroticism entailing security and calm) has demonstrated consistent relations with job performance ratings (Fullarton, Fuller-Tyszkiewicz, and von Treuer, 2014; Hogan and Holland, 2003; Salgado, 1997). For instance, the positive association between emotional exhaustion and job performance was found to be more pronounced in team environments (Mount, Barrick, and Stewart, 1998). Hence, the calm and pleasant attitude exhibited by low neurotic employees is likely to increase the success of the work team, thus resulting in an enhanced job performance. More recently, empirical findings suggest that the key facets of neuroticism – *volatility* and *withdrawal* – may predict different aspects of performance (DeYoung and Gray, 2009). Hence, employees reporting high levels of withdrawal are prone to experience negative affect that threatens the likelihood to complete job tasks successfully, thus their task performance is impaired.

The Mediation Role of Job Satisfaction

Somewhat curiously, despite a great deal of research on the direct link between neuroticism and job performance, previous studies failed to explore the indirect effects of this personality dimension on employees' performance. This chapter was interested in investigating how neuroticism modulates job performance through the mediation of job satisfaction.

Job satisfaction is conceptualized as an overall evaluative judgement regarding one's job that is caused by affective experiences on the job and beliefs about it (Brief, 1998; Brief and Weiss, 2002; Weiss, 2002). Considerable attention was given to the effect of neuroticism on job satisfaction. For instance, Judge, Heller and Mount (2002) found that low neuroticism is more strongly correlated to job satisfaction than all of the other personality traits in the five-factor model. Starting from the Theory of Core Self-Evaluation, neuroticism and emotional stability have been considered as opposite poles of the same continuum (Judge and Bono, 2001; Judge et al., 2002). Accordingly, neurotic employees tend to perceive the workplace more negatively, even if neuroticism displayed the lowest correlation with both satisfaction and performance in comparison to the other core self-evaluation traits (self-esteem, generalized self-efficacy, and locus of control). More recently, Cleare (2013) found that neuroticism was the core self-evaluation trait showing the highest correlation coefficient with overall score on job satisfaction although it explained a quite low percentage of variance. Judge and Larsen (2001) suggested that individuals with high level of neuroticism are likely to socially withdraw in response to dissatisfying job conditions allowing situations to get worse, while people with low level of neuroticism respond to the negative situation by proactively attempting to identify the source of the dissatisfaction and to improve the experience in the workplace.

Thus, neuroticism demonstrated to influence both job satisfaction and performance, but how to explain the relationship between job satisfaction and performance? This is a controversial issue. Reviewing past research, Judge and colleagues (2001) found that most of studies that included satisfaction and job performance treat them as separate variables that have no direct relationship to one another (Greenberger, Strasser, Cummings, and Dunham, 1989). However, in the past decades, there are an amount of studies that focused on the effect of job performance on satisfaction (Brown, Cron, and Leigh, 1993; MacKenzie, Podsakoff, and Ahearne, 1998). More recently, scholars tend to consider job satisfaction as an antecedent of job performance (Schleicher, Smith, Casper, Watt, and Greguras, 2015; Ziegler, Hagen, and Diehl, 2012). Indeed, they conceptualized job satisfaction as an individual's attitude toward his or her job and consequently, in line with Fishbein and Ajzen (1975), they assumed that job satisfaction should be predictive of job behaviours, measured as job performance. Hence, the results of previous studies lead us to formulate the following hypothesis:

Hypothesis 1. Neuroticism is related to job performance through the mediation of job satisfaction.

Workaholism and Job Performance

Following the suggestion of Judge et al., (2001), most recent research has incorporated moderating variables when connecting job performance to satisfaction (Schleicher et al., 2015; Ziegler et al., 2012).

As previously stated, work and organizational psychology now recognizes personality variables and behavioural styles as significant predictors of individual attitudes and performance in work settings (Judge, Klinger, Simon, and Yang, 2008). Among these factors, workaholism has been extensively investigated as an individual risk factor essentially entailing an overwhelming compulsion to work that propels employees to invest an excessive amount of time and energy to their occupation. Accordingly, Schaufeli, Taris, and Bakker (2008) defined workaholism as the combination of two underlying dimensions: working excessively and working compulsively. The behavioural component of the construct – *working excessively* – indicates that workaholics work beyond what would be reasonably expected to fulfil organizational or economic requirements; whereas the cognitive dimension of the construct – *working compulsively* – implies that workaholics are obsessed with their work and persistently think about work. This obsession with work is related to adverse consequences on individual well-being, such as higher levels of emotional exhaustion (Kubota et al., 2011) and health complaints (Andreassen, Hetland, Molde, and Pallesen, 2011). Moreover, given the extraordinary amount of time spent working, workaholics have insufficient time for recovery and have poor quality social relationship outside work (Bakker, Demerouti, Oerlemans, and Sonnentag, 2013), they report considerable levels of work-home conflict (Schaufeli, Shimazu, and Taris, 2009), and a higher occurrence of marital problems (Robinson, Flowers, and Carroll, 2001). In addition, a large body of empirical evidence points out that workaholism has a detrimental impact on the work domain (Ng, Sorensen, and Feldman, 2007).

At first glance, workaholics may appear to be an advantage for their organization in terms of their commitment and effort. The most evident feature of workaholics is their tendency to exhibit a great level of dedication to their jobs and to devote a greater amount of time to this activity as compared to their colleagues (Burke and Fiksenbaum, 2009). In addition, workaholic employees cultivate irrational beliefs regarding performance demands, so they set unattainable high performance standards and depend on social approval in the workplace (Van Wijhe, Peeters, and Schaufeli, 2013). Actually, these employees often make their work more complex than necessary, so they compromise organizational goals in subtle ways in order to maintain or increase their need for more work: in this sense, workaholic people work hard rather than smart (Schaufeli, Taris, and Bakker, 2006). Workaholism is related to negative emotions during and after carrying out one's job – guilt or feeling rushed – and frustration and agitation when prevented from engaging in this activity. Consequently, workaholics invest part of their cognitive resources in dealing with these negative emotions, thus exhibiting an impaired job performance (Gorgievski and Bakker, 2010).

Moreover, workaholism is positively related to psychophysical strain which, in turn, has a detrimental impact on one's job performance (Falco et al., 2013). To be specific, the tendency to devote an excessive amount of time to work displayed by workaholic employees entails having insufficient opportunity for recovery and the subsequent state of psychophysical strain has a negative impact on the quality of their performance at work. This evidence is in line with the Effort-Recovery (E-R) model (Meijman and Mulder, 1998), which posits that spending efforts during work activities leads to load reactions which involve physiological, behavioural and subjective correlates. If adequate possibilities for recovery are available these reactions are completely reversible, essentially because fatigue and other effects of stressful situations are reduced. In contrast, when recovery cannot occur, load reactions accumulate and may result in longer-term negative consequences, such as impaired well-being and health problems, that may even become irreversible (Sonnentag and Zijlstra, 2006). Additionally, the attitude of workaholic employees may imply a high potential for stress among co-workers, essentially due to the fact that workaholics tend to perceive their co-workers as being of lesser value than themselves to underestimate the quality of their colleagues' work if compared to their own work (Porter, 2001), and to exhibit recurrent interpersonal conflicts at work (Mudrack, 2006). The perfectionism exhibited by workaholic employees impede them to delegate tasks to other and, in turn, often have problematic relationships with their co-workers because they usually refuse to delegate tasks: in doing so, they also try to actively create more work for themselves (Taris, Schaufeli, and Verhoeven, 2005). The conflictual relationships in the workplace determine low social support and therefore an impaired job performance (Shimazu, Schaufeli, and Taris, 2010).

In view of the large amount of empirical results suggesting the presence of a negative association between workaholism and job performance, we predict that:

Hypothesis 2. In the relationship between neuroticism, job satisfaction and job performance, workaholism moderates the relationship between job satisfaction and job performance.

METHOD

Procedure

Data were collected in 2013 within an Italian company with branches all over the national territory. Employees were involved in a project aimed to investigate which personality and organisational variables could influence workaholism and work outcomes such as job performance. To this purpose, an e-mail sent by the head of the Human Resource Department provided them with a link to an online questionnaire. In the introduction to the survey participants received background information about the general aim of the study and their anonymity was emphasized and confidentiality guaranteed.

Participants

The final sample of the study included 295 employees. Most of them were female (75.4%). The mean age was 35.11 years old (*SD* = 8.67 years). Concerning educational qualification, most of the participants got a high school degree (76.9%), while 14.5% had an academic degree, 8.3% had a secondary school title and 0.3% had a post-graduate degree. Mean tenure was 5.32 (*SD* = 8.01), while employees reported a mean of 35.78 working hours per week (*SD* = 8.01).

Measures

Neuroticism has been measured through a short version of the Big Five Questionnaire (Van Emmerik, Jawahar, and Stone, 2004). The three items of the Likert scale ranged from 1 (never) to 7 (always). One example item was: "Emotions go way up and down".

Job Satisfaction was measured through a single item measure (Wanous, Reichers, and Hudy, 1997) ranged from 1 (not satisfied at all) to 5 (completely satisfied). The item is "Overall, how satisfied are you with your job?".

Job Performance was measured through one item used by Shimazu and colleagues (2010). Employees were asked to rate their overall job performance during the past four weeks on 11-point Likert scale ranging from 0 (worst possible job performance a person could have on this job) to 10 (top job performance).

Workaholism has been investigated using the 10-item Dutch Work Addiction Scale (DUWAS; Schaufeli, Bakker, Van der Heijden, and Prins, 2009). This dimension is composed by two subscales: Working Compulsively (e.g., "I feel that there's something inside me that drives me to work hard") and Working Excessively (e.g., "I seem to be in a hurry and racing against the clock"). Both subscales consisted of five items rated on a four-point frequency scale ranging from 1 "(almost) never" to 4 "(almost) always". According to the definition of workaholism as a syndrome, an overall workaholism score has been used (Schaufeli et al., 2009).

Strategy of Analysis

Preliminary, descriptive statistics, Cronbach's alpha and Pearson correlations have been computed for all the study variables. In order to investigate the study hypotheses, mediation and moderated mediation analyses have been conducted using PROCESS, a SPSS macro for bootstrapping developed by Hayes (2013). To be specific, moderated mediation effect was tested using Model 14, which corresponds to a simple mediation model with moderation of the indirect effect of X (neuroticism) on Y (job performance) through M (job satisfaction). The indirect effect of X (neuroticism) is conditional on V (workaholism) through moderation effect by V (workaholism) of the M → Y (job satisfaction → job performance). A graphical illustration of the hypothesized relationships is presented in Figure 1.

In all the analyses performed, gender, age and effective working hours reported by employees were included as covariates.

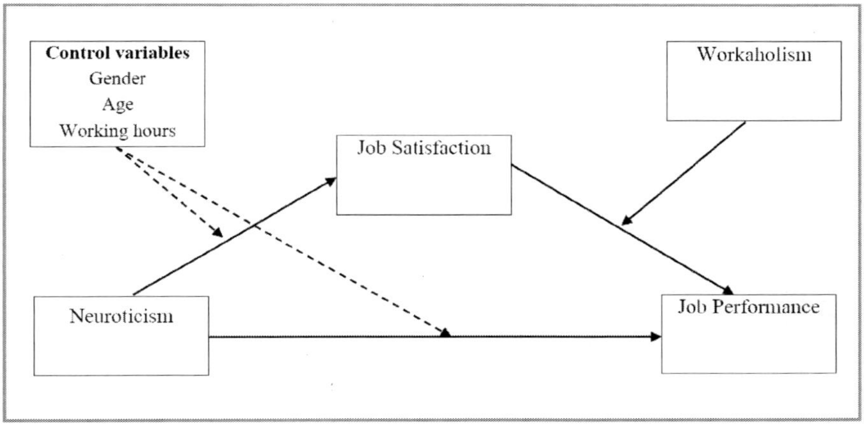

Figure 1. Model of study variables. Solid lines denote hypothesized effects. Dotted lines denote effects of control variables.

Results

In Table 1 descriptive results and Cronbach's alpha values (where applicable) of each variable has been reported. Pearson correlations results showed that neuroticism seems to not be related to any of the variables investigated (i.e., job satisfaction, workaholism and job performance). Also job performance doesn't report a significant correlation with the variables under investigation. Furthermore, job satisfaction shows a positive correlation with workaholism.

Table 1. Means, standard deviations, Pearson coefficients (Cronbach's Alpha)

	M; %	*SD*	1	2	3	4	5	6	7
1. Gender[1]	24.60	-	-						
2. Age	35.11	8.67	.06	-					
3. Working hours	35.78	8.01	$-.21^{***}$	.01	-				
4. Neuroticism	3.18	1.18	.07	.03	.08	(.79)			
5. Job Satisfaction	3.97	.80	.06	-.01	.05	-.09	-		
6. Workaholism	7.24	1.41	-.07	.11	$.14^{*}$	-.09	$.18^{**}$	(.67)	
7. Job performance	2.42	.43	.00	-.10	$.24^{*}$	.05	-.09	.04	-

Notes: $^{*}p < .05$; $^{**}p < .01$; $^{***}p < .001$; [1] male.

Table 2. Direct and indirect effects of the mediation of job satisfaction between neuroticism and job performance

	Path Coefficients		Indirect Effects	
	Job Performance (JP)	Job Satisfaction (JS)	Effect	Confidence Intervals
Neuroticism (*N*)	-.10	$-.08^{*}$		
Job Satisfaction (*JS*)	$.32^{**}$	-		
Gender[1]	-.16	.14		
Age	$.02^{*}$	-.00		
Working hours	$.02^{*}$	.01		
N → JS → JP			-.03	-.07; -.00

Notes: $^{*}p < .05$; $^{**}p < .01$; [1] male. Bootstrap confidence intervals were constructed using 5000 samples; Coefficients are not standardized.

A mediation analysis has been conducted in order to investigate whether job satisfaction could mediate the relationship between neuroticism and job performance. Despite limited results provided by the correlation coefficients presented in Table 2, our analyses indicate that neuroticism is related to job performance through the mediation of job satisfaction. In other words, neuroticism impacts on job satisfaction, which in turn affects job performance, although there is no direct effect of neuroticism on job performance. Therefore, *Hypothesis 1* was supported.

Table 3. Direct effects and interaction

	Job Satisfaction	Job Performance
Neuroticism	$-.08^{*}$	-.09
Job Satisfaction	-	$.31^{**}$
Workaholism	-	.77
Job satisfaction X Workaholism	-	$-.56^{*}$
Gender[1]	.14	-.20
Age	-.00	$.02^{*}$
Working hours	.01	.02

Notes. $^{*}p < .05$; $^{**}p < .01$; [1] male; Bootstrap confidence intervals were constructed using 5000 samples; Coefficients are not standardized.

Furthermore, results of the moderated mediation hypothesis (presented in Table 3) have been confirmed (Index of moderated mediation = .05; SE = .03; Boot LLCI = .00; Boot ULCI = .14). Specifically, job satisfaction mediates the relationship between neuroticism and job performance, and there is an interaction between job satisfaction and workaholism on job performance.

In addition, as shown in Figure 2, high job satisfaction was associated with high job performance only in case of low workaholism. In other words, employees reporting high levels of job satisfaction and lower levels of workaholism reported higher levels of job performance. On the other side, employees with low job satisfaction and low workaholism reported the lowest levels of job performance.

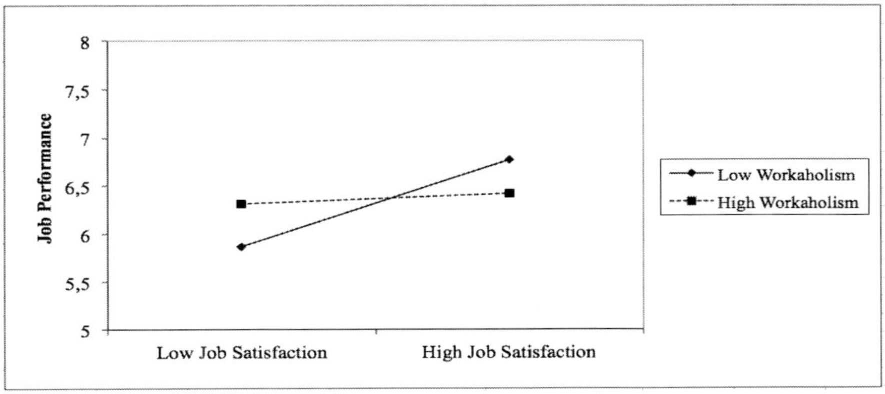

Figure 2. Interaction effect of job satisfaction and workaholism on job performance.

Conclusion

In this chapter we focused on the relevant role of neuroticism in triggering a process which leads to job performance through job satisfaction. In fact, our results showed that, despite neuroticism seems not to affect job performance directly, there is an indirect process through which neuroticism affects job satisfaction, which in turn impacts on job performance. In line with previous research (Judge and Bono, 2001; Judge et al., 2002), people with high level of neuroticism are less satisfied of their job and, consequently, have a poorer performance.

Furthermore, in this chapter we considered the role played by workaholism, in the path which leads from neuroticism to job performance. Workaholism is a construct composed by two main components, a behavioural and a cognitive one, respectively named working excessively and working compulsively (Schaufeli et al., 2008). Our results showed that high levels of job satisfaction are associated with high job performance when the level of workaholism is low. In contrast, high levels of workaholism do not engender a substantial variation in performance as the degree of job satisfaction changes. Considering workaholics as employees with ambiguous attitudes towards their jobs, this result is in line with Ziegler and colleagues (2012), who found that job satisfaction is a better predictor of job performance when individuals experience low job ambivalence. In other words, it is not enough to have satisfied employees to make certain to have good job performers too. It is fundamental to not encourage workaholic attitudes, erroneously considering them an advantage for organization in terms of their commitment and effort. Compelling strategies to successfully prevent and treat workaholism are: a) reinforcing appropriate behaviours; b) changing maladaptive thought patterns; c) involving in the intervention all work environment; d) designing comprehensive interventions able to treat both behavioural and compulsive component of workaholism (Van Wijhe, Peeters, and Schaufeli, 2010). Moreover, interventions aimed at combating workaholism should rely on three basic principles. First of all, although workaholism may be viewed by organizations as a desirable and advantageous conduct, efficacious interventions should raise the workaholics' awareness that their excessive work behaviour constitutes a problem that needs to be dealt with. In addition, the organizational and family environments should be involved in interventions aimed at reducing this obsession with work. On the one hand, it might be worthwhile for organizations and their representatives (i.e., managers, supervisors) to create an environment that does not reward compulsive work-related behaviour, on the other hand family members should also be included in prevention and treatment programs by exploring the role played in unconsciously supporting workaholism.

Lastly, interventions designed to reduce workaholism should pertain both its behavioural and cognitive dimensions. To date, preliminary evidences indicate that a cognitive-behavioural approach might represent the most efficient treatment when it comes to reduce the strong inner compulsion to work excessively hard displayed by workaholic employees (Burwell and Chen, 2002).

To conclude, the findings presented here added knowledge on how neuroticism could affect job performance and which variables are involved in this process. This is relevant especially because neuroticism is a personality trait, which cannot be easily modified. Thus it is useful to understand which factors could affect the relationship between neuroticism and job performance. Intervening on those factors (especially, enhancing job satisfaction and reducing workaholism) could then have an effect on employees' performance.

This study has some limitations that should be acknowledged. The first limitation concerns the use of self-report measures for job performance, which could be biased by subjectivity of the participants. Future studies should consider other types of measurements such as performance evaluation ratings of supervisors and other more objective organisational data concerning job performance. Moreover, two of the constructs under investigation have been assessed through single-items scales. Despite that validity of our single-item measure of job satisfaction has been widely acknowledged (Schaufeli et al., 2009), in future studies job performance could be measured with a wider scale, which could test potential different effects of neuroticism on different dimensions of job performance.

Furthermore, our study suggests that considering the role played by workaholism in the relationship between neuroticism and job performance could provide useful information in order to enhance job performance. In fact, based on our results, preventing or hindering workaholism through appropriate organizational interventions may not only help employees to better care for their health, but also contribute to enhanced levels of job performance. Although personality traits are not the main predictors of job performance, a quite impressive amount of research suggests that there is room for improve the fit between individual trait-based characteristics and job positions. One of the tools could be keeping control on factors which can modulate the relationship between personality and performance, mainly the negative ones. Our study indirectly suggests for instance that organisational climates tolerating (or even encouraging) workaholic behaviours may improve non adaptive responses to workload, creating preconditions for lower levels of job performance in people with coping styles affected by neuroticism.

References

Andreassen, C. S., Hetland, J., Molde, H. and Pallesen, S. (2011)."Workaholism" and potential outcomes in well-being and health in a cross-occupational sample. *Stress and Health*, *27*, e209–e214. doi:10.1002/smi.1366.

Bakker, A. B., Demerouti, E., Oerlemans, W. and Sonnentag, S. (2013). Workaholism and daily recovery: A day reconstruction study of leisure activities. *Journal of Organizational Behavior*, *34*(1), 87-107. doi:10.1002/job.1796.

Barlow, D. H., Ellard, K. K., Sauer-Zavala, S., Bullis, J. R. and Carl, J. R. (2014). The origins of neuroticism. *Perspectives on Psychological Science*, *9*(5), 481-496. doi:10.1177/1745691614544528.

Barlow, D. H., Sauer-Zavala, S., Carl, J. R., Bullis, J. R. and Ellard, K. K. (2014). The nature, assessment, and treatment of neuroticism: Back to the future? *Clinical Psychological Science*, *2*, 344-365. doi: 10.1177/2167702613505532.

Barrick, M. R., Mount, M. K. and Judge T. A. (2001). Personality and performance at the beginning of the new millennium: What do we know and where do we go next? *International Journal of Selection and Assessment*, *9*, 9-30. doi:10.1111/1468.2389.00160.

Berry, C. M., Carpenter, N. C. and Barratt, C. L. (2012). Do other-reports of counterproductive work behavior provide an incremental contribution over self-reports? A meta-analytic comparison. *Journal of Applied Psychology*, *97*, 613-636. doi:10.1037/a0026739.

Berry, C. M., Kim, A., Wang, Y., Thompson, R. and Mobley, W. H. (2013). Five-factor model personality measures and sex based differential prediction of performance. *Applied Psychology*, *62*, 13-43. doi:10.1111/j.1464-0597.2012.00493.x.

Berry, C. M., Ones, D. S. and Sackett, P. R. (2007). Interpersonal deviance, organizational deviance, and their common correlates: A review and meta-analysis. *Journal of Applied Psychology*, *92*, 410-424. doi:10.1037/0021-9010.92.2.410.

Brief, A. P. (1998). *Attitudes in and around organizations*. Thousand Oaks, CA: Sage.

Brief, A. P. and Weiss, H. M. (2002). Organizational behavior: Affect in the workplace. *Annual Review of Psychology*, *53*, 279-307. doi:0084-6570/02/0201-0279.

Brown, S. P., Cron, W. L. and Leigh, T. W. (1993). Do feelings of success mediate sales performance-work attitude relationships? *Journal of the Academy of Marketing Science*, *21*, 91-99.

Burke, R. J. and Fiksenbaum, L. (2009). Work motivations, satisfactions, and health among managers: Passion versus addiction. *Cross-Cultural Research: The Journal of Comparative Social Science*, *43*(4), 349-365. doi:10.1177/1069397109336990.

Burwell, R. and Chen, C. P. (2002). Applying REBT to workaholic clients. *Counselling Psychology Quarterly*, *15*(3), 219-228.

Chiaburu, D. S., Oh, I. S., Berry, C. M., Li, N. and Gardner, R. G. (2011). The five-factor model of personality traits and organizational citizenship behaviors: A meta-analysis. *Journal of Applied Psychology*, *96*, 1140-1166. doi:10.1037/a0024004.

Cleare, L. (2013). Personality as a predictor of job satisfaction: Study of the relationship between personality and job satisfaction amongst workers in the Bahamas. *Journal of Management Research*, *5*(3), 200-229. doi:10.5296/jmr.v5i3.3936.

Conard, M. A. and Matthews, R. A. (2008). Modeling the stress process: Personality eclipses dysfunctional cognitions and workload in predicting stress. *Personality and Individual Differences*, *44*, 171-181. doi:10.1016/j.paid.2007.07.023.

DeYoung, C. G. and Gray, J. R. (2009). Personality neuroscience: Explaining individual differences in affect, behavior, and cognition. In P. J. Corr and G. Matthews, (Eds.), *The Cambridge handbook of personality psychology* (pp. 323-346). New York: Cambridge University Press.

Falco, A., Girardi, D., Kravina, L., Trifiletti, E., Bartolucci, G. B., Capozza, D. and Nicola, A. (2013). The mediating role of psychophysic strain in the relationship between workaholism, job performance, and sickness absence: A longitudinal study. *Journal of Occupational and Environmental Medicine*, *55*(11), 1255-1261. doi:10.1097/JOM.0000000000000007.

Fishbein, M. and Ajzen, I. (1975). *Belief, attitude, intention, and behavior: An introduction to theory and research*. Reading, MA: Addison-Wesley.

Fullarton, C., Fuller-Tyszkiewicz, M. and Von Treuer, K. (2014). The mediating role of work climate perceptions in the relationship between personality and performance. E*uropean Journal of Work and Organizational Psychology*, *23*(4), 525-536. doi:10.1080/1359432X.2013.764601.

Gorgievski, M. J. and Bakker, A. B. (2010). Passion for work: Work engagement versus workaholism. In S. L. Albrecht (Ed.), *Handbook of employee engagement: Perspectives, issues, research and practice* (pp. 264–271). Glos, UK: Edward Elgar.

Greenberger, D. B., Strasser, S., Cummings, L. L. and Dunham, R. B. (1989). The impact of personal control on performance and satisfaction. *Organizational Behavior and Human Decision Processes*, *43*, 29-51.

Hayes, A. F. (2013). *Introduction to mediation, moderation, and conditional process analysis.* New York: The Guilford Press.

Hogan, J. and Holland, B. (2003). Using theory to evaluate personality and job performance relations: A socioanalytic perspective. *Journal of Applied Psychology, 88*(1), 100-112. doi:10.1037/0021-9010.88.1.100.

Hough, L. M. and Ones, D. S. (2001). The structure, measurement, validity, and use of personality variables in industrial, work, and organizational psychology. In N. Anderson, D. S. Ones, H. K. Sinangil, and C. Viswesvaran (Eds.), *Handbook of industrial, work and organizational psychology*. (Vol. 1, pp. 233-277). London, UK: Sage.

Judge, T. A. and Bono, J. E. (2001). Relationship of core self-evaluations traits – self-esteem, generalized self-efficacy, locus of control, and emotional stability – with job satisfaction and job performance: A meta-analysis. *Journal of Applied Psychology*, *86*, 80-92. doi:10.1037/0021-9010.86.1.80.

Judge, T. A., Heller, D. and Mount, M. K. (2002). Five-Factor Model of Personality and Job Satisfaction: A Meta-Analysis. *Journal of Applied Psychology, 87(3)*, 530-541. doi:10.1037/0021-9010.87.3.530.

Judge, T. A. and Ilies, R. (2002). Relationship of personality to performance motivation: A meta-analytic review. *Journal of Applied Psychology*, *87*, 797-807. doi:10.1037/0021-9010.87.4.797.

Judge, T. A., Klinger, R., Simon, L. S. and Yang, I. W. F. (2008). The contributions of personality to organizational behavior and psychology: Findings, criticisms, and future research directions. *Social and Personality Psychology Compass*, *2*(5), 1982-2000. doi:10.1111/j.1751-9004.2008.00136.x.

Judge, T. A. and Larsen, R. J. (2001). Dispositional affect and job satisfaction: A review and theoretical extension. *Organizational Behavior and Human Decision Processes*, *86*(1), 67-98. doi:10.1006/obhd.2001.2973.

Judge, T. A., Thoresen, C. J., Bono, J. E. and Patton, G. K. (2001). The job satisfaction – job performance relationship: A qualitative and quantitative review. *Psychological Bulletin*, *127*, 376-407. doi:10.1037/0033-2909.127.3.376.

Krueger, R. F. and Markon, K. E. (2006). Reinterpreting comorbidity: A model-based approach to understanding and classifying psychopathology. *Annual Review of Clinical Psychology*, *2*, 111-133. doi:10.1146/annurev.clinpsy.2.022305.095213.

Kubota, K., Shimazu, A., Kawakami, N., Takahashi, M., Nakata, A. and Schaufeli, W. B. (2011). Association between workaholism and sleeping problems among hospital nurses. *Industrial Health*, *48*, 864-871.

MacKenzie, S. B., Podsakoff, P. M. and Ahearne, M. (1998). Some possible antecedents of in-role and extra-role salesperson performance. *Journal of Marketing*, *62*, 87-98.

Meijman, T. F. and Mulder, G. (1998). Psychological aspects of workload. In P. J. D. Drenth, H. Thierry, and C. J. de Wolff (Eds.), *Handbook of work and organisational psychology* (2nd ed., pp. 5-33). Hove, England: Psychology Press/Erlbaum.

Mount, M., Barrick, M. and Stewart, G. (1998). Five-factor model of personality and performance in jobs involving interpersonal interaction. *Human Performance*, *11*, 145-165.

Mudrack, P. E. (2006). Understanding workaholism: The case of behavioral tendencies. In R. J. Burke (Ed.), *Research companion to working time and work addiction* (pp. 108-128). Cheltenham: Edward Elgar.

Ng, T. W. H., Sorensen, K. and Feldman, D. (2007). Dimensions, antecedents, and consequences of workaholism: A conceptual integration and extension. *Journal of Organizational Behavior*, *28*, 111-136. doi:10.1002/job.424.

Porter, G. (2001). Workaholic tendencies and the high potential for stress among co-workers. *International Journal of Stress Management*, *8*(2), 147-164. doi:10.1023/A:1009581330960.

Robinson, B. E., Flowers, C. and Carroll, J. (2001). Work stress and marriage: A theoretical model examining the relationship between workaholism and marital cohesion. *International Journal of Stress Management*, *8*(2), 165-175. doi:10.1023/A:1009533415030.

Salgado, J. F. (1997). The five factor model of personality and job performance in the European Community. *Journal of Applied Psychology*, *82*, 30-43.doi:10.1037/0021-9010.82.1.30.

Schaufeli, W. B., Bakker, A. B., Van der Heijden, F. M. and Prins, J. T. (2009). Workaholism, burnout and well-being among junior doctors: The mediating role of role conflict. *Work and Stress*, 23, 155-172. doi:10.1080/02678370902834021.

Schaufeli, W. B., Shimazu, A. and Taris, T. W. (2009). Being driven to work excessively hard: The evaluation of a two-factor measure of workaholism in the Netherlands and Japan. *Cross-Cultural Research*, *43*(4), 320-348. doi:10.1177/1069397109337239.

Schaufeli, W. B., Taris, T. W. and Bakker, A. B. (2006). Dr. Jekyll and Mr. Hyde: On the differences between work engagement and workaholism. In R. J. Burke (Ed.), *Research companion to working time and work addiction* (pp. 193–217). Northampton: Edward Elgar.

Schaufeli, W. B., Taris, T. W. and Bakker, A. B. (2008). It takes two to tango: Workaholism is working excessively and working compulsively. In R. J. Burke and C. L. Cooper (Eds.), *The long work hours culture. Causes, consequences and choices* (pp. 203-226). Bingley, UK: Emerald.

Schleicher, D. J., Smith, T. A., Casper, W. J., Watt, J. D. and Greguras, G. J. (2015). It's all in the attitude: The role of job attitude strength in job attitude – outcome relationships. *Journal of Applied Psychology*, *100*(4), 1259-1274. doi:10.1037/a0038664.

Shimazu, A., Schaufeli, W. B. and Taris, T. W. (2010). How does workaholism affect worker health and performance? The mediating role of coping. *International Journal of Behavioral Medicine*, *17*, 154-160. doi: 10.1007/s12529-010-9077-x.

Shipley, B. A., Weiss, A., Der, G., Taylor, M. D. and Deary, I. J. (2007). Neuroticism, extraversion, and mortality in the UK health and lifestyle survey: A 21-year prospective cohort study. *Psychosomatic Medicine*, *69*, 923-931. doi:10.1097/PSY.0b013e31815abf83.

Smith, T. W. and MacKenzie, J. (2006). Personality and risk of physical illness. *Annual Review of Clinical Psychology*, *2*, 435-467. doi:10.1146/annurev.clinpsy.2.022305.095257.

Sonnentag, S. and Zijlstra, F. R. H. (2006). Job characteristics and off-job activities as predictors of need for recovery, well-being, and fatigue. *Journal of Applied Psychology*, *91*(2), 330-350. doi:10.1037/0021-9010.91.2.330.

Suls, J. and Bunde J. (2005). Anger, anxiety, and depression as risk factors for cardiovascular disease: The problems and implications of overlapping affective dispositions. *Psychological Bulletin*, *131*, 260-300. doi:10.1037/0033-2909.131.2.260.

Taris, T. W., Schaufeli, W. B. and Verhoeven, L. C. (2005). Workaholism in the Netherlands: Measurement and implications for job strain and work-nonwork conflict. *Applied Psychology: An International Review*, *54*(1), 37-60. doi:10.1111/j.1464-0597.2005.00195.x.

Van Emmerik, I. J. H., Jawahar, J. and Stone, T. H. (2004). The relationship between personality and discretionary helping behaviors. *Psychological Reports*, *95*, 355-365. doi:10.2466/pr0.95.1.355-365.

Van Wijhe, C., Peeters, M. C. W. and Schaufeli, W. B. (2010). Understanding and treating workaholism: Setting the stage for successful interventions. In C. Cooper and R. Burke (Eds.), *Psychological and behavioural risks at work*. Farnham: Ashgate.

Van Wijhe, C., Peeters, M. C. W. and Schaufeli, W. B. (2013). Irrational beliefs at work and their implications for workaholism. *Journal of Occupational Rehabilitation*, *23*(3), 336-346. doi:10.1007/s10926-012-9416-7.

Wanous, J. P., Reichers, A. E. and Hudy, M. J. (1997). Overall job satisfaction: How good are single-item measures? *Journal of Applied Psychology*, *82*, 247-252. doi:10.1037/0021-9010.82.2.247.

Wayne, J. H., Musisca, N. and Fleeson, W. (2004). Considering the role of personality in the work-family experience: Relationships of the big five to work-family conflict and facilitation. *Journal of Vocational Behavior*, *64*, 108-130. doi:10.1016/S0001-8791(03)00035-6.

Weinstock, L. M. and Whisman, M. A. (2006). Neuroticism as a common feature of the depressive and anxiety disorders: A test of the revised integrative hierarchical model in a national sample. *Journal of Abnormal Psychology, 115*, 68-74. doi:10.1037/0021-843X.115.1.68.

Weiss, H. M. (2002). Deconstructing job satisfaction: Separating evaluations, beliefs and affective experiences. *Human Resource Management Review, 12*, 173-194. doi:10.1016/S1053-4822(02)00045-1.

Wright, T. A. and Staw, B. M. (1999). Affect and favorable work outcomes: two longitudinal tests of the happy–productive worker thesis. *Journal of Organizational Behaviour, 20*, 1-23. doi:10.1002/(SICI)1099-1379(199901)20:1<1::AID-JOB885>3.0.CO;2-W.

Ziegler, R., Hagen, B. and Diehl, M. (2012). Relationship between job satisfaction and job performance: Job ambivalence as a moderator. *Journal of Applied Social Psychology, 42*, 2019-2040. doi:10.1111/j.1559-1816.2012.00929.x.

In: Neuroticism
Editor: Annamaria Di Fabio
ISBN: 978-1-63485-323-1

Chapter 3

WORKAHOLISM: HEALTH RISK AND PREVENTION IN THE ORGANIZATIONS

Marco Giannini**, and Yura Loscalzo
University of Florence, School of Psychology, Florence, Italy
Department of Health Sciences, Florence, Italy

ABSTRACT

In this chapter, we will present some of the many definitions proposed for workaholism, highlighting the lack of a shared conceptualization by the scientific community and discussing the recent proposal related to the Heavy Work Investment model. Next, we will present all studies that have analyzed the relationship between neuroticism and workaholism, demonstrating major support for the association between neuroticism and the cognitive dimension of workaholism. Then, we will describe the negative consequences associated to workaholism, including physical and psychological health, as well as workplace and family wellbeing. Finally, we will discuss the lack of studies related to preventive interventions and mention the few studies that do provide some insights into prevention, in particular a recent study emphasizing the role of overwork climate in fueling workaholism.

INTRODUCTION

In the 70's, Oates (1971) created the term "workaholism" for people who seem addicted to work and who consequently experience negative effects in their lives. Since then many researchers studied this as a behavioral addiction and proposed various definitions. For example, Robinson (1998) defined workaholism as an obsessive-compulsive disorder, while Mosier (1983) proposed a behavior-based definition, working more than 50 hours in a week. Ng, Soresen, and Feldman (2007) added two other dimensions, characterizing workaholism as not only as spending many hours working (behavioral factor), but also being obsessed with

* Corresponding author: Marco Giannini, e-mail: giannini@psico.unifi.it.

work (cognitive factor) and enjoying it (emotional factor). Another three-factor definition is that of Spence and Robbins (1992): they defined workaholics as being highly involved in their work, feeling an inner pressure to work and having low enjoyment in work, differentiating them from "enthusiastic workaholics", who also score high on work enjoyment. They also created an instrument to measure these three factors (the Workaholism Battery; Spence and Robbins, 1992).

There are also authors who proposed to consider workaholism purely as an addiction, such as Andreassen, Griffiths, Hetland, and Pallesen (2012), who create an instrument to measure workaholism based on the core components of addiction: salience, tolerance, mood modification, relapse, withdrawal, conflict and problems. Finally, Snir and Harpaz (2012) proposed to define workaholism as a dispositional subtype of the construct of heavy work investment (which is characterized by heavy investment in both time and effort) characterized by addiction to work. They also proposed three other dispositional types: the work devoted, who has passion for work; the intimacy-avoider, who works in order to keep away from intimacy and relationships; the leisure-low-interested, for whom work is an alternative to leisure time, which is experienced as annoying. On the other side, they suggest the existence of situational "hard workers," namely people who work hard for economic needs (needy) or who work hard because of employer pressures (employer-directed). In line with this view that not all hard workers are workaholics, van Beek, Taris, and Schaufeli (2011) crossed work engagement and workaholism and found three types of hard workers: workaholic employees, engaged employees, and engaged workaholics.

As highlighted in a review of recent literature (Loscalzo and Giannini, 2015), currently there is no a shared definition of workaholism in the scientific community. This has prevented the accumulation of knowledge about workaholism, and there was not sufficient scientific evidence to allow its classification as a mental disorder in the latest edition of the Diagnostic and Statistical Manual of Mental Disorders (DSM-5, American Psychiatric Association, 2013).

Neuroticism as a Personal Antecedent of Workaholism

Although workaholism is not recognized as a mental disorder by DSM-5 (APA, 2013), many researchers have nevertheless analyzed its possible antecedents and its relation to health outcomes, aiming to increase the knowledge of this addiction. The most studied personal factors are motivation (Stoeber, Davis, and Townley, 2013; van Beek, Hu, Schaufeli, von Taris, and Schreurs, 2012; van Beek et al., 2011; van Beek, Taris, Schaufeli, and Brenninkmeijer, 2014; van den Broeck et al., 2011); cognitive aspects, such as enough continuation rule (i.e., working long time in order to do enough work), coping styles and irrational beliefs (Andreassen, Hetland, and Pallesen, 2012; van Wijhe, Peeters, and Schaufeli, 2011, 2013, 2014; van Wijhe, Peeters, Schaufeli, and van den Hout, 2 011); and, personality factors, primarily perfectionism (Bovornusvakool, Vodanovich, Ariyabuddhiphongs, and Ngamake, 2012; Mazzetti, Schaufeli, and Guglielmi, 2012; Tziner and Tanami, 2013; Stoeber et al., 2013; Falco, Piccirelli, Girardi, Di Sipio, and De Carlo, 2014).

However, some researchers have also been also interested into the relationship between workaholism and the Big Five personality traits (McCrae and Costa, 1987), pointing out that neuroticism has a significant role in predicting workaholism. Burke, Matthiesen, and Pallesen conducted the first study involving personality traits in 2006 in a sample of 496 Norwegian health care employees (mostly female nurses). They found that neuroticism is strongly and positively correlated with one of the three workaholism components proposed by Spence and Robbins (1992), Work Drive, but no relationship was found with Work Involvement or Work Enjoyment. In 2010, a second study on a sample of 661 Norwegian employees from different job sectors and with a balanced male female proportion confirmed that neuroticism was positively correlated with Work Drive, but it also found a negative correlation with Work Enjoyment. In addition, regression analysis showed that neuroticism was positively associated with Work Involvement, even if most variance was accounted for by Work Drive (Andreassen, Hetland, and Pallesen, 2010). Aziz and Tronzo (2011) replicated Burke et al.'s study in an American sample, with participants from various occupational settings (e.g., education, health, business) and also with a more equal distribution of males and females, although with a smaller sample (202 participants). Specifically regarding neuroticism, they hypothesized a positive relationship with Work Drive and negative correlations with both Work Involvement and Work Enjoyment. Contrary to their expectations, the results showed only a low negative correlation between neuroticism and work enjoyment that was, however, not supported by their hierarchical regression analysis, which did not show any significant relationship. In another study on 252 Pakistani workers from three occupational areas (education, health, banks), with a majority of males and youths (133 participants were aged between 25 and 30, and 102 between 31 and 40), neuroticism was significantly and positively correlated only with the Work Drive component. However, a hierarchical regression analysis showed that neuroticism positively predicted Work Involvement, contrary to their hypothesis but in agreement with Andreassen et al.'s (2010) study. In addition they found that neuroticism also positively predicted Work Drive and, in contrast to their hypothesis and previous studies, Work Enjoyment. In sum, this study found that neuroticism positively predicted all the three workaholism components, with the highest correlation for Work Drive (Hameed, Amjad, and Hameed, 2013).

Some other studies have also analyzed the relationship between the Big Five personality traits and workaholism, using different instruments to assess workaholism: the Work Addiction Risk Test (WART; Robinson, 1999), the Bergen Work Addiction Scale (BWAS; Andreassen et al., 2012) and the Dutch Work Addiction Scale (DUWAS; Schaufeli, Shimazu, and Taris, 2009). Clark, Lelchook, and Taylor (2010) in their study analyzed the relationship between workaholism and other personality traits, namely perfectionism, narcissism, positive and negative affect, over and above the effect of the Big Five personality traits. The participants of this study were 323 American working students, predominantly female, with a mean age of 24; this represents a lower age than other studies. They used the WART (Robinson, 1999) to measure workaholism; for the analysis they used the overall score and the following three factors: impatience, internal compulsion to work, polychronic control (or being in control of many tasks at once). The noteworthy result relating to the focus of this chapter is that only Neuroticism was a significant predictor of all four workaholism measures, while Extraversion was not a significant predictor of any of the workaholism dimensions and the other three personality Big five traits were significant predictors of only one of the four dimensions. In addition, when they added the additional personality variables to the hierarchical multiple regression analysis, neuroticism remained a significant positive predictor of all the four workaholism scores, while for conscientiousness and agreeableness the previous relationships disappeared.

Sharma and Sharma (2011) and Guédon and Bernaud (2015) evaluated workaholism by means of the DUWAS, which includes two dimensions: Working Excessively (behavioral component) and Working Compulsively (cognitive component), and a total score. In Sharma and Sharma's study, the participants were 145 Indian academics; the findings indicated that neuroticism is negatively correlated with (and a negative predictor of) all the three workaholism dimension. Guédon and Bernaud (2015), using the DUWAS short version (Libano, Llorens, Salanova, and Schaufeli, 2010), found that in their sample of 304 French University employees (mostly females), as hypothesized, neuroticism positively predicted the workaholism total score, as well as its two components (working excessively and working compulsively). Finally, Andreassen et al. (2014) analyzed the prevalence of workaholism in 1124 Norwegian employees by means of the BWAS, a 7-item scale based on the addiction criteria. For what concerns neuroticism, they found that it is positively associated with workaholism.

Taken together these studies highlight the finding that neuroticism is a significant predictor of workaholism and some of its components; the specific components differ based on the instrument used to assess workaholism and based on the sample. The majority of studies showed that neuroticism positively predicts the workaholism total score (Andreassen et al., 2014; Clark et al., 2010; Guédon and Bernaud, 2015), despite the fact that Sharma and Sharma (2011) instead found that neuroticism is a negative predictor. There is also major evidence for neuroticism's role in positively predicting workaholism's cognitive components, Work Drive, Working Compulsivity and Internal Compulsion to Work (Andreassen et al., 2010; Burke et al., 2006; Clark et al., 2013; Guédon and Bernaud; 2015; Hameed et al., 2013). Sharma and Sharma (2014) who found a negative relationship, are again an exception.

However, although these findings support the existence of an association between neuroticism and workaholism, some additional studies need to be undertaken in order to clarify some of the discrepancies among the studies. Future researchers should utilize the conceptualization of workaholism as a form of heavy work investment that may or may not be associated with work enjoyment, hence differentiating these diverse kinds of workers, in analyzing the association between neuroticism and workaholism and its components. This could help in understanding why some studies found positive and some negative association for the same variables. We speculate that this is due to varying percentages of workaholics with and without work enjoyment in the samples in these studies, with a resulting difficulty in directly comparing their results, as they could refer to different type of workaholics.

What Are the Effects of Workaholism on Health?

Even though there is not yet a shared definition of workaholism, many researchers have tried to examine the negative consequences that workaholism has on both workaholics themselves and their families. This means that these studies have predominantly adopted a negative conceptualization of workaholism, probably referring only to workaholics with low work enjoyment. Hence, in order to evaluate the following studies critically, the reader should be aware that not all hard workers are necessarily workaholics; as a consequence, these negative outcomes should be considered as a correlate in the 'negative' workaholics (those without work enjoyment) and not as characteristics of all hard workers. We reaffirm what we suggested in a previous contribution (Loscalzo and Giannini, 2015) that future studies should analyze the different health outcomes associated with engaged workaholics, workaholics employees and engaged employees, referring to van Beek et al.'s (2011) classification of hard workers. Van Beek et al. (2011) indeed found that engaged workaholics have lower levels of burnout than workaholic employees, but higher levels than engaged employees.

Keeping this warning in mind, we are going to present the main findings regarding the effect of workaholism on health. At a general level many studies showed a negative association between workaholism and well-being and health (Andreassen, Hetland, Molde, and Pallesen, 2011; Avanzi, van Dick, Fraccaroli, and Sarchielli, 2012; Falco et al., 2013; Guglielmi, Simbula, Schaufeli, and Depolo, 2012; Shimazu, Schaufeli, Kamiyama, and Kawakami, 2015; Simbula and Guglielmi, 2013; Wojdylo, Baumann, Fischbachm and Engester, 2014). Regarding more specific aspects recent studies of workaholics found exhaustion (van den Broeck et al., 2011), lower levels of psychological detachment from work (Innanen, Tolvanen, and Salmela-Aro, 2014; Shimazu, De Jonge, Kubota, and Kawakami, 2014), higher psychological distress (Shimazu, Demerouti, Bakker, Shimada, and Kawakami, 2011), sleep problems (Caesens, Stinglhamber, and Luypaert 2014; Andreassen et al., 2011; Kubota, Shimazu, Kawakami, and Takahashi, 2014), depressive mood (Matsudaira et al., 2013; Wojdylo, Baumann, Buczny, Owens, and Kuhl, 2013), disabling back pain, and work absences due to illness, particularly due to mental health problem (Matsudaira et al., 2013). Workaholism is also associated with work overload (Del Líbano, Llorens, Salanova, and Schaufeli, 2012), lower job satisfaction (Caesens et al., 2014; van Beek et al., 2014; Simbula and Guglielmi, 2013), less equality perception (Simbula and Guglielmi, 2013) and less sense of sufficient rewards (Innanen et al., 2014). As we can see, there appear to be many negative consequences of workaholism for both the physical and psychological health of the individual; there is impairment of wellbeing at work as well.

With regard to negative consequences for the individual there are also studies pointing out the impact of workaholism on the family due to work-family conflict (Del Líbano et al., 2012; Simbula and Guglielmi, 2013; Clark, Michel, Stevens, Howell, and Scruggs, 2013). Recently some researchers studied this conflict by means of the spillover-crossover model. The spillover model (or work-family conflict) is based on the idea that there is a bidirectional relationship between work and family life, with the consequence that not only can family life impair the work role, but also that work can impair family life (Frone, 2000). Hence, the spillover model takes a person-centered perspective which examines the conflict between two role domains in the same person. The spillover-crossover model also takes into account the crossover perspective that examines how the individual's work strain is experienced by his/her partner and relatives at home (Westman, 2001). These studies found a positive relationship between workaholism and work-to-family conflict (Bakker, Shimazu, Demerouti, Shimada, and Kawakami, 2014; Shimatzu et al., 2011; Andreassen, Hetland, and Pallesen, 2013). In addition, Shimazu et al. (2011) reported that the husbands of workaholic women are more likely to experience family-to-work conflict, while the wives of workaholic men were not. Thus, workaholism in women may have a negative impact both on their own and their partners' family and work functioning.

Prevention in Organizations

Since workaholism is associated with many negative effects for the individual, it would be worthwhile to implement prevention programs in order to avoid the onset or persistence of workaholism. Although this is an understudied area, Mazzetti et al. (2014) provide some important insights. They highlight an interaction between person characteristics and environmental factors. In particular, they found that conscientiousness and self-efficacy are individual characteristics associated with workaholism, but only if the worker perceives an overwork climate; achievement motivation and perfectionism have both an interaction effect and direct effects on workaholism. Therefore, they point out that it is worthwhile to act on the organizational climate. Indeed, while personality characteristics are more generally considered stable, organizational factors are modifiable. These authors proposed that managers should act as model for their employees, showing how to attain good outcomes by adequate time-management and a healthy work-life balance, not by working in one's free time.

Some other contributions relevant to prevention programs can be found in two recent studies on leisure time. Bakker, Demerouti, Oerlemans, and Sonnentag (2013) found that practicing a sport or doing exercise is a useful recovery strategy for workaholics. Hence, they proposed that organizations should encourage the employees not to work in their leisure time, but to dedicate themselves to a sport or exercise. Again in this case the focus is on the organizations that, instead of promoting an overwork climate, should encourage its employees to enjoy their leisure time instead of dedicating free time to the job. In a different vein, De Bloom, Radstaak, and Geurts (2014) analyzed the effect of long vacations. They found that workaholics experience a high improvement in emotional well-being during vacations, but that they also have a large decrease in well-being when they come back work. They concluded that a long vacation has a positive effect on workaholics, but that preventive interventions are necessary to avoid their great decline in affective well-being on returning to work. Preventive interventions should be done in the organizational setting in order to both incentivize workers to go on holidays and to reduce the negative effect of the vacationer coming back to work.

In sum, these studies stress the importance of preventive intervention in the workplace. However, studies on organizational antecedents of workaholism are still lacking, and further ones could help in understanding which components are the best to modulate in order to prevent or reduce workaholism. In addition, it will be crucial to develop intervention programs to implement and evaluate them in organizations where there are workaholics or employees at-risk for this behavioral addiction.

CONCLUSION

The present chapter has highlighted that workaholism is a construct that it is widely studied but still lacking a shared definition. There are some authors (as well instruments) that assess only the addiction factor of workaholism, while others outline the importance of other related dimensions (such as cognitive and emotional factors). Consequently, this is a behavioral addiction not yet classified in the DSM-5 (2013, APA) as there is not yet adequate evidence supporting its inclusion.

Despite the lack of a definition of workaholism shared by the scientific community, there is great interest in the literature for studying its antecedents and consequences. In this chapter, we reviewed publications related to neuroticism as a possible antecedent of workaholism. There are not many studies on this topic; however, they have shown an association between this personality factor and addiction to work. In general, it seems that the majority of studies agree in demonstrating a relationship between neuroticism and the cognitive factors of workaholism (Work Drive, Working Compulsivity or Internal Compulsion to Work). However, must note that these studies also showed some contrasting findings; this could be due to methodological issues, such as the differences in the participants (which vary by age, heterogeneity of workers, sample size and country).

With regard to the effects on workers' wellbeing, there is much more literature examining different negative correlates. These negative correlates are related to both physical and psychological wellbeing, including sleep problems, exhaustion, depressive mood and disabling back pain. Most interestingly, some negative consequences are also job-related, including a lower level of wellbeing in the workplace. Finally, family health may also be damaged, as some studies have described the presence of a family-work conflict and a negative impact on the workaholic's partner. As we can see, all the life's domains are affected by workaholism: physical, psychological, work context and family.

Given the many negative outcomes associated to workaholism, it will be important to implement and evaluate preventive interventions in the workplace, a place where the individual stays for long hours and which, if characterized by an overwork climate, could fuel work addiction, as highlighted by Mazzetti et al. (2014). However, this area is understudied, as are its organizational antecedents; these are important to address, as they could be informative regarding which work-related factors might be the most effective to modify in order to prevent workaholism.

As a final consideration, this chapter outlined how workaholism is a behavioral addiction generally considered only in its negative dimensions, even though some recent publications have suggested there might also be a positive form of workaholism, which could be better conceptualized with reference to heavy work investment. The definition of workaholism is only one of the aspects that deserves more attention in order to reach a shared conceptualization. Other areas in need of further study include organizational antecedents and interventions to prevent or avoid the persistence of workaholism.

References

American Psychiatric Association (2013). DSM-5. *Diagnostic and statistical manual of mental disorders* – 5th ed. Washington, DC: Author.

Andreassen, C. S., Griffiths, M. D., Hetland, J., Kravina, L., Jensen, F. and Pallesen, S. (2014). The prevalence of workaholism: A survey study in a nationally representative sample of Norwegian employees. *PLoS ONE,* 9(8), 1-10.

Andreassen, C. S., Hetland, J., Molde, H. and Pallesen, S. (2011). 'Workaholism' and potential outcomes in well-being and health in a cross-occupational sample. *Stress and Health*, 27, 209-214.

Andreassen, C. S., Griffiths, M. D., Hetland, J. and Pallesen, S. (2012). Development of a work addiction scale. *Scandinavian Journal of Psychology*, 53, 265-272.

Andreassen, C. S., Hetland, J. and Pallesen, S. (2010). The relationship between 'workaholism', basic need satisfaction at work and personality. *European Journal of Personality*, 24, 3-17.

Andreassen, C. S., Hetland, J. and Pallesen, S. (2012). Coping and workaholism. Results from a large cross-occupational sample. TPM-Testing, Psychometrics, *Methodology in Applies Psychology*, 19(4), 281-290.

Andreassen, C. S.; Hetland, J. and Pallesen, S. (2013). Workaholism and work-family spillover in a cross-occupational sample. *European Journal of Work and Organizational Psychology*, 22(1), 78-87.

Avanzi, L., van Dick, R., Fraccaroli, F. and Sarchielli, G. (2012). The downside of organizational identification: Relations between identification, workaholism and well-being. *Work and Stress*, 26(3), 589-307.

Aziz, S. and Tronzo, C. L. (2011). Exploring the relationship between workaholism facets and personality traits: A replication in American workers. *The Psychological Record*, 61, 269-286.

Bakker, A. B., Demerouti, E., Oerlemans, W. and Sonnentag, S. (2013). Workaholism and daily recovery: A day reconstruction study of leisure activities. *Journal of Organizational Behavior*, 34, 87-107.

Bakker, A. B., Shimazu, A., Demerouti, E., Shimada, K. and Kawakami, N. (2014). Work engagement versus workaholism: A test of the spillover-crossover model. *Journal of Managerial Psychology*, 29(1), 63-80.

Bovornuskavool, W., Vodanovich, S. J., Ariyabuddhiphongs, K. and Ngamake, S. T. (2012). Examining the antecedents and consequences of workaholism. *The Psychologist-Manager Journal*, 15(1), 56-70.

Burke, R. J., Matthiesen, S. B. and Pallesen, S. (2006). Personality correlates of workaholism. Personality and Individual Differences, 40, 1223-1233.

Caesens, G., Stinglhamber, F. and Luypaert, G. (2014). The impact of work engagement and workaholism on well-being. *Career Development International,* 19(7), 813-835.

Clark, M. A., Lelchook, A. M. and Taylor, M. L. (2010). Beyond the Big Five: How narcissism, perfectionism, and dispositional affect relate to workaholism. *Personality and Individual Differences*, 48, 786-791.

Clark, M. A., Michel, J. S., Stevens, G. W., Howell, J. W. and Scruggs, R. S. (2013). Workaholism, work engagement and work-home outcomes: Exploring the mediating role of positive and negative emotions. *Stress and Health,* 30, 287-300.

De Bloom, J., Radstaak, M. and Geurts, S. (2014). Vacation effects on behaviour, cognition and emotions of compulsive and non-compulsive workers: Do obsessive workers go 'Cold Turkey'?. *Stress and Health*, 30, 232-243.

Del Líbano, M., Llorens, S., Salanova, M. and Schaufeli, W. B. (2012). About the dark and bright sides of self-efficacy: Workaholism and work engagement. *The Spanish Journal of Psychology*, 15(2), 688-701.

Falco, A., Piccirelli, A., Girardi, D., Di Sipio, A., De Carlo, N. A. (2014). "The best or nothing": The mediating role of workaholism in the relationship between perfectionism and burnout. TPM-Testing, Psychometrics, Methodology in Applied Psychology, 21(2), 213-232.

Frone, M. R. (2000). Work-family conflict and employee psychiatric disorders: The national comorbidity survey. *Journal of Applied Psyhcology*, 85, 888-895.

Guédon, D. and Bernaud, J.-L. (2015). Le workaholism danse une université française: Une perspective transactionelle. *Pratiques Psychologiques*, 21, 71-85.

Guglielmi, D., Simbula, S., Schaufeli, W. B. and Depolo, M. (2012). Self-efficacy and workaholism as initiators of the job demands-resources model. *Career Development International*, 17(4), 375-389.

Hameed, F., Amjad, S. and Hameed, A. (2013). The relationship between workaholism and personality. *Middle East Journal of Scientific Research,* 17(7), 898-907.

Innanen, H., Tolvanen, A. and Salmela-Aro (2014). Burnout, work engagement and workaholism among highly educated employees: Profiles, antecedents and outcomes. *Burnout Research*, 1, 38-49.

Kubota, K., Shimazu, A., Kawakami, N. and Takahashi, M. (2014). Workaholism and sleep quality among Japanese employees: A prospective cohort study. International Journal of Behavioral Medicine, 21(1), 66-76.

Libano, M., Llorens, S., Salanova, M. and Schaufeli, W. (2010). Validity of a brief workaholism scale. *Psicothema,*22, 143-150.

Loscalzo Y. and Giannini, M. (2015). Workaholism: Cosa c'è di nuovo?. Counseling, 8(3) – *Digital Journal.*

Matsudaira, K., Shimazu, A., Fujii, T., Kubota, K., Sawada, T., Kikuchi, N. and Takahashi, M. (2013). Workaholism as a risk factor for depressive mood, disabling back pain, and sickness absence. *PLoS ONE*, 8(9), 1-8.

Mazzetti, G., Schaufeli, W. B. and Guglielmi, D. (2014). Are workaholics born or made? Relations of workaholism with person characteristics and overwork climate. *International Journal of Stress Management*, 23(1), 227-254.

McCrae, R. R. and Costa, P. T. (1987). Validation of the five-factor model of personality across instruments and observers. *Journal of Personality and Social Psychology*, 52, 81-90.

Mosier, S. K. (1983). *Workaholic: An analysis of their stress, success and priorities.* Unpublished Master's Thesis, University of Texas, Austin.

Ng, T. H. W., Sorensen, K. L. and Feldman, D. C. (2007). Dimensions, antecedents, and consequences of workaholism: A conceptual integration and extension. *Journal of Organizational Behavior*, 28, 111-136.

Oates, W. (1971). Confession of a workaholic. New York, NY: Abingdon.

Robinson, B. E. (1998). Chained to the desk: A guidebook for workaholics, their parents and children and the clinicians who treat them. New York University Press: New York, USA.

Robinson, B. E. (1999). The work addiction risk test: Development of a tentative measure of workaholism. *Perceptual and Motor Skills*, 88, 199-210.

Schaufeli, W. B., Shimazu, A. and Taris, T. W. (2009). Being driven to work excessively hard. The evaluation of a two-factor measure of workaholism in the Netherlands and Japan. *Cross Cultural Research*, 43, 320-348.

Sharma, J. and Sharma, P. (2011). Workaholism and its correlates: A study of academicians. *International Journal of Management and Business Research,* 1(3)151-160.

Shimazu, A., De Jonge, J., Kubota, K. and Kawakami, N. (2014). Psychological detachment from work during off-job time: Predictive role of work and non-work factors in Japanese employees. *Industrial Health*, 52, 141-146.

Shimazu, A., Demerouti, E., Bakker, A. B., Shimada, K. and Kawakami, N. (2011). Workaholism and well-being among Japanese dual-earner couples: A spillover-crossover perspective. *Social Science and Medicine,* 73, 399-409.

Shimazu, A., Schaufeli, W. B., Kamiyama, K. and Kawakami, N. (2015). Workaholism vs. work engagement: The two different predictors of future well-being and performance. *International Journal of Behavioral Medicine*, 22(1), 18-23.

Simbula, S. and Guglielmi, D. (2013). Engaged sì, workaholic no: Il ruolo di engagement e workaholism sulla salute e il benessere dei dirigenti scolastici. *Giornale Italiano di Psicologia*, 40(1), 195-207.

Snir, R. and Harpaz, I. (2012). Beyond workaholism: Towards a general model of heavy work investment. *Human Resource Management Review*, 22, 232-243.

Spence, J. T. and Robbins, A. S. (1992). Workaholism: Definition, measurement, and preliminary results. *Journal of Personality Assessment*, 58, 160-178.

Stoeber, J., Davis, C. R. and Townley, J. (2013). Perfectionism and workaholism in employees: The role of work. *Personality and Individual Differences,* 55, 733-738.

Tziner, A. and Tanami, M. (2013). Examining the links between attachment, perfectionism, and job motivation potential with job engagement and workaholism. *Journal of Work and Organizational Psychology*, 29, 65-74.

Van Beek, I., Taris, T. W. and Schaufeli, W. B. (2011). Workaholic and work engaged employees: Dead ringers or worlds apart?. *Journal of Occupational Health Psychology*, 16(4), 468-482.

Van Beek, I., Hu, Q., Schaufeli, W. B., Taris, T. W. and Schreurs, B. H. J. (2012). For fun, love, or money: What drives workaholic, engaged, and burned-out employees at work? *Applied Psychology: An International Review, 61(1), 30-55.*

Van Beek, I., Taris, T. W., Schaufeli, W. B. and Brenninkmeijer (2014). Heavy work investment: its motivational make-up and outcomes. *Journal of Managerial Psychology*, 29(1), 46-62.

Van den Broeck, A., Schreurs, B., De Witte, H., Vansteenkiste, M., Germeys, F. and Schaufeli, W.(2011). Understanding workaholics' motivations: A self-determination perspective. *Applied Psychology: An International Review,* 60(4), 600-621.

Van Wijhe, C. I., Peeters, M. C. W. and Schaufeli, W. B. (2011). To stop or not to stop, that's the question: About persistence and mood of workaholics and work engaged employees. *International Journal of Behavioral Medicine,* 18, 361-372.

Van Wijhe, C. I, Peeters, M. C. W. and Schaufeli, W. B. (2013). Irrational belief at work and their implications for workaholism. *Journal of Occupational Rehabilitation*, 23, 336-346.

Van Wijhe, C. I., Peeters, M. C. W. and Schaufeli, W. B. (2014). Enough is enough: Cognitive antecedents of workaholism and its aftermath. *Human Resource Management,* 53(1), 157-177.

Van Wijhe, C. I., Peeters, M. C. W., Schaufeli, W. B. and van den Hout, M. (2011). Understanding workaholism and work engagement: The role of mood and stop rules. *Career DevelopmentInternational*, 16(3), 254-270.

Westman, M. (2001). Stress and strain crossover. *Human Relations*, 54, 557-591.

Wojdylo, K., Baumann, N., Buczny, J., Owens, G. and Kuhl, J. (2013). Work craving: A conceptualization and measurement. *Basic and Applied Social Psychology,* 35, 547-568.

Wojdylo, K., Baumann, N., Fischbach, L. and Engeser, S. (2014). Live to work or love to work: work craving and work engagement. *PLoS ONE*, 9(10), 1-7.

In: Neuroticism
Editor: Annamaria Di Fabio

ISBN: 978-1-63485-323-1

Chapter 4

THE INDIRECT RELATIONSHIP BETWEEN NEUROTICISM AND JOB PERFORMANCE IN ITALIAN TRADE WORKERS: A CROSS-SECTIONAL STUDY

Riccardo Sartori*, Arianna Costantini and Andrea Ceschi

Department of Philosophy,
Education, Psychology,
University of Verona, Verona, Italy

ABSTRACT

Since *Neuroticism* is the only negative personality trait out of the so-called Big Five (the other four are *Agreeableness*, *Conscientiousness*, *Extraversion* and *Openness*), researchers often reverse it into the complementary one of *Emotional Stability* (Jeronimus, Riese, Sanderman, and Ormel, 2014). *Emotional Stability* is considered to be one of the two Big Five (the other one is *Conscientiousness*; Le et al., 2011), if not the only one (Tett, Jackson, and Rothstein, 1991), to be a valid predictor of job performance regardless of gender and occupational group (Barrick, Mount and Judge, 2001; Shaffer and Postlethwaite, 2013). In addition, *Emotional Stability* is the only one Big Five that improves over the length of service (Williams et al., 2006). On the other hand, the strength and type of correlations between the Big Five and job performance also depend on the specific job considered (Judge, Rodell, Klinger, Simon, and Crawford, 2013). For example, *Extraversion* has been found to be particularly related to job performance in sales (Barrick and Mount, 1991; Mount, Barrick, and Stewart, 1998), and a study carried out by Warr, Bartram and Martin (2005) on the relationship between personality and sales performance finds that high job performance is related to low *Agreeableness*. In the specific case of the study here presented, the sample was composed of 220 trade agents (16 females). A cross-sectional survey design was used. The personality traits were measured by a new Italian personality test named FLORA, which is based on the Big Five and covers 24 dimensions (Sartori, Ceschi, Costantini, and Scalco, 2015). Job

* Corresponding author: Riccardo Sartori, E-mail: riccardo.sartori@univr.it.

performance was expressed in terms of sales figures. Results show statistically significant positive correlations of job performance to *Conscientiousness*, *Extraversion* and *Openness*, a statistically significant negative correlation to *Agreeableness* and an indirect positive relationship between *Emotional Stability* (*Neuroticism*) and job performance passing through the length of service. Results are discussed in the light of literature.

INTRODUCTION

The chapter presents the results of a study carried out with 220 Italian trade agents (salespeople) in order to determine the relationship between their personality traits, in particular *Emotional Stability*, the positive side of *Neuroticism*, and their job performance.

The relationship between personality and job performance has interested research in work and organizational psychology for the last fifty years, but before the Eighties "no well-accepted taxonomy existed for classifying personality traits" (Barrick and Mount, 1991, p. 2), different instruments and approaches, both idiographic and nomothetic, were used to measure personality (Sartori, 2010) and, therefore, it was difficult to determine whether there were consistent, meaningful relationships between particular personality constructs and performance criteria in different occupations (Barrick et al., 2001).

Nowadays, there is general agreement about the existence of five robust factors of personality (the so called Big Five: *Agreeableness*, *Conscientiousness*, *Extraversion*, *Openness* and *Neuroticism/Emotional Stability*) which can serve as a meaningful taxonomy for classifying personality attributes (Digman, 1990). In fact, the Big Five are personality traits that have shown to be relevant to different cultures (De Fruyt, McCrae, Szirmák, and Nagy, 2004; McCrae and Costa, 1997; McCrae, Terracciano, and 79 Members of the Personality Profiles of Cultures Project, 2005) and have been recovered consistently in factor analyses of peer- and self-ratings of trait descriptors involving diverse conditions and samples (Soto, John, Gosling, and Potter, 2011) and diverse factor extraction and rotation methods (Grucza and Goldberg, 2007).

However, while there is general agreement about the existence of the Big Five, there is some disagreement about their precise meaning, that is to say, the type and number of lower order traits (facets) defining them (Judge et al., 2013), which makes it difficult to estimate the exact shape and strength of the relationship between each Big Five and job performance (Le et al., 2011). For example, the lower order traits (facets) defining the Big Five currently range from 12 (the PCI by Mount, Barrick, Laffitte, and Callans, 1999) to 45 (the AB5C by Hofstee, de Raad, and Goldberg, 1992) passing through 18 (Saucier and Ostendorf, 1999), 30 (the NEO-PI by Costa and McCrae, 1992), 32 (the GPI by Schmit, Kihm, and Robie, 2000) and 44 (the HPI by Hogan and Hogan, 1992), only to consider the most famous frameworks based on construct valid measures of the Big Five and not considering all the local versions available in different countries all over the world. In this way:

- *Agreeableness* can refer to kindness, care and empathy (which are mostly personal characteristics) but also to cooperation, collaboration and teamwork (which are more relational);
- *Conscientiousness* can refer to precision, accuracy and order (which are quite specific) but also to constancy, perseverance and reliability (which are more general);

- *Extraversion* can refer to interactivity, persuasion and influence (which are the typical relational aspects of extraversion) but also to energy, activity and speed (which are more personal);
- *Openness* can refer to imagination, inventiveness and originality (which have to do with adaptability, creativity and innovation) but also to intelligence, curiosity and learning (which have to do with schooling, education, training and culture);
- *Neuroticism*, which is the tendency to experience such negative emotions as anger, anxiety, or depression (Norris, Larsen, and Cacioppo, 2007), is often called *Emotional Stability* (Jeronimus et al., 2014) and can refer to calm, tranquility and serenity (typical connotations of emotional stability) but also to stress and emergency management (which relate more to soundness).

As personality traits, the Big Five are generally found to be quite stable (Cobb-Clark and Schurer, 2012). In fact, even if some research finds differences in the Big Five across the life span (Donnellan and Lucas, 2008), they generally do not show variations according to either gender or education level (Donnellan and Lucas, 2008). Besides, they appear to be quite stable among working-age adults (Cobb-Clark and Schurer, 2012). Nevertheless, the only exception to this trend is *Neuroticism* that is generally found to be negatively related to age (Steunenberg, Twisk, Beekman, Deeg, and Kerkhof, 2004), while *Emotional Stability*, the construct which is considered to be opposite to *Neuroticism*, is found to improve over age (Williams et al., 2006). In addition, age generally varies with the length of service (Sarker, Crossman, and Chinmeteepituck, 2003). Consequently, it is possible to conclude that *Emotional Stability* tends to improve with the length of service (Williams et al., 2006) and positively affects job performance (Tett et al., 1991).

As for job performance, literature in personality traits finds that its first consistently valid predictor regardless of gender and occupational group is *Conscientiousness* (Barrick and Mount, 1991; Barrick et al., 2001; Shaffer and Postlethwaite, 2013). Second comes *Emotional Stability* (Le et al., 2011; Tett et al., 1991). *Conscientiousness* and *Emotional Stability* are in fact called the Big Two (Le et al., 2011) and are considered to be the best predictors of job performance. As it is possible to read in the meta-analysis by Barrick et al. (2001, p. 22), "individuals who are not temperamental, not stress-prone, not anxious and not worrisome (emotional stability), and those who are hard-working, persistent, organized, efficient and achievement-oriented (conscientious), are most likely to perform well." Also Salgado (1997) and Anderson and Viswesvaran (1998) find that *Conscientiousness* and *Emotional Stability* are the only personality traits consistently related to job performance. Nevertheless, the strength and type of correlations between the Big Five and job performance also depend on the specific job considered (Judge et al., 2013) and this is the reason why not every study finds that *Conscientiousness* and *Emotional Stability* are the main personality traits related to job performance. Typical examples of these studies are the ones carried out in the field of sales, where *Extraversion*, and not *Conscientiousness* or *Emotional Stability*, is usually found to be particularly related to job performance (Barrick and Mount, 1991; Mount et al., 1998). In another meta-analysis by Barrick and Mount (1991), the authors write that most correlations between *Emotional Stability* (*Neuroticism*) and job performance are likely to be relatively low because individuals who are highly neurotic are unable to function effectively and, as a result, are not likely to be in the labor force (Barrick et al., 2001). They also add that, as long as an individual possesses enough *Emotional Stability*, the predictive value of any differences is minimized. As for *Agreeableness* and *Openness*, they generally tend to show weak relationships with job performance (Barrick, Stewart, Neubert, and Mount, 1998; Mount, Barrick, and Stewart, 1998), but again a study carried out by Warr et al., (2005) on the relationship between personality and sales performance finds that high job performance is related to low *Agreeableness*. In addition, the relationship between job performance and *Conscientiousness* is found to be not contingent on the level of the other Big Five. On the contrary, Witt, Burke, Barrick and Mount (2002) find that the relationship between *Conscientiousness* and job performance is stronger for people high in *Agreeableness* than for those low in *Agreeableness*, but this is true only in jobs characterized by cooperative interactions with others (which is not the case of sales where in fact high *Extraversion* and low *Agreeableness* are more typical). As for *Openness*, a study by Bing and Lounsbury (2000) finds that *Openness* predicts job performance for workers and employees who are above and beyond both cognitive aptitude and the other four Big Five. Finally, a study carried out by Rothmann and Coetzer (2003) with employees of a pharmaceutical company finds that all the Big Five are somehow related to job performance and this result is said to be consistent with the findings of several other studies, among which one by Dunn, Mount, Barrick and Ones (1995).

Apart from being attributed to the different situational characteristics of the jobs for which the studies cited have been carried out, these mixed results point to the two issues of the (in)validity and the variety of the personality tests used to measure the Big Five (Morgeson et al., 2007) with their different number of lower order traits (facets). In general, valid and reliable tests need to be based on empirically supported theoretical models (Sartori and Pasini, 2007). In the specific case of personality tests for organizational contexts, they also need to be appropriately developed according to a procedure leading to identify the traits involved in successful performance and express them in an understandable language for users in organizations (Sartori, Ceschi, Cubico, and Favretto, 2014). Indeed, the needs for psychological assessment in organizational contexts are different from the needs that are felt in clinical and educational fields (Sartori and Ceschi, 2013; Sartori et al., 2014), even when it comes to personality inquiry (Sartori, 2010). For example, personality measures for the assessment of candidates or employees should be at least related to job performance (Rothmann and Coetzer, 2003; van der Linden, te Nijenhuis, and Bakker, 2010). Even strong correlations between personality tests and job performance might not be sufficient though, because some tests make use of a language people working in organizations are not accustomed to and therefore the personality profiles obtained by those tests may sound meaningless or even abstruse to organizational managers and decision makers (Hogan, Hogan, and Roberts, 1996; Sartori and Rolandi, 2013). Since Italy lacked a personality test which was both specifically designed for organizations and based on the Big Five, and given the decision to give birth to an instrument composed of an evidence-based number of lower order traits (facets), a new personality test named FLORA was developed (Sartori et. al., 2015).

The chapter reports the results of a study carried out by administering FLORA to 220 trade agents in order to put in relation their performance (in terms of sales figures) with the 24 lower order traits (facets) measured by this personality test based on the Big Five. The hypotheses of the study were the following:

H1: positive correlations are expected between *Conscientiousness*, *Emotional Stability*, *Extraversion*, *Openness* and job performance, since the first two are considered to be the best predictors of job performance regardless of gender and occupational group, while the second two are typical of the specific professional group here considered;

H2: as for *Emotional Stability* in particular, a positive relation between this Big Five and the length of service is expected, since *Emotional Stability* is the only one Big Five to show changes over age and age is in general positively related to the length of service;

H3: a negative correlation is expected between *Agreeableness* and job performance, since in sales, where interactions are not cooperative, high job performance is found to be related to low *Agreeableness*.

THE STUDY

Participants

Participants are 220 Italian trade agents (16 female) working in the Italian branch of a large European group of direct sales companies operating in the market of small items for professional use in the field of automotive, crafts and industry. Ages vary between 21 and 63 years. The majority (51%) has been working in the company for a period of time between 1 year and 5 years (length of service).

Measures and Procedure

In line with research by Rothmann and Coetzer (2003) and van der Linden et al., (2010), the study here presented tests the hypothesis of correlations between the Big Five personality traits, in particular *Emotional Stability*, and job performance. A cross-sectional survey design was used.

The personality traits were measured by administering FLORA, a new Italian personality test expressly developed for the assessment of specific professional profiles in organizations and based on the Big Five (Sartori et. al., 2015). Starting point for the development of FLORA were interviews to workers and employees on the relationship between personality and job performance (for the 8 questions composing the interview grid, see Sartori et al., 2015). Thirty-two interviews with 16 different job profiles were carried out. Two work and organizational psychologists were involved for each interview, one as a conductor, the other one as an assistant taking notes. Each interview was audio-registered. Audio-registrations and notes were given to other five work and organizational psychologists who worked together for the extrapolation of the personal characteristics emerged in interviews and the categorization of the personal characteristics according to the Big Five (for further details on the procedure, see Barrick and Mount 1991, pp. 8-9). Such characteristics as abilities, capabilities, skills, competences, aptitudes and attitudes were eliminated in order to keep personality traits only (78% out of all the characteristics emerged). As for these ones, synonyms and antonyms referring to the same characteristic were unified under one label chosen according to literature. The personality traits not related to the Big Five, such as the ones referring to the *Honesty-Humility* dimension of the HEXACO model (Ashton and Lee, 2007), were eliminated. Content analyses of interviews led to the identification of 28 different personality dimensions grouped according to the Big Five and named and operationally defined according to both literature and the organizational aims of the test. For each dimension, 6 items, 3 positively and 3 negatively worded, were generated (7-point rating scale where: 1 = *Totally disagree*; 2 = *Strongly disagree*; 3 = *Tend to disagree*; 4 = *Neither agree nor disagree*; 5 = *Tend to agree*; 6 = *Strongly agree*; 7 = *Totally agree*) and a first version of the test was prepared.

Table 1. Final version of FLORA

Big Five	FLORA's dimensions	Number of items	Cronbach Alpha	Avarage total-item coefficient
EXTRAVERSION	Activism	10	.76	.56
	Interactivity	6	.81	.59
	Multitasking	6	.79	.58
	Initiative	6	.77	.58
	Influence	6	.72	.55
	Leadership	4	.70	.53
	Autonomy	4	.70	.52
Extraversion total items		42	.79	.57
AGREEABLENESS	Interpersonal sensitivity	6	.80	.60
	Collaboration	6	.70	.54
	Care	5	.71	.56
	Supportiveness	5	.63	.49
	Positive affectivity	5	.62	.50
Agreeableness total items		27	.85	.64
CONSCIENTIOUSNESS	Reliability	6	.79	.58
	Constancy	6	.77	.57
	Deliberateness	6	.71	.49
	Accomplishment	6	.60	.45
	Precision	5	.71	.50
Conscientiousness total items		29	.81	.60
EMOTIONAL STABILITY (NEUROTICISM)	Stress tolerance	10	.86	.66
	Frustration tolerance	6	.69	.48
	Self-control	5	.69	.47
Emotional stability total items		21	.76	.56
Big Five	FLORA's dimensions	Number of items	Cronbach Alpha	Avarage total-item coefficient
OPENNESS	Learning	8	.81	.60
	Deepening	6	.65	.55
	Flexibility	5	.60	.46
	Inventiveness	4	.77	.57
Openness total items		23	.79	.58
LIE SCALE		7	.77	-
FLORA Total items (with *Lie Scale*)		142 (149)		

It was administered to a validation sample of 407 workers and employees and, after changes due to explorative analyses, to a confirmation sample of other 418 workers and employees. After all the analyses, both explorative and confirmative, the final version of FLORA has taken the structure shown in Table 1 (the initial 28 dimensions have been reduced to 24). FLORA can currently count on norms calculated on 2366 workers and employees distributed into 16 different professional profiles.

Job performance was expressed in terms of the sales figures achieved by the trade agents. Even if previous studies evaluated job performance by considering self-assessment questionnaires or supervisory ratings (Asare, Yang, and Brashear, 2012), in the case of our study it was decided to adopt sales figures as a more objective measure. Each participant was assessed on a scale of 1 (= *Low performer*) to 5 (= *High performer*), based on the amount of the monthly sales revenue. The 5 different levels of job performance provided by organizational data were described as follow: 1 = 0-5000 € per month, low performance; 2 = 6000-10000 € per month, passing grade; 3 = 11000-15000 € per month, fair performance; 4 = 16000-20000 € per month, good performance; 5 > 20000 € per month, high performance.

Statistical Analyses

In order to test the hypothesis of correlations between the Big Five and job performance, Pearson correlation coefficients were calculated between the 24 dimensions of FLORA and the sales figures of the trade agents involved in the study.

RESULTS

Table 2 shows the Pearson correlation coefficients between the 8 dimensions of FLORA for which these coefficients are statistically significant ($p < .05$) and job performance in terms of sales figures. The first column reports the Big Five to which the dimensions of FLORA belong.

Table 2. Pearson correlation coefficients between 8 dimensions of FLORA and the job performance of 220 trade agents expressed in terms of sales figures

Big Five	Dimensions of FLORA	Job performance
Extraversion	Interactivity	.37 **
	Multitasking	.21 *
Agreeableness	Care	– .40 **
	Interpersonal sensitivity	– .19 *
Conscientiousness	Constancy	.31 **
Openness	Deepening	.28 **
	Flexibility	.23 **
	Learning	.20 *

* = correlation is significant for $p < .05$; ** = correlation is significant for $p < .001$.

According to hypotheses, *Conscientiousness*, *Extraversion* and *Openness* are positively related (H1) and *Agreeableness* is negatively related (H3) to job performance. *Emotional Stability* does not emerge as a Big Five directly related to job performance but the three dimensions of *Emotional Stability* measured by FLORA (*Stress tolerance*, *Frustration tolerance* and *Self-control*) are positively and significantly related to the length of service (with r coefficients varying from .21 to .24), while the length of service, in turn, is related to job performance with $r = .59$. Thus, even if a direct relation between *Emotional Stability* and job performance does not emerge, the amount of *Emotional Stability* in the salespeople involved in this study vary with their length of service, while their length of service, in turn, varies with their job performance, which would be in favor of an indirect relation between *Emotional Stability* and job performance passing through the length of service (H3). On the other hand, *Emotional Stability* improves with age (Williams et al., 2006) and in fact, in the study reported in this chapter, age and length of service are related with $r = .35$ ($p < .05$).

CONCLUSION

Given the importance of this kind of studies for personnel selection and assessment (see for example Rothstein and Goffin, 2006), much research in work and organizational psychology has been devoted to discover the relationship between personality and job performance, especially since the five traits of *Agreeableness*, *Conscientiousness*, *Emotional Stability* (*Neuroticism*), *Extraversion* and *Openness* (the so-called Big Five) were established and thoroughly investigated (Soto et al., 2011).

At the moment, *Emotional Stability* is considered to be one of the two Big Five (the other one is *Conscientiousness*; Le et al., 2011), if not the only one (Tett et al., 1991), to be a valid predictor of job performance regardless of gender and occupational group (Barrick et al., 2001; Shaffer and Postlethwaite, 2013). In addition, *Emotional Stability* is the only one Big Five improving over the length of service (Williams et al., 2006). On the other hand, as discussed in the introduction to this chapter, the strength and type of correlations between the Big Five and job performance also depend on the particular job considered (Judge et al., 2013).

In the specific case of the study here presented, the sample was composed of 220 trade agents (16 females). A cross-sectional survey design was used. The personality traits were measured by a new Italian personality test named FLORA, which is based on the Big Five and covers 24 dimensions (Sartori et al., 2015). Job performance was expressed in terms of sales figures. The results reflect the specificity of the professional field considered (sales) and show statistically significant correlations ($p < .05$) between 8 dimensions of FLORA and job performance (Table 1). Before analyzing the situation of *Emotional Stability* (*Neuroticism*), let us comment first on the relationships between the other four Big Five and job performance in the specific sample involved in the study.

Two dimensions, *Interactivity* and *Multitasking*, belong to the Big Five *Extraversion*. Literature on *Extraversion* has found that it is related to job performance in occupations where interactions with others are a significant portion of the job, such as sales (Barrick and Mount, 1991; Mount, Barrick, and Stewart, 1998), so this result is in line with evidence from literature. In the specific case of the study here reported, where participants are salespeople, it is interesting to point out that the dimension *Interactivity* (r = .37) refers to the typical relational aspects of *Extraversion*, while the dimension *Multitasking* (r = .21) is more related to energy, activity and speed.

Two dimensions, *Care* (r = – .40) and *Interpersonal sensitivity* (r = – .19), belong to the Big Five *Agreeableness*, which is hardly ever found to be related to job performance (Barrick et al., 1998; Mount et al., 1998). They both refer to such aspects as kindness and empathy. In the specific case of the study here reported, these two dimensions are negatively related to job performance, which is consistent with results obtained by both Warr et al. (2005) and Witt et al. (2002). In fact, in the case of sales, high *Extraversion* and low *Agreeableness* are typical. One possible explanation of this result summons the *Machiavellianism* personality trait (Christie and Geis, 1968). In literature, this trait has been found to be a main feature of salespeople (Robinson and Shaver, 1973). It seems to characterize workers and employees with a *cool detachment*, which would make them less emotionally involved with other people, with sensitive issues, or with saving face in embarrassing situations (and this has something to do with facets of *Emotional Stability*). Another explanation could deal with the social and cultural background of the specific organizational environment in which this study was carried out. In other words, the particular organizational climate in which salespeople operate might be a factor determining sales professionals' ethical decision making (Singhapakdi and Vitell, 1991) influencing the way sales agents would interpret and act their professional role.

The dimension of *Constancy* (r = .31) belongs to *Conscientiousness*. One possible explanation of this result could deal with the specific fact that the trade agents of this study, operating in the market of small items for professional use in the field of automotive, crafts and industry, must be particularly perseverant and constant in their efforts to sell such kind of products.

Three dimensions belong to *Openness*. They are *Deepening* (r = .28) and *Learning* (r = .20; they both have to do with schooling, education, training and culture) and *Flexibility* (r = .23; it has to do with adaptability, creativity and innovation). *Openness* generally tends to show weak relationships with job performance (Barrick et al., 1998; Mount et al., 1998), but in the specific case of the study here presented three dimensions belonging to *Openness* show positive and statistically significant correlations with job performance. This is in line with research by Bing and Lounsbury (2000) and probably depends on the particular products that the trade agents deal with (which require knowing lots of information about their characteristics and uses) and the particular environment they found themselves acting in when they try to sell their products (which requires to be flexible, adaptable and inventive).

Finally, no dimension of *Emotional Stability* (*Neuroticism*) has been found to be directly related to job performance in the specific case of the study here presented ($p > .05$), which is surprising in the light of the fact that *Emotional Stability* (*Neuroticism*) is claimed to be at least one of the two Big Five (Barrick et al., 2001; Le et al., 2011), if not the only one (Tett et al., 1991), to be a valid predictor of job performance. Nevertheless, in their meta-analysis, Barrick and Mount (1991) write that most correlations between *Emotional Stability* (*Neuroticism*) and job performance are relatively low and they explain this result by remembering that individuals who are highly neurotic are unable to function effectively and, as a result, are not likely to be in the labor force (Barrick et al., 2001). They also add that, as long as an individual possesses enough *Emotional Stability*, the predictive value of any differences is minimized. The participants to our study are at least mid-term workers and employees. This means, according to Barrick and Mount's reasoning, that they possess enough *Emotional Stability* to keep a job. Therefore, they could have taken for granted that, in order to simply be a worker or an employee, you must be emotionally stable and so, when answering the items of FLORA, they could have answered by focusing on those characteristics, apart from *Emotional Stability* (*Neuroticism*), that really make the difference in workers and employees' performance. On the other hand, the three dimensions of *Emotional Stability* measured by FLORA (*Stress tolerance*, *Frustration tolerance* and *Self-control*) are positively and significantly related to the length of service (with r coefficients varying from .21 to .24), while the length of service, in turn, is related to job performance with $r = .59$. Thus, even if a direct relation between *Emotional Stability* and job performance does not emerge, the amount of *Emotional Stability* in the salespeople involved in this study vary with their length of service, while their length of service, in turn, varies with their job performance, which would be in favor of an indirect relation between *Emotional Stability* and job performance passing through the length of service. Research points out that *Neuroticism* is generally negatively related to age (Steunenberg et al., 2004), while *Emotional Stability*, the opposite construct, improves over age (Williams et al., 2006), probably because of the decrease of impulses. In addition, age generally varies with the length of service (Sarker et al., 2003). Consequently, it is possible to conclude that *Emotional Stability* tends to improve with the length of service (Williams et al., 2006), probably because of the mastery acquired by experience, and positively affects job performance (Tett et al., 1991).

LIMITATIONS

The study is cross-sectional. Therefore, the sample, however wide, is not as wide as in meta-analyses. In addition, the test used for measuring the Big Five, however validated, is not so well-known as other measures of the same traits and cannot count, at the moment, on many studies supporting its validity and reliability. Replications of the study are welcome.

REFERENCES

Anderson, G. and Viswesvaran, C. (April, 1998). *An update of the validity of personality scales in personnel selection: A meta-analysis of studies published after 1992*. Paper presented at the 13th Annual Conference of the Society of Industrial and Organizational Psychology, Dallas.

Asare, A. K., Yang, J. and Brashear A. T. G. (2012). The state of research methods in personal selling and sales management literature. *Journal of Personal Selling and Sales Management*, *32*, 473-489.

Ashton, M. C. and Lee, K. (2007). Empirical, theoretical, and practical advantages of the HEXACO model of personality structure. *Personality and Social Psychology Review*, *11*, 150-166.

Barrick, M. R. and Mount, M. K. (1991). The Big Five personality dimensions and job performance: A meta-analysis. *Personnel Psychology*, *44*, 1-26.

Barrick, M. R., Stewart, G. L., Neubert, M. J. and Mount, M. K. (1998). Relating member ability and personality to work-team processes and team effectiveness. *Journal of Applied Psychology*, *83*, 377-391.

Barrick, M. R., Mount, M. K. and Judge, T. A. (2001). Personality and performance at the beginning of the New Millennium: What do we know and where do we go next? *International Journal of Selection and Assessment*, *9*, 9-30.

Bing, M. N. and Lounsbury, J. W. (2000). Openness and job performance in US-based Japanese manufacturing companies. *Journal of Business and Psychology*, *14*, 515-522.

Christie, R. and Geis, F. (1968). Some consequences of taking Machiavelli seriously. *Handbook of personality theory and research*, 959-973.

Cobb-Clark, D.A. and Schurer S. (2012). The stability of Big Five personality traits. *Economics Letters*, *115*, 11-15.

Costa, P. T., Jr. and McCrae, R. R. (1992). *Revised NEO Personality inventory and Five-Factor Model inventory professional manual*. Odessa, FL: Psychological Assessment Resources.

De Fruyt, F., McCrae, R. R., Szirmák, Z. and Nagy, J. (2004). The Five-Factor personality inventory as a measure of the Five-Factor Model: Belgian, American, and Hungarian comparisons with the NEO-PI-R. *Assessment*, *11*, 207-215.

Digman, J. M. (1990). Personality structure: Emergence of the five-factor model. *Annual Review of Psychology*, *41*, 417-440.

Donnellan, M. B. and Lucas, R. E. (2008). Age differences in the Big Five across the life span: Evidence from two national samples. *Psychology and Aging*, *23*, 558-566.

Dunn, W. S., Mount, M. K., Barrick, M. R. and Ones, D. S. (1995). Relative importance of personality and general mental ability in managers' judgments of applicant qualifications. *Journal of Applied Psychology*, *80*, 500-509.

Grucza, R. A. and Goldberg, L. R. (2007). The comparative validity of 11 modern personality inventories: Predictions of behavioral acts, informant reports, and clinical indicators. *Journal of Personality Assessment*, *89*, 167-187.

Hofstee, W. K. B., de Rand, B. and Goldberg, L. R. (1992). Integration of the Big Five and circumplex approaches to trait structure. *Journal of Personality and Social Psychology*, *63*, 146-163.

Hogan, R.T. and Hogan, J. (1992). *Hogan Personality Inventory Manual*. Tulsa, OK: Hogan Assessment Systems.

Hogan, R., Hogan, J. and Roberts, B. W. (1996). Personality measurement and employment decisions: Questions and Answers. *American Psychologist*, *51*, 469-477.

Jeronimus, B. F., Riese, H., Sanderman, R. and Ormel, J. (2014). Mutual reinforcement between neuroticism and life experiences: A five-wave, 16-year study to test reciprocal causation. *Journal of Personality and Social Psychology*, *107*, 751-64.

Judge, T. A., Rodell, J. B., Klinger, R. L., Simon, L. S. and Crawford, E. R. (2013). Hierarchical representations of the five-factor model of personality in predicting job performance: Integrating three organizing frameworks with two theoretical perspectives. *Journal of Applied Psychology*, *98*, 875-925.

McCrae, R. R. and Costa, P. T. (1997). Personality trait structure as human universal. *American Psychologist*, *52*, 509-516.

McCrae, R. R., Terracciano, A. and 79 Members of the Personality Profiles of Cultures Project (2005). Personality profiles of cultures: Aggregate Personality Traits. *Journal of Personality and Social Psychology*, *89*, 407-425.

Morgeson, F. P., Campion, M. A., Dipboye, R. L., Hollenbeck, J. R., Murphy, K. and Schmitt, N. (2007). Reconsidering the use of personality tests in personnel selection contexts. *Personnel Psychology, 60*, 683-729.

Mount, M. K., Barrick, M. R. and Stewart, G. L. (1998). Five-factor model of personality and performance in jobs involving interpersonal interactions. *Human Performance, 11*, 145-165.

Mount, M. K., Barrick, M. R., Laffitte, L. J. and Callans, M. C. (1999). *Personal Characteristics Inventory User's Manual*. Libertyville: Il: Wonderlic Consulting.

Norris, C. J., Larsen, J. T. and Cacioppo, J. T. (2007). Neuroticism is associated with larger and more prolonged electrodermal responses to emotionally evocative pictures. *Psychophysiology, 44*, 823-826.

Robinson, J.P. and Shaver, P.R. (1973). *Measures of social psychological attitudes*. Revised.

Rothmann, S. and Coetzer, E.P. (2003). The Big Five personality dimensions and job performance. *SA Journal of Industrial Psychology, 29*, 68-74.

Rothstein M. G. and Goffin, R. D. (2006). The use of personality measures in personnel selection: What does current research support? *Human Resource Management Review, 16*, 155-180.

Salgado, J. F. (1997). The five factor model of personality and job performance in the European Community. *Journal of Applied Psychology, 82*, 30-43.

Sarker, S. J., Crossman, A. and Chinmeteepituck, P. (2003). The relationships of age and length of service with job satisfaction: An examination of hotel employees in Thailand. *Journal of Managerial Psychology, 18*, 745-758.

Sartori, R. (2010). Face validity in personality tests: Psychometric instruments and projective techniques in comparison. *Quality and Quantity, 44*, 749-759.

Sartori R. and Ceschi A. (2013). Assessment and development centers: Judgment biases and risks of using idiographic and nomothetic approaches to collecting information on people to be evaluated and trained in organizations. *Quality and Quantity, 47*, 3277-3288.

Sartori, R., Ceschi, A., Costantini, A. and Scalco A. (2015). Big Five for work and organizations: FLORA (Role Related Personal Profile), an Italian personality test based on the Five-Factor Model and developed for the assessment of candidates and employees, *Quality and Quantity*. doi:10.1007/s11135-015-0250-9.

Sartori, R., Ceschi, A., Cubico, S. and Favretto, G. (2014). Quality and quantity in the construction and validation of a psychological test for the assessment and selection of aspiring volunteer rescuers: The action-research in an Italian health association. *Quality and Quantity, 48*, 3037-3051.

Sartori, R. and Pasini, M. (2007). Quality and quantity in test validity: How can we be sure that psychological tests measure what they have to? *Quality and Quantity. International Journal of Methodology, 41*, 359-374.

Sartori, R. and Rolandi, A. (2013). Validation study of a model for the assessment of potential in Italian Young Professionals working in medium-sized to large companies in different business sectors. *Quality and Quantity. 47*, 2729-2737.

Saucier, G. and Ostendorf, F. (1999). Hierarchical subcomponents of the Big Five personality factors: A cross-language replication. *Journal of Personality and Social Psychology, 76*, 613-627.

Schmit, M. J., Kihm, J. A. and Robie, C. (2000). The development of a global measure of personality. *Personnel Psychology, 1*, 153-193.

Shaffer J. A. and Postlethwaite, B.E. (2013). The validity of Conscientiousness for predicting job performance: A meta-analytic test of two hypotheses. *International Journal of Selection and Assessment*, 183-199.

Singhapakdi, A. and Vitell, S. J. (1991). Analyzing the ethical decision making of sales professionals. *Journal of Personal Selling and Sales Management*, *11*, 1-12.

Soto, C. J., John, O. P, Gosling, S. D. and Potter, J. (2011). Age differences in personality traits from 10 to 65: Big Five domains and facets in a large cross-sectional sample. *Journal of Personality and Social Psychology*, *100*, 300-348.

Steunenberg, B., Twisk, J. W. R., Beekman, A. T. F., Deeg, D. J. H. and Kerkhof, J. F. M. (2004). Stability and change of neuroticism in aging, *The Journal of Gerontology*, *60*, 27-33.

Tett, R. P., Jackson, D. N. and Rothstein, M. (1991). Personality measures as predictors of job performance: A meta-analytic review. *Personnel Psychology*, *44*, 703-742.

van der Linden, D., te Nijenhuis, J. and Bakker, A. B. (2010). The General Factor of Personality: A meta-analysis of Big Five intercorrelations and a criterion-related validity study. *Journal of Research in Personality*, *44*, 315-327.

Warr, P., Bartram, D. and Martin, T. (2005). Personality and sales performance: Situational variation and interactions between traits. *International Journal of Selection and Assessment*, *13*, 87-91.

Williams, L. M., Brown, K. J., Palmer, D., Liddell, B. J., Kemp, A. H., Olivieri, G., Gordon (2006). The mellow years?: Neural basis of improving emotional stability over age. *Journal of Neuroscience*, *26*, 6422-6430.

Witt, L., Burke, L. A., Barrick, M. A. and Mount, M. K. (2002). The interactive effects of conscientiousness and agreeableness on job performance. *Journal of Applied Psychology*, *87*, 164.

In: Neuroticism
Editor: Annamaria Di Fabio

ISBN: 978-1-63485-323-1

Chapter 5

THE INFLUENCE OF NEUROTICISM, PERSONALITY TRAITS AND MOTIVATION ON ORGANIZATIONAL EMOTIONAL INTELLIGENCE AND WORK-RELATED STRESS TOLERANCE

Giorgi Gabriele**, *Javier Fiz Perez and Melissa Morone

European University of Rome, Department of Psychology and Human Science, Business@Health laboratory, Rome, Italy

ABSTRACT

The book chapter aims to investigate the role played by neuroticism, personality traits and motivation in the development of the emergent concept of organizational emotional intelligence. The research was conducted in an Italian company among 139 employees. Employees compiled the ORG-EIQ, the WOMI and the BIG FIVE questionnaire Italian version. Findings point out that personality traits, over the effect of work motivation, impact on organizational emotional intelligence and work-related stress tolerance. The particular role played by neuroticism is highlighted in the results. Indeed, neuroticism may impede emotional intelligence, with particular reference to self-awareness and self-management. Implications of the results obtained are finally discussed.

INTRODUCTION

Neuroticism is defined as a tendency for experiencing anxiety, tension, self-consciousness, hostility, impulsiveness, timidity, illogical thinking, depression and low self-esteem (John, 1989; Mc Crae and John, 1992: Mc Crae and Costa, 1987). It is a personality trait that reflects pessimism, for the most part by negative emotions, and it is characterized by the tendency of people to negatively react to life and stressors (Watson and Clarke, 1982) in the knowledge that they will not be able to resolve the situation perceived as threatening. In

* Corresponding author: Gabriele Giorgi, e-mail: gabriele.giorgi@unier.it.

understanding relations of this type, McCrae and Costa (1991) confronted two personality-processing views. The first instrumental view contends that negativity is likely due to the greater frequency of harmful life events occurring among individuals high in neuroticism. The second temperamental view contends, instead, that neuroticism seems to enhance "arousability" and that such reactivity processes are likely to be the most important factors in understanding neuroticism's outcome-related correlates. Although the "views debate" is still ongoing, literature agreed that neuroticism is a significant predictor of negative emotional outcomes and health problems: depression (Clark, Watson, and Mineka, 1994), anger-motivated aggression (Wilkowski and Robinson, 2008), anxiety disorders (Hettema, Neale, Myers, Prescott, and Kendler, 2006), and somatic symptoms (Rosmalen, Neeleman, Gans, and de Jonge, 2007). In addition, literature on the harmful effects of neuroticism in workplace is growing. For instance, victims of workplace bullying, an acute form of stress, reported a leading personality trait characterized by excessive emotional sensitivity to adverse life events (neuroticism) (Brousse et al., 2008). Neuroticism then seems to have a pervasive effect in organizations and could play an important role in the context of working life, with particular reference to the inhibition of the development of job skills and of emotional intelligence (Giorgi et al., in press). According to a recent study conducted among Jamaican unattached youth, findings pointed out that certain individual characteristics such as neuroticism influence their workplace skills development (Chen, Johnson, Hull, and Reid, 2015).

Despite a number of studies demonstrating the negative outcomes of neuroticism, little research aimed at identifying how neuroticism and personality impedes the development of the abilities of emotional intelligence. Specifically, the present study aims to investigate the relationship between personality (neuroticism), work motivation and emotional intelligence.

Emotional Intelligence and BIG FIVE

The growing interest for the construct of EI is also due to the attempt to verify whether the introduction of this emergent variable permits to explain a percentage of incremental variance compared to cognitive intelligence and to personality (Fox and Spector, 2000).

Starting from the recognition of the existence of various theories of personality, the research that has been conducted to investigate this relation between IE and personality has mostly referred to the model of the "Big Five Factors" (BFQ) which has spread in the eighties. According to this model, personality can be divided into five dimensions: Energy-extraversion, Agreeableness, Conscientiousness, Emotional Stability or Neuroticism and Openness.

The empirical studies that have been conducted have found a positive correlation with the dimensions of Neuroticism, Extraversion, Agreeableness and Conscientiousness, but not with the dimension of mental openness. So, people who have a good emotional intelligence are likely to be socially balanced, expansive, empathetic, self-confident, responsible, have a rich emotional life, feel at ease with themselves and with others. Similarly, many of the skills studied by Goleman (1995, 1998), including empathy, self-control, self confidence measured by the ECI-360 were compared with the BFQ, highlighting significant correlations with Extraversion, Openness and Conscientiousness (r = from .22 to .49; Sala, 2002).

However, some researchers (Brackett and Mayer, 2003; Gignac, Palmer, Manocha, and Stough, 2005) have raised serious concerns about the extent to which self-report measures of EI correlate with some dimensions of personality, such as those the ones belonging to the model of the Big Five factors (Big Five), and in particular Extraversion and Neuroticism. The latter, according to Costa and McCrae (1992), it would be correlated with negative emotionality and anxiety. Therefore, intuitively, individuals who get high scores in Neuroticism are more likely to get low scores on self-report measures of EI (Zeidner, Matthews, and Roberts, 2002). In general, the interpretations of a correlation from high to moderate between EI and self-referred personality have been varied and contradictory.

Some researchers (Davies, Stankov, and Roberts, 1998) have argued that a correlation value close to .40 would be a full redundancy between the two constructs, while others (Petrides and Furnham, 2006) suggested that the self-perceived EI precisely coincides with a personality trait. Gignac and colleagues (2005) states that it would be difficult for any self-report instrument designed to measure individual differences to demonstrate the incremental validity more and better than how the Big Five Questionnaire already does, and recommends to use a statistical methodology based on factor analysis to test the redundancy between EI and personality.

For example, Gignac and colleagues (2005) suggests to extrapolate the effects of the Neuroticism component from the relationship between the TMMS (*Trait Meta-Mood Scale*) and the SREIS (*Self Report Emotional Intelligence Scale*) and determine whether the subscales of EI still form a general factor (EIg) after the extrapolation.

Measuring Organizational Emotional Intelligence

The link between emotional intelligence and personality appears complex and multifaceted and potential carrier of both methodological and theoretical bias. A strategy to better understand the relationship between constructs, in the opinion of who is writing, is to investigate emotional intelligence circumscribed in the workplace. If, in fact, highlighting significant relationships between the Big 5 factors and emotional organizational intelligence might help in reaching conclusive statements about the overlap or not of the two constructs.

According to Giorgi and Majer (2009, 2012) it in fact exists a specific and circumscribed emotional intelligence in the workplace. The basic assumption shared by the authors is the fact that emotional intelligence still depends on the context in which it applies and therefore is measured and declined in a specific setting. For example, you could have people with high emotional intelligence in varied contexts (eg. family, friendship groups, associations) but who do not apply it well at work or vice versa. By anchoring the measurement of the construct in question to the working setting it should be obtained a more specific and less elusive measure that can make better understand the connection of the EI with personality.

Another interesting factor to be investigated in relation with personality and emotional intelligence is motivation.

In 1998 Goleman published *Working with emotional intelligence*. According to Goleman, Emotional intelligence was made up of five core competencies: self-knowledge, self-regulation, motivation, empathy, social skills. The author pointed out how motivation was crucial to emotional intelligence. However, other scholars believe that the skills related to emotional intelligence are exclusively those linking emotions to cognition (Breso, Ferrer, and

Giorgi, 2013) or to the job skills (Giorgi, 2013). The study of Christie, Jordan, Troth and Lawrence (2007) investigates these two conceptualizations (motivation as part of emotional intelligence or not) and supports the position that sees motivation linked to EI without constituting it a factor. However ascertained the existence of a strong relationship between emotional intelligence and motivation it is interesting to highlight the additive effect of personality (with particular reference to neuroticism) on working motivation in predicting emotional intelligence. In view of the link between EI and motivation, which in some theories appears to be as part of a common construct, to investigate the additive effect of the personality appears to be a search track to tread with particular interest.

The Design

Knauf Case - Knauf is a well-known German company, leader in the production of plasterboard material. Knauf products consist mainly of plaster, tile, drywall, insulation, tiles and construction machinery. In Italy, Knauf was born in Treviso in 1977. Currently, three Knauf factories are located in Castellina Marittima, where slabs are produced and where there are quarries and gypsum's deposits, and in Gambassi Terme, site of production of the plaster. The Dry Construction Systems Knauf, modular and comprehensive, are the evolution of the simple concept of product. The company proposes a wide range of solutions for all requirements of contemporary building trade, going from gypsum coated profiles, to putty accessories. The quality of every single component is guaranteed by Knauf's technological know-how and reliability. Moreover, in Bolgheri, from 1998, Knauf created its own wine estate: Campo alla Sughera, 20 hectares of vineyards specialized in grapes for Cabernet Sauvignon, Cabernet Franc, Merlot, Petit Verdot, Vermentino, Sauvignon Blanc and Chardonnay. The company's objective is to produce great red wines that reflect the high vocation of the land while maintaining an excellent quality standard.

Assumptions and Objectives of Research

1) Gather empirical evidence that verify possible relationships between emotional and organizational skills, motivation and personality. In particular we expect moderate associations of Big Five with organizational emotional intelligence.

2) Highlight how the Big five, with particular reference to neuroticism, preach emotional intelligence and organizational and stress tolerance to be over the effect of working motivation. Indeed in light of Boyatzis (2009, p. 270) *"even though competencies are being described as a behavioral and functional approach to EI, they are part of an integrated, holistic theory of personality."*

METHODS

Participants

139 Knauf workers participated to the research. Specifically, 38 women and 101 men (W = 27%; M = 73%) to which were administered 3 tests. The subjects were divided into two categories: *white-collars* (32%) *blue-collars* (68%). They have been recruited in three Knauf's locations (Castellina Marittima: *n* = 129; Gambassi Terme: *n* = 4; Bolgheri: *n* = 6).

Instruments

- The *Organizational Emotional Intelligence Questionnaire (EIQ-Org,* Giorgi and Majer, 2009*)* evaluates emotional intelligence in relation to the working setting (*contextual performance*) and focuses on the vitality of the concept of organizational intelligence in the belief that organizations will provide as higher performance as higher their emotional competence will be at the level of aggregation. The Org-EIQ is composed of 99 items that converge into 4 macro-factors, each of which is divided into three factors:

1) *Awareness and Self-assessment*: it evaluates the individual's ability to discern and classify emotions at work and its self-evaluation about its inner resources and its limits and abilities. It is divided into the factors *Self-awareness* (α = .70), Self-*Confidence* (α = .72), Intrapersonal (α = .77);
2) *Self-management*: it measures the individual's ability to dominate impulses, moods and feelings to the extent to which they would have no impact on job performance and on the degree of flexibility and adaptability to new situations. It is divided into the factors of *Emotional self-control* (α = .76), *Tenacity* (α = .72), *Adaptability* (α = .73);
3) *Social competence*: it evaluates the ability in social relations and the degree of empathy that the person knows how to develop within the working environment. It includes factors of *Empathy* (α = .74), *Customer Orientation (internal and external costumer)* (α = .76), *Organizational awareness* (α = .58);
4) *Relationship Management*: it measures the ability to fluidly interact with others, developing cooperation and leadership skills. It is divided into the factors of *Teamwork* (α = .80), *Leadership* (α = .76) and *Catalyst for change* (α = .68).

The test is also accompanied by four constructs of *facilitators/correlates* to emotional intelligence: in this research the factor of Stress tolerance (α = .74) was used as theoretically linked to neuroticism.

Moreover the test has a control scale *(Positive impression)* to verify the quality of the administered questionnaire.

- *Work and Organizational Motivation Inventory (WOMI,* Giorgi and Majer, 2010*)* is a test that evaluates the motivation taking into account the nature of intrinsic variables and that of the extrinsic ones. The tool then provides a wide broad framework of the motivational dynamics that are the basis of the working behavior, enabling us to understand what are the motivational levers on which it is possible to intervene at an individual and organizational level. The test consists of 110 items divided into statements followed by a Likert scale from 1 to 5 where: 1 = *My motivation decreases greatly*; 2 = *My motivation tends to decrease*; 3 = *Has no effect on my motivation*; 4 = *My motivation tends to increase*; 5 = *My motivation increases a lot.*

The items converge into four macro-factors which, in turn, are divided into the factors of:

1) *Reward*: it refers to the motivation on the reward, which is a major push to get to the top of the organization. Specifically, for individuals particularly motivated by remuneration, compensation and incentives it carries great potential motivational. Factors: *Career* (α = .74), *Status* (α = .76), *Compensation* (α = .75), *Recognition* (α = .70).
2) *Success*: it indicates the push to do their work guided by the objective of arriving to obtain leading positions and organizational guide. Who feels the need to be successful, feels perfectly at ease in workplaces that require lots of activities characterized by considerable commitment to achieve the goals. Factors: *Management* (α = .77), *Activity* (α = .70), *Achievement* (α = .76), *Dominance* (α = .70).
3) *Competence*: it indicates a willingness to work following a continuing effort to improve and enhance skills in order to have full command of activities. Factors: *Psychological climate* (α = .70), *Ethics* (α = .75), *Freedom/flexibility* (α = .67), *Self-realization/Growth* (α = .84), *Customer (internal and external)* (α = .70).
4) *Stability*: it points out the need to ensure the protection of physical integrity and stable and secure social dimension. The presence of these elements is capable of producing satisfaction. Factors: *Interest* (α = .70), *Security* (α = .76), *Comfort* (α = .65), *Physical Environment* (α = .69), *Home/Work Balance* (α = .70).

The *Big Five Model* identifies five key dimensions for the description and evaluation of each individual's personality. The five major personality factors proposed by this model included in the Italian Version of the questionnaire of 132 items (Caprara, Barbaranelli and Borgogni, 1993; Majer and D'Amato, 1997). are: *Energy* (α = .72), which is inherent to a confident and enthusiastic approach towards the various circumstances of life, most of which are interpersonal; *Agreeableness* (α = .70), which includes, at one pole, features such as altruism, being caring, giving emotional support, and, at the opposite pole, features such as hostility, indifference to others, selfishness; *Conscientiousness* (α = .71), which refers to characteristics such as precision and accuracy, reliability, responsibility, the will to succeed and perseverance; *Neuroticism* (α = .81), that is a dimension comprising a very wide variety of features related to anxiety and the presence of emotional problems, such as depression, mood instability, irritability, etc. Finally, *Open-mindedness* (α = .77), which refers to the openness to new ideas, to the values of others and their feelings.

Procedure

The participants to the research were recruited through the participation to training courses for skills development organized by the company and held at the turn of the years 2013-2014. During the training they were administered psychometric instruments by personnel specialized in Work and Organizational Psychology. The participants subsequently completed three tests that were all valid and reliable without omissions of items. The percentage of response rate was superior to 90%.

Data Analysis

Correlational analysis and hierarchical regression analysis were used. The regression is a statistical tool that allows making a prediction about the values supposedly assumed by the two variables of the correlational analysis, depending on the value assumed by the other.

RESULTS

The correlational analysis showed that the factors and macro-factors of emotional intelligence are significantly correlated with motivation:

Relationship management correlates with *Remuneration* (r = .443), with *Success* (r = .453) and *Growth* (r = .472) and with *Stability* (r = .244);

Self-management correlates with *Remuneration* (r = .377), with *Success* (r = .319) and *Growth* (r = .515) and with *Stability* (r = .276);

Social skills correlates with *Remuneration* r=.354, with *Success* r=.376 and *Growth* r=.323, and with *Stability* r=.137;

Self-awareness correlates with *Remuneration* (r = .388), with *Success* (r = .343), Growth (r = .392) and with *Stability* (r = .330);

The correlational analysis showed that the factors and macro factors of emotional intelligence are significantly correlated with personality, but only at a certain extent confirming our first hypothesis:

Relationship management correlates with *Energy* (r = .485) and *Neuroticism* (r = -.311), with *Agreeableness* (r = .254), *Conscientiousness* (r = .273) and *Openness* (r = .210);

Self-management correlates with *Energy* (r = .379) and *Agreeableness* (r = .379), with *Conscientiousness* (r = .298), with *Neuroticism* (r = .195) and *Openness* (r = .199);

Social skills correlates with *Energy* (r = .413) with *Neuroticsm* (r = .469), with *Agreeableness* (r = .250), with *Conscientiousness* (r = .269) and *Openness* (r = .168).

Self-awareness correlates with *Energy* (r = .413), with *Conscientiousness* (r = .318), with *Emotional Stability* (r = .257) and *Openness* (r = .239) while it does not correlate with *Agreeableness* (r = .087).

The results from regression models are shown in Tables 1-2-3-4-5.

Table 1. Hierarchical regression Self-awareness

	Self-awareness		
Predictors	Block 1	Block 2	Block3
Gender	.08	.08	.08
Job position	-.01	-.01	-.04
Remuneration	-	.10	.08
Stability	-	.10	.16
Achievement	-	.15	.01
Growth	-	.18	.15
Neuroticism			-.18*
Agreeableness			.25*
Openness			.07
Conscientiousness			.07
Extraversion			-.18
R^2	.00	.17***	.27***
ΔR^2	-	.17***	.10***

Examination of the regression indicates that the proposed models are significant.

After having controlled the demographic variables for all, we found that motivational factors together explained the additional variance in emotional competencies ($p < .001$). To test the incremental contribution of personality on emotional intelligence, we added a third block to the hierarchical multiple regressions. A closer look to each tested model is given.

As far as model 1 is concerned, results show that big five personality factors explain self-awareness over motivation and demographics. In the final model (block 3) only neuroticism and agreeableness resulted significant ($p < .05$).

The empirical evidence validates our second model that show neuroticism particularly impacts on self-management ($\beta = .34$, $p < .001$). Indeed, in block three, when big five factors are added, the only significant factor in the entire model is neuroticism.

Table 2. Hierarchical regression Self-management

	Self-management		
Predictors	Block 1	Block 2	Block3
Gender	-.07	-.06	-.02
Job position	-.15	-.12	-.08
Remuneration	-	.11	.10
Stability	-	-.18	.00
Achievement	-	.19	.12
Growth	-	.30*	.10
Neuroticism			-.34***
Agreeableness			.17
Openness			-.10
Conscientiousness			.07
Extraversion			.08
R^2	.00	.16***	.31***
ΔR^2	-	.16***	.15***

Table 3. Hierarchical regression Social-awareness

	Social-awareness		
Predictors	Block 1	Block 2	Block3
Gender	-.08	-.10	-.12
Job position	-.13	-.12	-.10
Remuneration	-	.06	.17
Stability	-	-.24	-.09
Achievement	-	.06	.02
Growth	-	.58***	.40**
Neuroticism			.04
Agreeableness			.24*
Openness			-.11
Conscientiousness			.01
Extraversion			.25**
R^2	.00	.26***	.33***
ΔR^2	-	.26***	.7**

The third model confirms our hypothesis. Personality explains social-awareness over motivators and demographics (growth β = .44, $p < .001$; achievement β = .16, $p < .05$). In the final model (block 3) growth motivation remains significant, as well as extraversion and agreeableness. Neuroticism is not significant.

Table 4. Hierarchical regression Relationship management

	Relationship management		
Predictors	Block 1	Block 2	Block3
Gender	-.08	-.08	-.08
Job position	-.14	-.11	-.10
Remuneration	-	.06	.07
Stability	-	-.16	-.06
Achievement	-	.24*	.12
Growth	-	.43***	.32*
Neuroticism			-.10
Agreeableness			.32**
Openness			-.06
Conscientiousness			-.05
Extraversion			.07
R^2	.00	.28***	.36***
ΔR^2	-	.28***	.8**

Table 5. Hierarchical regression Work-related stress tolerance

	Work-related stress tolerance		
Predictors	Block 1	Block 2	Block3
Gender	-.07	-.11	-.08
Job position	.00	-.02	-.01
Remuneration	-	.45**	.46**
Stability	-	-00	.07

Table 5. (Continued)

	Work-related stress tolerance		
Achievement	-	.15	.09
Growth	-	.46**	.37**
Neuroticism			-.28**
Agreeableness			.11
Openness			.04
Conscientiousness			.05
Extraversion			-.04
R^2	.00	.10**	.17***
ΔR^2	-	.10**	.7*

The fourth model shows that the intrinsic motivators growth and achievement well explain the relationship-management (growth $\beta = .43$, $p < .001$; achievement $\beta = .24$, $p < .05$). In block three, when personality factors are added, achievement is not significant anymore, whereas agreeableness predicts relationship management ($\beta = .32$, $p < .001$).

Finally the fifth model with work-related stress as dependent variable points out remuneration, growth and in the third block neuroticism which are the significant variables in the stress tolerance prediction.

Conclusion

Findings from the results are discussed according to with previous researches.

The work sheds light on how neuroticism is an important variable in the development of emotional intelligence and can represent an impediment. In particular, the negative thoughts and arousal linked to neuroticism may inhibit a full awareness of emotions in the workplace, contributing to a less stable, secure and uncertain vision of self-awareness. Even the area of self-management seems particularly linked to neuroticism. Regression analysis has in fact shown that neuroticism is the only variable of significant prediction. Even in this case, negativity associated with the possession of neurotic traits is likely to inhibit the management of emotions at work, especially of the negative ones. It could be developed less adaptability to working changes, less perseverance in the pursuit of tasks and objectives and a general difficulty to handle negative situations at work.

It is interesting to notice that the link between neuroticism and social skills (social competence and relationship management) is rather weak. Other personality factors (such as Agreeableness and Extraversion) and motivating factors seem to be more meaningful.

For instance; extraversion stimulates workers to experience positive emotions. These situations can help workers to be more skilled in interpersonal and social interactions (Boyatzis, 2008).

These results are still of interest. The enucleating of some bonds of neuroticism with only some dimensions of emotional intelligence cannot suggest an extrapolation of the component of neuroticism, as previously noted by other authors, in the study of the relationship between personality and emotional intelligence. Neuroticism seems to be a promising construct to be tested also in the workplace and its overlap with organizational emotional intelligence appears limited.

The research also pointed out that the effects of personality are over those of motivation. This result seems important, in the opinion of the writer, as motivation and emotional intelligence in the workplace have a special link. Therefore additive effects of personality to those of motivation appear of relevant theoretical and empirical significance. In addition the comprehension of what encourages and what impedes development of emotional intelligence at work is important, because its development seems to be connected to the success of an individual as well as of an organization (Boyatzis, 1982; Giorgi, 2013; Giorgi, Mancuso, and Fiz Perez, 2014).

Results also confirmed the role of neuroticism in predicting work-related stress tolerance. As Balducci, Alfano, and Fraccaroli (2009) noted, individuals characterized by the neurotic triad on MMPI seem to manifest, particularly when under stress, dysfunctional defensive mechanisms such as somatization, denial, and repression which decrease their ability in stress management and resilience.

However, it should be stressed that there are methodological limitations in this study. Firstly, the sample was composed of employees of a single company. For instance, personality traits and motivational traits might be differently linked in public and private organization sectors (Giorgi and Majer, 2010). The generalization of the results appears therefore limited. Secondly, the research design is cross-sectional and future studies are therefore desired with longitudinal analysis techniques.

In conclusion we believe that our study may be a new avenue to be considered for the applied use in the field of neuroticism, suggesting that this personality factor is critical for the employees' organizational emotional intelligence and work-related stress tolerance.

References

Balducci, C., Alfano, V. and Fraccaroli, F. (2009). Relationships between mobbing at work and MMPI-2 personality profile, posttraumatic stress symptoms, and suicidal ideation and behavior. *Violence and Victims*, *24*, 52-67.

Boyatzis, R. (1982). *The competent manager: A model for effective performance*. New York, NY: Wiley and Sons.

Boyatzis, R. (2008). Competencies in the 21st century. *Journal of Management Development*, *27*, 5-12.

Boyatzis, R. (2009). Competencies as a behavioral approach to emotional intelligence. *Journal of Management Development*, *28*, 749-770.

Brackett, M. A. and Mayer, J. D. (2003). Convergent, discriminant, and incremental validity of competing measures of emotional intelligence. *Personality and Social Psychology Bulletin*, *9*, 1147- 1158.

Breso, E. Ferrer, A. and Giorgi, G. (2013). Meit (Mobile emotional intelligence test): Una novedosa metodologia para evaluar la percepcion de emociones haciendo uso de dispositivos moviles. *Ansiedad Y Estres*, *19*, 185-200.

Brousse, G., Fontana, L., Ouchchane, L., Boisson, C., Gerbaud, L., Bourguet, D., Chamoux, A. (2008). Psychopathological features of a patient population of targets of workplace bullying. *Occupational Medicine*, *58*, 122-128.

Caprara, G. V., Barbaranelli, C. and Borgogni, L. (1993). *Big Five Questionnaire* (scientific manual). Firenze: Giunti O. S., Organizzazioni Speciali.

Chen, D., Johnson, U., Hull, D. and Reid, J. (2015). Workplace skills development: A multilevel study of Jamaican unattached youth. *Journal of Career Assessment*. doi:10.1177/1069072715580416.

Christie, A., Jordan, P. J., Troth, A. C. and Lawrence, S. A. (2007). Testing the links between emotional intelligence and motivation. *Journal of Management and Organization*, *13*, 212-226.

Clark, L. A., Watson, D. and Mineka, S. (1994). Temperament, personality, and the mood and anxiety disorders. *Journal of Abnormal Psychology*, *103*, 103-116.

Costa, P. T. Jr. and McCrae, R. R. (1992). *Revised NEO Personality Inventory (NEO-PI-R) and NEO Five-Factor Inventory (NEO-FFI) manual*. Odessa, FL: Psychological Assessment Resources.

Davies, M., Stankov, L. and Roberts, R. D. (1998). Emotional intelligence: In search of an elusive construct. *Journal of Personality and Social Psychology, 75*, 989-1015.

Fox, S., Spector, P. and Miles, D. (2001). Counterproductive Work Behavior (CWB) in response to job stressors and organizational justice: Some mediator and moderator tests for autonomy and emotions. *Journal of Vocational Behavior*, *59*, 291-309.

Gignac, G. E., Palmer, B. R., Manocha, R. and Stough, C. (2005). An examination of the factor structure of the Schutte Self-Report Emotional Intelligence (SSREI) scale via confirmatory factor analysis. *Personality and Individual Differences*, *39*, 1029-1042.

Giorgi, G. (2013). Organizational emotional intelligence: Development of a model. *International Journal of Organization analysis*, *21*, 4-18.

Giorgi, G. and Majer, V. (2009). *Organizational Emotional Intelligence Questionnaire (scientific manual)*. Firenze Italy: Giunti O.S., Organizzazioni Speciali.

Giorgi, G. and Majer, V. (2010). *Work and Organizational Motivation Inventory (scientific manual)*. Firenze: Giunti O. S., Organizzazioni Speciali.

Giorgi, G. and Majer, V. (2012). *Intelligenza organizzativa*. Firenze Italy: Giunti O.S., Organizzazioni speciali.

Giorgi, G., Mancuso, S. and Fiz Perez, J. (2014). Organizational Emotional Intelligence and Top Selling. *Europe's Journal of Psychology*, *10*, 712-725.

Giorgi, G., Premineme, M., Montani, F., Fiz Perez J., Mucci, N., Arcangeli G. (in press). Detrimental effects of workplace bullying: Impediment of self-management competence via psychological distress. *Frontiers in Psychology*.

Goleman, D. (1995). *Emotional intelligence*. New York: Bantam Books.

Goleman, D. (1998). *Working with emotional intelligence*. New York: Bantam Books.

Hettema, J. M., Neale, M. C., Myers, J. M., Prescott, C. A. and Kendler, K. S. (2006). A population-based twin study of the relationship between neuroticism and internalizing disorders. *American Journal of Psychiatry*, *163*, 857-864.

John, O. P. (1989). Towards a taxonomy of personality descriptors. In D. M. Buss, and N. Cantor (Eds.), *Personality psychology: Recent trends and emerging directions* (pp. 261-271). New York: Springer.

Majer, V. and D'Amato, A. (1997). Contributo alla taratura del Big Five Questionnaire. Confronto tra soggetti in situazione competitiva -selezione- e soggetti in situazione non competitiva -orientamento. *Risorsa Uomo*, *3*, 325-340.

McCrae, R. R. and John, O. P. (1992). An introduction to the five-factor model and its application. Special Issue: The five-factor model: Issues and applications. *Journal of Personality*, *60*, 175-215.

McCrae, R. R. and Costa, Jr, P. T. (1987). Validation of the five-factor model of personality across instruments and observers. *Journal of Personality and Social Psychology*, *52*, 81-90.

McCrae, R. R. and Costa, P. T. (1991). Adding Liebe und Arbeit: The full five-factor model and well-being. *Personality and Social Psychology Bulletin*, *17*, 227-232.

Petrides, K. V. and Furnham, A. (2006). The role of trait emotional intelligence in a gender-specific model of organizational variables. *Journal of Applied Social Psychology*, *36*, 552-569.

Rosmalen, J. G. M., Neeleman, J., Gans, R. O. B. and de Jonge, P. (2007). The association between neuroticism and self-reported common somatic symptoms in a population cohort. *Journal of Psychosomatic Research*, *62*, 305-311.

Sala, F. (2002). *Emotional Competence Inventory (ECI): Technical manual*. Boston: Hay/Mcber Group.

Watson, D. and Clark, L. A. (1992). On traits and temperament: General and specific factors of emotional experience and their relation to the five-factor model. *Journal of Personality*, *60*, 441-476.

Wilkowski, B. M. and Robinson, M. D. (2008). The cognitive basis of trait anger and reactive aggression: An integrative analysis. *Personality and Social Psychology Review*, *12*, 3-21.

Zeidner, M., Roberts, R. D. and Matthews, G. (2002). Can emotional intelligence be schooled? A critical review. *Educational Psychology*, *37*, 215-231.

In: Neuroticism
Editor: Annamaria Di Fabio

ISBN: 978-1-63485-323-1

Chapter 6

FOCUS ON NEUROTICISM AND STRENGTHS OF WORKERS: EMPIRICAL RESULTS IN DIFFERENT ORGANIZATIONAL CONTEXTS

Annamaria Di Fabio* ***and Letizia Palazzeschi***
Department of Education and Psychology (Psychology Section),
University of Florence, Florence, Italy

ABSTRACT

Previous research has demonstrated relationships between personality and both resilience and life satisfaction, particularly in adolescents and young adults. This study aims to verify the association between the Big Five personality traits and both resilience and life satisfaction in organizational contexts, with participants from three Italian organizational realities: 117 physicians, 123 nurses, and 101 employees of an insurance company. The participants filled out the Big Five Questionnaire (BFQ), the Connor-Davidson Resilience Scale (CD-RISC), and the Satisfaction with Life Scale (SWLS). The results of the present study showed that Neuroticism in particular consistently inversely explained a significantly larger percentage of variance both in resilience and life satisfaction in all three groups. The results contribute to the in-depth exploration of both the constructs of resilience and life satisfaction, broadening our understanding of their associations with personality traits, and in particular with neuroticism, in different organizational contexts.

INTRODUCTION

Positive psychology (Seligman, 2002; Seligman and Csikszentmihalyi, 2000) is centered on strengths promotion and on the study of well-being and mental health. Since the introduction of the positive psychology perspective, the importance of developing personal resources and resilience has been underlined in a preventive framework (Hage et al., 2007;

* Corresponding author: Annamaria Di Fabio, e-mail: adifabio@psico.unifi.it.

Kenny and Hage, 2009) that highlights the relevance of building individual strengths (Di Fabio, 2015a; Di Fabio and Blustein, 2010; Di Fabio and Kenny, 2012a, 2012b, 2015, 2016; Di Fabio, Kenny, and Claudius, in press; Di Fabio and Palazzeschi, 2008a, 2008b, 2009, 2012b; Di Fabio, Palazzeschi, and Bar-On, 2012; Di Fabio, Palazzeschi, Asulin-Peretz, and Gati, 2013; Di Fabio and Saklofske, 2014a, 2014b). Resilience is a fundamental variable in the positive psychology perspective (Luthar, Lyman, and Crossman, 2014). It can be defined as the perceived ability of individuals to confront and overwhelm difficulties in an adaptive manner (Campbell-Sills and Stein, 2007; Luthar, Cicchetti, and Becker, 2000). It can be also considered as the implementation by individuals of adaptive approaches to deal with uneasiness and hardship (Tugade and Fredrickson, 2004). Furthermore, resilience concerns a set of resources that permit individuals to convert critical experiences into opportunities for personal growth (Malaguti, 2005). Resilience is also studied in organizational contexts (Harland, Harrison, Jones, and Reiter-Palmon, 2005; Jackson, Firtko, and Edenborough, 2007) as capacity to resist and respond to difficulties, imposed changes and external requirements.

Life satisfaction is another fundamental variable in the positive psychology perspective, representing an essential component of hedonic well-being (Kahneman, Diener, and Schwarz, 1999). Life satisfaction in fact represents the cognitive component of hedonic well-being (Kahneman, Diener, and Schwarz, 1999), which also includes an affective component characterized by the prevalence of positive rather than negative emotions (Kahneman et al., 1999) in addition to life satisfaction. To be more precise, life satisfaction constitutes a broad cognitive judgment about one's own life: it doesn't concern the emotional aspects, but regards the cognitive aspects of judgment (Diener, Emmons, Larsen, and Griffin, 1985). Specifically, it is the average result of satisfaction, taking into account every aspect of one's own life (Andrews and Withey, 1976). Life satisfaction is studied in the organizational field (Demerouti, Bakker, Nachreiner, and Schaufeli, 2000; Di Fabio and Palazzeschi, 2014; Ernst Kossek and Ozeki, 1998; Mafini and Dlodlo, 2014; Vanaki and Vagharseyyedin, 2009) because workers' satisfaction is associated with many positive outcomes, such as fewer work-family conflicts (Adams, King, and King, 1996; Ernst Kossek and Ozeki, 1998; Goh, Ilies, and Wilson, 2015), fewer negative psychological conditions such as depression, anxiety, and hopelessness (Guney, Kalafat, and Boysan, 2010), high subjective health (Straume and Vittersø, 2015), high perceived workplace support (Newman, Nielsen, Smyth, and Hooke, 2015), and high levels of organizational commitment (Sharma and Sharma, 2015; Sood, Bakhshi, and Singh, 2015).

Both resilience and life satisfaction are studied in relation to personality traits. Regarding resilience, in the literature, relationships with personality traits emerge, and in particular an inverse relationship between resilience and neuroticism (i.e., Annalakshmi, 2007; Campbell-Sills, Cohan, Murray, and Stein, 2006; Di Fabio, 2014, 2015; Friborg, Barlaug, Martinussen, Rosenvinge, and Hjemdal, 2005; Nakaya, Oshio and Kaneko, 2006). In a study carried out on adults, Friborg et al., (2005) found above all a negative relationship between resilience and neuroticism, and to a lesser extent a positive relationship between resilience and extraversion, and even positive relations of lower intensity with the conscientiousness and agreeableness dimensions of the Five Factors Model (McCrae and Costa, 1987). In a study carried out on young adults (Campbell-Sills et al., 2006), resilience was negatively associated to neuroticism and positively associated to extraversion, but also to conscientiousness on the Five Factors Model (McCrae and Costa, 1987). A study conducted on Japanese adolescents (Nakaya et al.,

2006) showed a marked negative relationship between resilience and neuroticism of the Five Factors Model (McCrae and Costa, 1987). In a subsequent study conducted on Italian high school students (Di Fabio and Palazzeschi, 2015), an inverse relation emerged between resilience and neuroticism investigated in terms of its opposite (emotional stability). This same inverse association between resilience and neuroticism also emerged with nurses and physicians in the Italian context (Di Fabio, 2014), as did relations between extraversion and resilience, albeit to a lesser extent.

Regarding the relations between resilience and Eysenck personality model dimensions (Eysenck, 1981), one study (Annalakshmi, 2007) showed negative relations of resilience with neuroticism and psychoticism and a positive relation with extraversion in young adults. This inverse relation demonstrated between resilience and neuroticism according to the Eysenck model is in line with findings presented in the literature underlining the relation between resilience and neuroticism according to the Big Five model, with similar associations between resilience and neuroticism thus emerging for both models. Individuals with lower levels of neuroticism thus seem to be more resilient and therefore able to face difficulties and adversity with a greater degree of adaptability (Campbell-Sills and Stein, 2007; Luthar et al., 2000). However, in the existing literature there is no comprehensive study of the relations between resilience and personality, particularly in the organizational field, and as such it is a subject which warrants further investigations.

With regard to the relation between life satisfaction and personality traits, the literature indicates in particular a negative relation between life satisfaction and neuroticism and a positive relation with extraversion (i.e., Diener et al., 1985; Diener and Lucas, 1999; Di Fabio and Palazzeschi, 2014, Di Fabio and Saklofske, 2014a; Gannon and Ranzijn, 2005; Haslam, Whelan, and Bastian, 2009; Quevedo and Abella, 2011; Schimmack, Diener, and Oishi, 2002). In 1999, Diener and Lucas underlined that life satisfaction is negatively associated above all with neuroticism, and also to a lesser extent positively associated with extraversion in the Five Factors Model (McCrae and Costa, 1987). In university students, Schimmack et al. (2002) found a particularly marked negative association between life satisfaction and neuroticism, and positive associations to a lesser extent between life satisfaction and both the extraversion and conscientiousness dimensions of the Five Factors Model (McCrae and Costa, 1987). The inverse relationship between life satisfaction and neuroticism and the positive relation of life satisfaction with extraversion on the Five Factors Model (McCrae and Costa, 1987) were also found in adults in a study by Gannon and Ranzijn (2005), which showed a strong association between life satisfaction and neuroticism. This strong association has also emerged with Australian university students (Haslam et al., 2009), Spanish university students (Quevedo and Abella, 2011), and Italian high school students (Di Fabio and Saklofske, 2014a). In Italian nurses (Di Fabio and Palazzeschi, 2014), the inverse relation of life satisfaction with neuroticism in terms of its contrary (emotional stability) and the positive relation of life satisfaction with extraversion according to the Five Factors Model (McCrae and Costa, 1987) also emerged, underling in particular the contribution of neuroticism. Regarding the relations between life satisfaction and Eysenck personality model dimensions (Eysenck, 1981), Diener et al. (1985) underlined a negative relationship between resilience and neuroticism and a positive relationship with extraversion. These relations of life satisfaction, above all negative with neuroticism and with a lesser extent positive with extraversion emerged also in Italian nurses (Di Fabio, 2014). However, study of the relationships between life satisfaction and personality traits has not been extensively carried out in the organizational field, where instead job satisfaction has been the primary focus of attention (Judge, Heller, and Mount, 2002; Mehrad, Redzuan, and Abdullah, 2015). In sum, analysis of the literature showed in particular an inverse relation between life satisfaction and neuroticism. Individuals with lower levels of neuroticism seem to have a greater overall level of satisfaction with their lives (Diener et al., 1985).

Aim and Hypotheses

Since previous research has shown that personality is associated both with resilience and life satisfaction, particularly in adolescents and young adults, the aim of the present study was to examine these relations in more detail in the organizational field, investigating the contribution of personality to resilience and life satisfaction among the three groups of Italian workers (physicians, nurses, and employees of an insurance company). Specifically, the following hypotheses were formulated:

H1. In all three groups, among personality traits the stronger association will emerge between resilience and neuroticism (Annalakshmi, 2007; Campbell-Sill et al., 2006; Di Fabio, 2014; Di Fabio and Palazzeschi, 2015; Friborg et al., 2005; Nakaya et al., 2006)

H2. In all three groups, among personality traits the stronger association will emerge between life satisfaction and neuroticism (Diener et al., 1985; Diener and Lucas, 1999; Di Fabio and Palazzeschi, 2014, Di Fabio and Saklofske, 2014a; Gannon and Ranzijn, 2005; Haslam et al., 2009; Quevedo and Abella, 2011; Schimmack et al., 2002).

Material and Methods

Participants

The first group was composed of 117 Italian physicians who worked in local healthcare organizations in the Tuscany region (66 men, 56.40%; 51 women, 43.60%). The second group comprised 123 Italian nurses who worked in local healthcare organizations in the Tuscany region (41 men, 33.30%; 82 women, 66.70%). The third group included 101 Italian employees of an insurance company in the Tuscany region (43 men, 42.60%; 58 women, 57.40%).

Measures

Big Five Questionnaire (BFQ)

To evaluate personality traits, the Italian version of Big Five Questionnaire (BFQ, Caprara, Barbaranelli, and Borgogni, 1993) was used. The questionnaire comprises 132 items with response options on a 5-point Likert scale ranging from 1 = *Absolutely false* to 5 = *Absolutely true*. The questionnaire measures five personality traits. The Cronbach's alpha coefficients were: .82 for Extraversion, .76 for Agreeableness, .83 for Conscientiousness, .91 for Emotional Stability, and .77 for Openness.

Connor-Davidson Resilience Scale (CD-RISC)

To evaluate resilience, the Connor-Davidson Resilience Scale (CD-RISC, Campbell-Sills and Stein, 2007) in the Italian version by Di Fabio and Palazzeschi (2012a) was used. The scale was composed of 10 items with response options on a 5-point Likert scale ranging from *Not true at all* (0) to *True nearly all the time* (4). The Cronbach's alpha coefficient was .90.

Satisfaction with Life Scale (SWLS)

To evaluate life satisfaction, the Satisfaction with Life Scale (SWLS, Diener et al., 1985) in the Italian version by Di Fabio and Gori (2015) was used. The questionnaire has 5 items on a 7-point Likert scale ranging from 1 = *Strongly disagree* to 7 = *Strongly agree*. The Cronbach's alpha coefficient was .89.

Procedure and Data Analysis

The questionnaires were filled out in groups of 10-30 participants, and administered by trained psychologists. The order of the questionnaires was counterbalanced during administration to control the possible effects of presentation. The administration followed the requirements of privacy and informed consent specified in Italian law (Law Decree DL-196/2003). Pearson's *r* correlations and stepwise regressions were carried out.

Results

Correlations between BFQ, CD-RISC, SWLS for the three groups of workers are reported in Tables 1 and 2.

Table 1. Correlations between CD-RISC, SWLS and BFQ among physicians (*N* = 117, below diagonal) and nurses (*N* = 123, above diagonal)

	1	2	3	4	5	6	7
1. CD-RISC	-	.33**	.46**	.19	.16	-.51**	.11
2. SWLS	.34**	-	.37**	.19	.15	-.42**	.19
3. BFQ E	.45**	.36**	-	.15	.11	-.30**	.20*
4. BFQ A	.11	.15	.20*	-	.11	-.25**	.11
5. BFQ C	.17	.11	.21*	.20*	-	-.27**	.20*
6. BFQ N	-.49**	-.40**	-.32**	-.31**	-.30**	-	-.35**
7. BFQ O	.12	.17	.20*	.37**	.30**	-.34**	-

Note: * $p < .05$. ** $p < .01$.

CD-RISC = Resilience; SWLS = Life satisfaction; BFQ E = Extraversion; BFQ A = Agreeableness; BFQ C = Conscientiousness; BFQ N = Neuroticism; BFQ O = Openness to Experience.

Table 2. Correlations between CD-RISC, SWLS and BFQ among employees of an insurance company (N = 101, above diagonal)

	1	2	3	4	5	6	7
1. CD-RISC	-	.26**	.44	.12	.17	-.48**	.12
2. SWLS		-	.34**	.20*	.20*	-.39**	.21**
3. BFQ E			-	.29	.14	.30**	.16
4. BFQ A				-	.28*	.30**	.38**
5. BFQ C					-	.31**	.31**
6. BFQ N						-	.33**
7. BFQ O							-

Note. * $p < .05$. ** $p < .01$.

CD-RISC = Resilience; SWLS = Life satisfaction; BFQ E = Extraversion; BFQ A = Agreeableness; BFQ C = Conscientiousness; BFQ N = Neuroticism; BFQ O = Openness to Experience.

To further assess the association between the BFQ and both CD-RISC and SWLS, we carried out a stepwise multiple regression analysis using both CD-RISC and SWLS as the dependent variables and the Big Five factors that are correlated (neuroticism – in terms of its contrary: emotional stability – and extraversion) as the independent variables, separately for each of the three groups. A summary of these analyses is presented in Table 3.

Table 3. Results of Multiple Regression Analysis

	Physicians N = 117		Nurses N = 123		Employees N = 101	
	CD-RISC	SWLS	CD-RISC	SWLS	CD-RISC	SWLS
BFQ	β ΔR^2	β ΔR^2	β ΔR^2	β ΔR^2	β ΔR^2	β ΔR^2
BFQ E	.31*** .10	.27*** . .09	.33*** .11	.30** .10	.26** .09	.25** .09
BFQ N	-36*** .23	.-.32*** .22	-38*** .24	-.35** .23	-.34*** .22	.-.30** .21
Adjusted R^2	.33***	.31***	.35***	.33***	.31***	.30***

** p< .01. *** p< .001.

Resilience. Similar results emerged for the explanation of resilience among the three groups of participants, with only two out of the five BFQ factors explaining resilience (*Adjusted* R^2= .33; *Adjusted* R^2= .35; *Adjusted* R^2 = .31, for physicians, nurses, and insurance company employees respectively). These factors were Neuroticism (in terms of its contrary: emotional stability) and Extraversion: for physicians (β = -.36, ΔR^2 = .23; β = .31, ΔR^2 = .10; for Neuroticism and Extraversion, respectively), for nurses (β = -.38, ΔR^2 = .24; β = .33, ΔR^2 = .11; for Neuroticism and Extraversion, respectively), and for employees of an insurance company (β = -.34, ΔR^2 = .22; β = .25, ΔR^2 = .09; for Neuroticism and Extraversion respectively).

Life satisfaction. Similar patterns of results also emerged for the explanation of life satisfaction (*Adjusted* R^2 = .31; *Adjusted* R^2 = .35; *Adjusted* R^2 = .31, for physicians, nurses, and insurance company employees, respectively), again with only two out of the five BFQ factors explaining life satisfaction. These factors were Neuroticism (in terms of its contrary:

emotional stability) and Extraversion: for physicians (β = -.32, ΔR^2 = .22; β = .27, ΔR^2 = .09, for Neuroticism and Extraversion respectively), for nurses (β = -.35, ΔR^2 = .23; β = .30, ΔR^2 = .10, for Neuroticism and Extraversion respectively), and for insurance company employees (β = -.30, ΔR^2 = .21; β = .25, ΔR^2 = .09, for Neuroticism and Extraversion respectively).

DISCUSSION

The present study aimed to examine the contribution of personality to resilience and life satisfaction among the three groups of Italian workers studied. The results confirmed the first hypothesis, since, in all three groups, among personality traits the stronger association emerged between resilience and neuroticism in terms of its contrary (emotional stability), which is in line with the literature (Annalakshmi, 2007; Campbell-Sill et al., 2006; Di Fabio, 2014; Di Fabio and Palazzeschi, 2015; Friborg et al., 2005; Nakaya et al., 2006). Individuals with low neuroticism, more able to control their emotions and impulses, also appear more resilient and thus seem to perceive themselves as more able to adaptively face and overcome adversities (Campbell-Sills and Stein, 2007; Luthar et al., 2000). Furthermore, an association emerged between resilience and extraversion, underlining that individuals who are more dynamic and open to interpersonal relationships perceive themselves as more resilient, again consistent with the literature, which has indicated this same association (Annalakshmi, 2007; Campbell-Sill et al., 2006; Di Fabio, 2014; Di Fabio and Palazzeschi, 2015; Friborg et al., 2005; Nakaya et al., 2006).

The results of the present study also confirmed the second hypothesis, since in all three groups of workers, among personality traits the stronger association emerged between life satisfaction and neuroticism in terms of its contrary (emotional stability), again in line with previous studies (Diener et al., 1985; Diener and Lucas, 1999; Di Fabio and Palazzeschi, 2014, Di Fabio and Saklofske, 2014a; Gannon and Ranzijn, 2005; Haslam et al., 2009; Quevedo and Abella, 2011; Schimmack et al., 2002). Individuals with low neuroticism who perceive themselves as more able to control their emotions and impulses also seem to have a greater level of overall satisfaction with their lives (Diener et al., 1985). Furthermore – and again, in line with the literature – an association emerged between life satisfaction and extraversion, underlining that individuals who perceived themselves as more dynamic and oriented toward interpersonal relationships also perceive themselves as having a greater overall satisfaction with life (Diener et al., 1985; Diener and Lucas, 1999; Di Fabio and Palazzeschi, 2014, Di Fabio and Saklofske, 2014a; Gannon and Ranzijn, 2005; Haslam et al., 2009; Quevedo and Abella, 2011; Schimmack et al., 2002).

Overall, the results of the present study confirm the strong contribution of neuroticism both to resilience and to life satisfaction across different groups of Italian workers, thus expanding on results presented in the existing literature which mainly relate to adolescents and young adults.

The results of the present study should be interpreted with an awareness of limitations vis-à-vis the generalizability of results obtained among specific Italian groups of physicians, nurses, and insurance company employees. Future research should include a broader range of participants more representative of Italian society, and results verified in other international contexts as well. In addition, future studies should use a longitudinal approach to investigate causality among the studied variables.

CONCLUSION

Limitations notwithstanding, the findings of this study add to and extend the literature on the constructs of resilience and life satisfaction, underlining their inverse associations above all with neuroticism – in this study in terms of its contrary (emotional stability) – confirming these relationships also in different organizational contexts. On the basis of the relationships between neuroticism and both resilience and life satisfaction, if the results of this study are confirmed in future research it may be possible to consider opportunities for identifying individuals at risk of high neuroticism and thus to intervene accordingly. From a preventive perspective (Hage et al., 2007; Kenny and Hage, 2009) emphasizing the importance of developing personal resources, it may help to deal with neuroticism early in terms of job tasks or through training focused on promoting resilience and life satisfaction. Taking such considerations into account to promote to the development of individual attributes such as resilience and life satisfaction also promotes higher levels of well-being both in individuals and in organizations.

REFERENCES

Adams, G. A., King, L. A. and King, D. W. (1996). Relationships of job and family involvement, family social support, and work-family conflict with job and life satisfaction. *Journal of Applied Psychology*, *81*(4), 411-420.

Andrews, F. M. and Withey, S. B. (1976). *Social indicators of well-being*. New York: Plenum Press.

Annalakshmi, N. (2007). Resilience in relation to extraversion-introversion, psychoticism, and neuroticism. *Indian Journal of Psychometry and Education, 38*, 51-55.

Campbell-Sills, L., Cohan, S. L. and Stein, M. B. (2006). Relationship of resilience to personality, coping, and psychiatric symptoms in young adults. *Behaviour research and therapy*, *44*(4), 585-599.

Campbell-Sills, L. and Stein, M. B. (2007). Psychometric analysis and refinement of the Connor-Davidson Resilience Scale (CD-RISC): Validation of a 10-item measure of resilience. *Journal of Traumatic Stress*, *20*(6), 1019-1028.

Caprara, G. V., Barbaranelli, C. and Borgogni, L. (1993). *BFQ: Big Five Questionnaire* (2nd ed.). Firenze, Italy: Giunti O.S.

Demerouti, E., Bakker, A. B., Nachreiner, F. and Schaufeli, W. B. (2000). A model of burnout and life satisfaction amongst nurses. *Journal of advanced nursing*, *32*(2), 454-464.

Diener, E., Emmons, R. A., Larsen, R. J. and Griffin, S. (1985). The satisfaction with life scale. *Journal of Personality Assessment*, *49*(1), 71-75.

Diener, E. and Lucas, R. E. (1999). Personality and subjective well-being. *Well-being: Foundations of Hedonic Psychology, 213.*

Di Fabio, A. (2014, February). *In light of the changing work scene: New challenges for research and intervention*. Invited Keynote at the Symposium sponsored by Linch School of Education of Boston College, in D. L. Blustein (Chair). Career Development and the Psychology of Working. Boston College, Boston.

Di Fabio, A. (2015). Beyond fluid intelligence and personality traits in social support: The role of ability based emotional intelligence. *Frontiers in Psychology*, *6*, 395. doi: 10.3389/fpsyg.2015.00395.

Di Fabio, A. and Blustein, D. L. (2010). Emotional intelligence and decisional conflict styles: Some empirical evidence among Italian high school students. *Journal of Career Assessment*, *18*(1), 71-81.

Di Fabio, A. and Gori, A. (2015). Measuring adolescent life satisfaction: Psychometric properties of the Satisfaction With Life Scale in a sample of Italian adolescents and young adults. *Journal of Psychoeducational Assessment*. Advance online publication. doi: 10.1177/0734282915621223.

Di Fabio, A. and Kenny, M. E. (2012a). The contribution of emotional intelligence to decisional styles among Italian high school students. *Journal of Career Assessment*, *20*, 404-414.

Di Fabio, A. and Kenny, M. E. (2012b). Emotional intelligence and perceived social support among Italian high school students. *Journal of Career Development*, *39*, 461-475.

Di Fabio, A. and Kenny, M. E. (2015). The contributions of emotional intelligence and social support for adaptive career progress among Italian youth. *Journal of Career Development*, *42*, 48-49.

Di Fabio, A. and Kenny, E. M. (2016). From decent work to decent lives: Positive Self and Relational Management (PS&RM) in the 21st century. In A. Di Fabio and D. L. Blustein (Eds.), "From meaning of working to meaningful lives: The challenges of expanding decent work". Research topic in *Frontiers in Psychology. Section Organizational Psychology.*

Di Fabio, A., Kenny, M. E. and Claudius, M. (in press). Preventing distress and promoting psychological well-being in uncertain times through career management intervention. In M. Israelashvili and J. L. Romano (Eds.), *Cambridge handbook of international prevention science*. Cambridge: Cambridge University Press.

Di Fabio, A. and Palazzeschi, L. (2008a). Emotional intelligence and self-efficacy in a sample of Italian high school teacher. *Social Behavior and Personality*, *36*(3), 315-326.

Di Fabio, A. and Palazzeschi, L. (2008b). Indécision vocationnelle et intelligence émotionnelle: Quelques données empiriques sur un échantillon d'apprentis italiens. *Pratiques Psychologiques*, *14*(4), 213-222.

Di Fabio, A. and Palazzeschi, L. (2009). Emotional intelligence, personality traits and career decision difficulties. *International Journal for Educational and Vocational Guidance*, *9*(2), 135-146.

Di Fabio, A. and Palazzeschi, L. (2012a). Connor-Davidson Resilience Scale: Proprietà psicometriche della versione italiana [Connor-Davidson Resilience Scale: Psychometric properties of the Italian version]. *Counseling. Giornale Italiano di Ricerca e Applicazioni*, *5*, 101-110.

Di Fabio, A. and Palazzeschi, L. (2012b). Incremental variance of the core self-evaluation construct compared to fluid intelligence and personality traits in aspects of decision-making. *Personality and Individual Differences*, *53*, 196-201.

Di Fabio, A. and Palazzeschi, L. (2014). Emotional intelligence and life satisfaction: An empirical study on Italian nurses. *European Journal of Management*, *14*(2), 109-111.

Di Fabio, A. and Palazzeschi, L. (2015, June). *Resilienza: dai tratti di personalità all'intelligenza emotiva* [*Resilience: From personality traits to emotional intelligence*]. In A. Delle Fave (Chair). Thematic session on work conducted at the 8th Italian Conference on Positive Psychology *Nutrire positività. Ricerche e interventi per la promozione del benessere* [*Nurture positivity. Researches and interventions for the promotion of the well-being*]. University of Bergamo, 12-13 June 2015, Bergamo, Italy.

Di Fabio, A., Palazzeschi, L., Asulin-Peretz, L. and Gati, I. (2013). Career indecision versus indecisiveness: Associations with personality traits and emotional intelligence. *Journal of Career Assessment*, *21*, 42-56.

Di Fabio, A., Palazzeschi, L. and Bar-On, R. (2012). The role of personality traits, core self-evaluation and emotional intelligence in career decision-making difficulties. *Journal of Employment Counseling*, *49*, 118-129.

Di Fabio, A. and Saklofske, D. H. (2014a). Comparing ability and self-report trait emotional intelligence, fluid intelligence, and personality traits in career decision. *Personality and Individual Differences*, *64*, 174-178.

Di Fabio, A. and Saklofske, D. H. (2014b). Promoting individual resources: The challenge of trait emotional intelligence. *Personality and Individual Differences*, *65*, 19-23.

Ernst Kossek, E. and Ozeki, C. (1998). Work-family conflict, policies, and the job-life satisfaction relationship: A review and directions for organizational behavior-human resources research. *Journal of Applied Psychology*, *83*(2), 139-149.

Eysenck, H. J. (Ed.). (1981). *A model for personality*. New York: Springer.

Friborg, O., Barlaug, D., Martinussen, M., Rosenvinge, J. H. and Hjemdal, O. (2005). Resilience in relation to personality and intelligence. *International Journal of Methods in Psychiatric Research*, *14*(1), 29-42.

Gannon, N. and Ranzijn, R. (2005). Does emotional intelligence predict unique variance in life satisfaction beyond IQ and personality? *Personality and Individual Differences*, *38*(6), 1353-1364.

Goh, Z., Ilies, R. and Wilson, K. S. (2015). Supportive supervisors improve employees' daily lives: The role supervisors play in the impact of daily workload on life satisfaction via work-family conflict. *Journal of Vocational Behavior*, *89*, 65-73.

Hage, S. M., Romano, J. L., Conyne, R. K., Kenny, M., Matthews, C., Schwartz, J. P. and Waldo, M. (2007). Best practice guidelines on prevention practice, research, training, and social advocacy for psychologists. *The Counseling Psychologist*, *35*, 493-566.

Haslam, N., Whelan, J. and Bastian, B. (2009). Big Five traits mediate associations between values and subjective well-being. *Personality and Individual Differences*, *46*(1), 40-42.

Harland, L., Harrison, W., Jones, J. R. and Reiter-Palmon, R. (2005). Leadership behaviors and subordinate resilience. *Journal of Leadership and Organizational Studies*, *11*(2), 2-14.

Jackson, D., Firtko, A. and Edenborough, M. (2007). Personal resilience as a strategy for surviving and thriving in the face of workplace adversity: A literature review. *Journal of advanced nursing*, *60*(1), 1-9.

Judge, T. A., Heller, D. and Mount, M. K. (2002). Five-factor model of personality and job satisfaction: A meta-analysis. *Journal of Applied Psychology*, *87*(3), 530-541.

Kahneman, D., Diener, E. and Schwarz, N. (Eds.). (1999). *Well-being: The foundations of hedonic psychology*. New York, NY: Russell Sage Foundation.

Kenny, M. E. and Hage, S. M. (2009). The next frontier: Prevention as an instrument of social justice. *The Journal of Primary Prevention*, *30*, 1-10.

Luthar, S. S., Cicchetti, D. and Becker, B. (2000). The construct of resilience: A critical evaluation and guidelines for future work. *Child Development*, *71*(3), 543-562.

Luthar, S. S., Lyman, E. L. and Crossman, E. J. (2014). Resilience and positive psychology. In *Handbook of developmental psychopathology* (pp. 125-140). Springer US.

Mafini, C. and Dlodlo, N. (2014). The relationship between extrinsic motivation, job satisfaction and life satisfaction amongst employees in a public organisation. *SA Journal of Industrial Psychology*, *40*(1), 1-12.

Malaguti, E. (2005). *Educarsi alla resilienza: Come affrontare crisi e difficoltà e migliorarsi* [Educate yourself on resilience: How to deal with crises and difficulties and improve]. Trento, Italy: Erickson.

McCrae, R. R. and Costa, P. T. (1987). Validation of the five-factor model of personality across instruments and observers. *Journal of Personality And Social Psychology*, *52*(1), 81-90.

Mehrad, A., Redzuan, H. H. M. R. B. and Abdullah, H. (2015). The role of personality factors on job satisfaction among academic staff at public research university. *Journal of Educational, Health and Community Psychology*, *4*(1), 16-22.

Nakaya, M., Oshio, A. and Kaneko, H. (2006). Correlations for adolescent resilience scale with big five personality traits. *Psychological Reports*, *98*(3), 927-930.

Newman, A., Nielsen, I., Smyth, R. and Hooke, A. (2015). Examining the relationship between workplace support and life satisfaction: The mediating role of job satisfaction. *Social Indicators Research*, *120*(3), 769-781.

Quevedo, R. J. M. and Abella, M. C. (2011). Well-being and personality: Facet-level analyses. *Personality and Individual Differences*, *50*(2), 206-211.

Schimmack, U., Diener, E. and Oishi, S. (2002). Life-satisfaction is a momentary judgment and a stable personality characteristic: The use of chronically accessible and stable sources. *Journal of Personality*, *70*(3), 345-384.

Seligman, M. E. P. (2002). Positive psychology, positive prevention, and positive therapy. In C. R. Snyder and S. J. Lopez (Eds.), *Handbook of positive psychology* (pp. 3-9). New York: Oxford University Press.

Seligman, M. E. and Csikszentmihalyi, M. (2000). *Positive psychology: An introduction*. Washington, DC: American Psychological Association.

Sharma, R. and Sharma, S. (2015). Life satisfaction: A study of public sector employees by affective commitment. *American International Journal of Contemporary Scientific Research*, *2*(7), 32-39.

Sood, S., Bakhshi, A. and Singh, K. (2015). Gratitude and life satisfaction as Predictors of organizational commitment in Anganwadi workers. *Prabandhan: Indian Journal of Management*, *8*(3), 48-56.

Straume, L. V. and Vittersø, J. (2015). Well-being at work: Some differences between life satisfaction and personal growth as predictors of subjective health and sick-leave. *Journal of Happiness Studies*, *16*(1), 149-168.

Tugade, M. M. and Fredrickson, B. L. (2004). Resilient individuals use positive emotions to bounce back from negative emotional experiences. *Journal of Personality and Social Psychology*, *86*, 320-333.

Vanaki, Z. and Vagharseyyedin, S. A. (2009). Organizational commitment, work environment conditions, and life satisfaction among Iranian nurses. *Nursing and health sciences*, *11*(4), 404-409.

WIDENING THE HORIZON

In: Neuroticism
Editor: Annamaria Di Fabio

ISBN: 978-1-63485-323-1

Chapter 7

NEUROTICISM, ATTENTION, AND EYE MOVEMENTS

Sowon Hahn* and Yumin Chung
Department of Psychology, Seoul National University,
Seoul, South Korea

ABSTRACT

A great deal of research has indicated attention as a central mechanism to account for the relationship between neuroticism and various task performances. For instance, high levels of neuroticism are associated with a decreased attentional control and increased automatic orienting of attention. Increased negative emotionality linked with neuroticism is also related with decreased attentional control and reduced cue utilization. This chapter outlines theories and experimental findings that are related to the attentional control deficits associated with neuroticism. Research examining saccadic eye movements also reveals the relation between neuroticism and attentional mechanisms. We included in our discussion the studies investigating the relationship between neuroticism and various attentional performance including the orienting, RSVP, and change detection paradigms as well as pro- and anti-saccade tasks. Despite the general belief that neuroticism has a negative impact on performance, recent studies also highlight the benefits of neuroticism in task performance.

INTRODUCTION

Neuroticism is a personality trait that is linked to negative affect, tendency to worry, and proneness to general psychopathology. Neuroticism appears in almost all personality theories, but research has only limited success predicting its behavioral outcomes. One of the mechanisms to account for the task performance associated with neuroticism is attentional control. There are several reasons why attention can be a critical factor in understanding performance variance linked to neuroticism. First, classical theories of personality provide arousal as a central explanatory construct for biological bases of personality (Eysenck, 1967; Gray, 1981; Wallace and Newman, 1998). Based on the arousal theory, individual differences

* Corresponding author: Sowon Hahn, e-mail: swhahn@snu.ac.kr.

of personality can predict various cognitive performances. For instance, extraversion is associated with low arousal level, so extraverts tend to perform better than introverts in stimulating environments (Avila, Furnham, and McClelland, 2011; Furnham, Trew, and Sneade, 1999). Individuals high in neuroticism level are associated with higher arousal levels, and can be more overwhelmed in stressful environments; certainly, previous research shows that individuals high in neuroticism show a negative reaction toward change in the work place, be it work load or the work environment itself (Cox-Fuenzalida, Swickert, and Hittner, 2004; Moyle and Parkes, 1999). Second, heightened negative emotionality of neuroticism can be linked to decreased attentional capacity. According to the Easterbrook's cue-utilization theory, suboptimal affective states such as tension lead to a decreased number of cues utilized from the environment (Easterbrook, 1959). In the visual field, a reduction of flexible cue utilization can be equivalent to a narrowed attentional scope. Research examining affect-related personality traits showed that positive mood and optimism were associated with global bias, while anxiety and depression were associated with local bias (Basso, Schefft, Ris, and Dember, 1996). More recent studies have also supported that positive affect broadens and negative affect narrows the scope of attention (Fredrickson and Branigan, 2005; Gasper and Clore, 2002; Rowe, Hirsh, and Anderson, 2007). These results are consistent with people's everyday experiences of narrowed attentional focus under stress (Derryberry and Tucker, 1991). Thus, negative emotionality associated with neuroticism can predict a decreased scope of attention.

Research also supports that higher levels of neuroticism are associated with increased automatic orienting of attention and decreased attentional control (Wallace and Newman, 1998). This can also provide an alternative view on the relationship between neuroticism and negative emotionality. Wallace and Newman (1998) proposed that neurotic individuals would experience more difficulty in performing controlled evaluation and correction of maladaptive cognition, and hence would be more prone to experiencing negative affect and psychopathology. According to this view, neuroticism reflects individual differences in the activity of the non-specific arousal system. Highly neurotic individuals are known to show strong emotional responses to all sorts of stimuli, resulting in a facilitation of automatic orienting of attention (Eysenck, 1967). This suggests that the controlled use of attention to support self-regulatory processes would be compromised. Therefore, neurotic individuals would experience more difficulty in controlling maladaptive cognitions, hence be prone to experiencing negative affect and psychopathology.

Neuroticism and Attention

Variety of Attention

To discuss the relationship between neuroticism and attention, it is important to clearly differentiate various attentional mechanisms. Attentional paradigms are frequently used in personality research, but many studies neglected the distinction between functionally and anatomically separate attentional mechanisms (MacLean and Arnell, 2010). Attention usually refers to a focused activation of the cerebral cortex that is related to enhanced information processing (Mesulam, 1990; Posner and Petersen, 1990). For instance, shifting the 'spotlight' of attention or facilitating the processing of the stimulus to which attention is directed, is supported by the activation of the posterior parietal cortex (Posner and Petersen, 1990). On the other hand, selective enhancement of perceptual discrimination is supported by the enhanced activation of the anterior cortex (Posner and Petersen, 1990). Executive attention, a construct related with working memory and fluid intelligence, is associated with increased activation of the prefrontal cortex (Kane and Engle, 2002). Sustained attention, or vigilance that has been used to describe an ability to sustain attention to a task for a period of time, is primarily connected with subcortical structure (Parasuraman, 1998). Vigilance is closed related with alertness; however, while there are many modulatory systems that impact alertness, vigilance is dependent on multiple brainstem-thalamo-cortical pathways (Oken, Salinsky, and Elsas, 2006).

Another construct that combine attention and long-term memory is the distinction between automatic and controlled processing. Posner and Snyder (1975) define automatic processing as processing that occurs without intention, without conscious attention, and without interfering with other mental activities. Schneider, Dumais, and Shiffrin (1984) define automatic processing as a fast, parallel, fairly effortless processing. Logan (1988) argues that, as a process becomes more automatic through practice, it becomes faster and less variable. When people perform a skill repeatedly, according to Logan (1988), processing becomes based on direct retrieval from long-term memory and bypasses short-term memory altogether. Controlled processing, by contrast, requires attentional resources, is relatively slow, and is impaired under conditions of cognitive load (Schneider et al., 1984). In the series of classic experiments, Schneider and Shiffrin (1977) investigated visual search tasks either involved varied mapping (VM) or consistent mapping (CM) of stimuli and responses. Under the VM condition, target and non-target stimuli changed their roles across trials whereas under the CM condition, target and non-target stimuli never interchanged roles. The results show that CM training can direct participants' attention to the target automatically regardless of concurrent input or memory load, while the VM condition required participants to search the display in a voluntary or controlled manner.

Neuroticism and Attentional Control

Wallace and Newman (1998) proposed that neurotic individuals were more likely to show facilitated automatic orienting of attention in the presence of distractors, compromising controlled self-regulation of attention. The difficulty in performing the controlled regulation of attention can lead to negative affect and maladaptive cognition. In other words, facilitation of automatic orienting of neurotic individuals can underlie negative emotionality. Certain types of affective phenomena may occur in the absence of controlled processing. Instead, once primed, valenced information may even influence our behavior in reflexive ways; emotionally salient stimuli – particularly fear and anxiety inducing stimuli – are processed automatically. Neurotic individuals have a reduced ability to control attentional set, as the attention of individuals may be already tuned into anxiety or fear related stimuli.

Although neuroticism and anxiety are theoretically separate, researchers often use them interchangeably since these dimensions overlap significantly. Numerous studies suggest a link between anxiety and attentional deficits. According to the attentional control theory, anxiety alters the balance between the stimulus-driven attentional system and the top-down, goal-driven attentional system, reducing the influence of the latter (Eysenck, Derakshan, Santos, and Calvo, 2007). This mechanism is similar to the proposal of Wallace and Newman (1998) that neuroticism is associated with facilitated automatic orienting and inefficient controlled processing.

Putting together, a substantial amount of research used atttentional control as a key mechanism to understand the performance variance related with neuroticism. In the following section, we will overview some of the experimental findings that support the relationship between neuroticism and attentional performance.

Experimental Findings

Using the visual orienting paradigm, Derryberry and Reed (1994) investigated the influence of extraversion and neuroticism in the covert shift of attention. They used a pre-cueing paradigm and found that costs of attentional shift were greater for neurotic individuals. Avila (1995) found that highly neurotic individuals manifested greater inhibition of return (i.e., an increased latency to return attention to a previously attended location). Poy, del Carmen Eixarch, and Avila (2004) found that anxiety facilitated covert visual orienting guided by peripheral cues. In their study, anxious individuals were faster to detect peripheral cues, which can facilitate detection of potentially dangerous stimuli. Burton et al., (2010) showed that higher neuroticism is associated with higher vigilance and interpreted the results based on the biological link between personality and cognitive assessment such as arousal.

Another line of research with RSVP paradigms reported that highly neurotic individuals show longer attentional blink (Bredemeier, Berenbaum, Most, and Simons, 2011). The attentional blink (AB) is observed when reported accuracy for a second target (T2) is reduced as the T2 is presented within approximately 500 ms of a first target (T1); accuracy is relatively unimpaired at longer T1–T2 separations. The AB is thought to represent a transient cost of attending to a target, and reliable individual differences have been observed in its magnitude. Researchers found that individual differences of personality can predict temporal attentional costs in the attentional blink paradigm (MacLean, Arnell, and Busseri, 2010). Anxiety and depression are often associated with difficulties in attentional disengagement from negative emotional stimuli.

Researchers have also used change detection paradigm to investigate the relationship between anxiety, conscious awareness and attentional performance (Gregory and Lambert, 2012). In this study, anxious patients were given a change detection task; participants detected change more rapidly when negative stimuli were presented subliminally, than when positive or negative stimuli were presented in a supraliminal manner. Gregory and Lambert (2010) proposed that for anxious participants, subliminal presentation of emotionally negative distractor scenes stimulated attention into a dynamic state in the absence of attentional engagement. Presentation of the same scenes at longer exposure times was accompanied by conscious awareness, attentional engagement, and slower change detection. Hahn, Buttaccio, Hahn, and Lee (2015) also showed that higher levels of neuroticism would predict less efficient change detection accuracies.

ATTENTION AND EYE MOVEMENTS

Derakshan, Ansari, Hansard, Shoker, and Eysenck (2009) investigated the effect of anxiety on the antisaccade task. Attentional control theory predicts that anxiety affects top-down processes involved in updating, maintenance, and goal activation in working memory. There is evidence that low working memory capacity (WMC) show increased saccade latencies on the antisaccade task (Kane, Bleckley, Conway, and Engle, 2001). They found that high and low anxiety groups did not differ in terms of the saccade effectiveness antisaccade error rate. However, high anxiety participants showed longer correct antisaccade latencies than low-anxiety participants. Antisaccade performance effectiveness reflects a conflict between volitional and reflexive responses. However, latency of the correct saccade reflects processing efficiency – relationship between performance effectiveness and use of resources.

Another researcher investigated the volitional attentional control of anxiety disorder using an emotional saccade task; Wieser, Pauli, and Mühlberger (2009) found that socially anxious individuals have difficulties inhibiting themselves from reflexively attending to facial expressions. Socially anxious individuals made more error saccades towards emotional facial expression stimuli when an antisaccade was required. Their study showed that anxiety is associated with inhibiting the reflexive orienting to neutral as well as emotional facial expression stimuli. Wieser et al., (2009) concluded that this result might be due to dysfunction of prefrontal areas being involved in attentional control.

Ettinger et al., (2005) investigated the relationship between saccadic eye movements, schizotypy and the role of neuroticism, by measuring anti- and prosaccades. Neuroticism is a personality dimension with negative emotionality and general psychopathology. Schizotypy refers to temporally stable signs and symptoms that are phenomenologically similar to, but lesser severe than the full-blown symptoms of schizophrenia. A number of studies have observed an association between levels of neuroticism and schizotypal traits amongst healthy individuals (Eysenck and Barrett, 1993; Lipp, Arnold, and Siddle, 1994). Increased levels of neuroticism are observed as a consequence of distressing psychosis-like symptoms (Claridge and Broks, 1984). Alternatively, neuroticism may be a non-specific predictor of many different types of psychopathology, not specific to psychosis (Claridge and Davis, 2001). Ettinger et al., (2005) showed that an antisaccade error rate was predicted by a measure of positive schizotypy (reality distortion or disorganization), but this relationship was not accounted for by individual differences of neuroticism.

NEUROTICISM AND PERFORMANCE

Neuroticism is connected to decreased performance especially when the task is cognitively demanding or the environmental condition is stressful (Judge and Illies, 2002). Smillie, Yeo, Furnham, and Jackson (2006) suggested that this attentional account of neuroticism could be used to explain the relationship between attentional resource allocation and job performance. For instance, when individuals put much effort in a given task or the environment is engaging, leaving less resource available to be distracted elsewhere, neurotic individuals may be able to gain larger performance improvement, as compared to being in less busy situations or otherwise disengaged from work, as it leads to a disruption of performance due to negative thoughts (Smillie et al., 2006). This is based on the model of Wallace and Newman (1998) of neuroticism and attention. Since neurotic individuals are more vulnerable to automatic orienting of attention and attentional dysregulation, fewer resources being available to be redirected elsewhere reduces the likelihood of dysregulation.

Arousal and Performance

The relationship between neuroticism and attention stems from the biological theory of personality and the Yerkes-Dodson law of performance. According to the Yerkes-Dodson law, performance increases with physiological arousal up to a certain point before decreasing with higher levels of arousal, often illustrated graphically as a bell-shaped curve. For instance, neurotics show worse performance in more demanding attentional tasks. In general, neurotics tend to be chronically highly aroused (Eysenck, Eysenck, and Barrett, 1985). Using the arousal account only, neurotic individuals' performance would be best when the task is not demanding. However, the model needs to also account for the effort people put in the task or attentional set. If a task is less demanding and monotonous, neurotic individuals perform better than controls. When the task is demanding, neurotics are at a disadvantage since the overall level of stimulation surpasses the optimal level of arousal. However, not all high demanding tasks cause the impaired attentional performance for neurotics. Szymura and Wodniecka (2003) showed that neurotics were impaired when the speed of the stimulus presentation was increased, but not when the task complexity increased. Neurotics show impaired performance in the dual task condition compared to their stable counterparts, unless the stimulus presentation is relatively slow; at a very slow speed of stimuli presentation, it is possible to switch attention between two tasks without losing efficiency of the selective attention processes.

Boundary Conditions

Neuroticism has been considered as a fundamental dimension of temperament, and therefore is likely to show as an enduring facet of human behavior (Eysenck, 1967). Although results that have shown the relationship between neuroticism and cognitive performance are not consistent, recent research provides explanations based on predictions under specific circumstances (Costa and McCrae, 1980; Szalma and Teo, 2010; Tamir, 2005). Thus, looking for boundary conditions can be more useful than making a prediction that can be applied to all situations (Smillie et al., 2006).

Following the hedonic principle of affective regulation, people are generally motivated to increase positive emotion and decrease negative emotion. However, when negative emotion is instrumental to facilitate job performance, neurotic individuals are motivated to experience negative emotion (Tamir, 2005).

CONCLUSION

The deficit of voluntary control of attention is possibly the most prominent mechanism to account for the behavioral outcomes of neuroticism. Selective attention can function as a 'spotlight' to facilitate the processing of information towards which it is oriented. Highly neurotic individuals are prone to worrying and making pessimistic interpretations of events; selective attentional mechanisms of neurotic individuals may mediate negative affect and maladaptive cognition.

Neuroticism is a personality dimension based on emotional reactivity, tendency to worry, and susceptibility to negative mood (Costa and McCrae, 1980; Eysenck, 1967). Neuroticism is also correlated with massive symptoms of psychopathology, influencing its expression of the disorder-specific characteristics to produce the clinical conditions. However, neuroticism is orthogonal to other personality dimensions such as introversion-extraversion, thus potentially indicating a broader range of emotionality. In the case of anxiety – the most commonly quoted expression of neuroticism – neurotic extraverts can be related with anxiety while neurotic introverts can be connected with depression. Neuroticism can function as an emotional amplifier, and transform normality into abnormality in the form of anxiety, depression, anger, or the pathological need for novelty. In that sense neuroticism could be regarded as a truly heterogeneous construct, with multiple connections across personality matrix (Claridge and Davis, 2001).

REFERENCES

Avila, C. (1995). Facilitation and inhibition of visual orienting as a function of personality. *Personality and Individual Differences, 18*(4), 503-509.

Avila, C., Furnham, A. and McClelland, A. (2011). The influence of distracting familiar vocal music on cognitive performance of introverts and extraverts. *Psychology of Music, 40*(1), 84-93.

Basso, M. R., Schefft, B. K., Ris, M. and Dember, W. N. (1996). Mood and global-local visual processing. *Journal of the International Neuropsychological Society, 2*(3), 249-255.

Bredemeier, K., Berenbaum, H., Most, S. B. and Simons, D. J. (2011). Links between neuroticism, emotional distress, and disengaging attention: Evidence from a single-target RSVP task. *Cognition and Emotion, 25*(8), 1510-1519.

Burton, L., Pfaff, D., Bolt, N., Hadjikyriacou, D., Silton, N., Kilgallen, C. and Allimant, J. (2010). Effects of gender and personality on the Conners Continuous Performance Test. *Journal of Clinical and Experimental Neuropsychology, 32*(1), 66-70.

Claridge, G. and Broks, P. (1984). Schizotypy and hemisphere function—I: Theoretical considerations and the measurement of schizotypy. *Personality and Individual Differences*, 5(6), 633-648.

Claridge, G. and Davis, C. (2001). What's the use of neuroticism? Personality. *Personality and Individual Differences, 31*, 383-400.

Costa, P. T. and McCrae, R. R. (1980). Influence of extraversion and neuroticism on subjective well-being: happy and unhappy people. *Journal of Personality and Social Psychology, 38*(4), 668-678.

Cox-Fuenzalida, L., Swickert, R. and Hittner, J. B. (2004). Effects of neuroticism and workload history on performance. *Personality and Individual Differences, 36*(2), 447-456.

Derakshan, N., Ansari, T. L., Hansard, M., Shoker, L. and Eysenck, M. W. (2009). Anxiety, inhibition, efficiency, and effectiveness: An investigation using the antisaccade task. *Experimental Psychology, 56*(1), 48-55.

Derrberry, D. and Reed, M. A. (1994). Temperament and attention: Orienting toward and away from positive and negative signals. *Journal of Personality and Social Psychology, 66*(6), 1128-1139.

Derryberry, D. and Tucker, D. M. (1991) Motivating the focus of attention. In P. Niedenthal and S. Kitayama (Eds.), *The heart's eye: Emotional influences in perception and attention* (pp. 167-196). San Diego, CA: Academic Press.

Easterbrook, J. A. (1959). The effect of emotion on cue utilization and the organization of behavior. *Psychological Review, 66*(3), 183-201.

Ettinger, U., Kumari, V., Crawford, T. J., Flak, V., Sharma, T., Davis, R. E. and Corr, P. J. (2005). Saccadic eye movements, schizotypy, and the role of neuroticism. *Biological Psychology, 68*, 61-78.

Eysenck, H. J. (1967). *The biological basis of personality.* Springfield, IL: Thomas.

Eysenck, H. J. and Barrett, P. (1993). The nature of schizotypy. *Psychological Reports, 73*, 59-63.

Eysenck, M. W., Derakshan, N. Santos, R. and Calvo, M. G. (2007). Anxiety and cognitive performance: Attentional control theory. *Emotion, 7*(2), 336-353.

Eysenck, S. B., Eysenck, H. J. and Barrett, P. (1985). A revised version of the psychoticism scale. *Personality and individual differences, 6*(1), 21-29.

Fredrickson, B. L. and Branigan, C. (2005). Positive emotions broaden the scope of attention and thought-action repertoires. *Cognition and Emotion, 19*(3), 313-332.

Furnham, A., Trew, S. and Sneade, I. (1999). The distracting effects of vocal and instrumental music on the cognitive test performance of introverts and extraverts. *Personality and Individual Differences, 27*(2), 381-392.

Gasper, K. and Clore, G. L. (2002). Attending to the big picture: Mood and global versus local processing of visual information. *Psychological Science, 13*(1), 34-40.

Gray, J. A. (1981). A critique of Eysenck's theory of personality. In H. J. Eysenck (Ed.), *A model for personality* (pp. 246–276). Berlin: Springer-Verlag.

Gregory, S. M. and Lambert, A. (2012). Anxiety, conscious awareness and change detection. *Consciousness and Cognition, 21*, 69-79.

Hahn, S., Buttaccio, D., Hahn, J. and Lee, T. (2015). Personality and attention: Levels of neuroticism and extraversion can predict attentional performance during a change detection task. *Quarterly Journal of Experimental Psychology, 68*(6), 1041-1048.

Judge, T. A. and Illies, R. (2002). Relationship of personality to performance motivation: A meta-analytic view. *Journal of Applied Psychology, 87*(4), 797-807.

Kane, M. J, and Engle, R. W. (2002). The role of prefrontal cortex in working-memory capacity, executive attention, and general fluid intelligence: An individual-differences perspective. *Psychonomic Bulletin and Review, 9*, 637-671.

Kane, M. J., Bleckley, M. K., Conway, A. R. A. and Engle, R. W. (2001). A controlled-attention view of working-memory capacity. *Journal of Experimental Psychology: General, 130,* 169-183.

Lipp, O. V., Arnold, S. L. and Siddle, D. A. T. (1994). Psychosis proneness in a non-clinical sample. Part I. A psychometric study. *Personality and Individual Differences, 17,* 395-404.

Logan, G. D. (1988). Toward an instance theory of automatization. *Psychological Review, 95*(4), 492-527.

MacLean, M. H. and Arnell, K. M. (2010). Personality predicts temporal attention cost in the attentional blink paradigm. *Psychonomic Bulletin and Review, 17*(4), 556-562.

MacLean, M. H., Arnell, K. M. and Busseri, M. (2010). Dispositional affect predicts temporal attention costs in the attentional blink paradigm. *Cognition and Emotion, 24*, 1431–1438.

Mesulam, M. (1990). Large scale neurocognitive networks and distributed processing for attention, language, and memory. *Annual Neurology, 19,* 597-613.

Moyle, P. and Parkes, K. (1999). The effects of transition stress: A relocation study. *Journal of Organizational Behavior, 20*, 625-646.

Oken, B. S., Salinsky, M. C., and Elsas, S. M. (2006). Vigilance, alertness, or sustained attention: Physiological basis and measurement. *Clinical Neurophysiology, 117*, 1885-1901.

Parasuraman, R. (1998). *The attentive brain.* In R. Parasuraman (Ed.), *The attentive brain* (pp. 3-15). Cambridge, MA: The MIT Press.

Posner, M. I. and Petersen, S. E. (1990). The attention system of the human brain. *Annual Review of Neuroscience, 13*, 25-42.

Posner, M. I. and Snyder, C. R. R. (1975). Facilitation and inhibition in the processing of signals. In P. M. A. Rabbitt and S. Domic (Eds.), *Attention and performance: V* (pp. 669-682). New York: Academic Press.

Poy, R., del Carmen Eixarch, M. and Avila, C. (2004). On the relationship between attention and personality: Covert visual orienting of attention in anxiety and impulsivity. *Personality and Individual Differences, 36*(6), 1471-1481.

Rowe, G., Hirsh, J. B. and Anderson, A. K. (2007). Positive affect increases the breadth of attentional selection. *Proceedings of the National Academy of Sciences, 104*, 383-388.

Schneider, W. and Shiffrin, R. M. (1977). Controlled and automatic human information processing: I. *Detection, search, and attention. Psychological Review, 84*, 1-66.

Schneider, W., Dumais, S. T. and Shiffrin, R. M. (1984). Automatic and controlled processing and attention. In R. Parasuraman and D. R. Davies (Eds.), *Varieties of attention* (pp. 1-27). Orlando, FL: Academic Press.

Smillie, L. D., Yeo, G. B., Furnham, A. F. and Jackson, C. J. (2006). Benefits of all work and no play: The relationship between neuroticism and performance as a function of resource allocation. *Journal of Applied Psychology, 91*(1), 135-155.

Szalma, J. L. and Teo, G. W. (2010). The joint effect of task characteristics and neuroticism on the performance, workload, and stress of signal detection. *Proceedings of the Human Factors and Ergonomics Society Annual Meeting, 54*(14), 1052-1056.

Szymura, B. and Wodniecka, Z. (2003). What really bothers neurotics? In search for factors impairing attentional performance. *Personality and Individual Differences, 34*, 109-126.

Tamir, M. (2005). Don't worry, be happy? Neuroticism, trait consistent affect regulation, and performance. *Journal of Personality and Social Psychology, 89*(3), 449-461.

Wallace, J. P. and Newman, J. F. (1998). Neuroticism and the facilitation of the automatic orienting of attention. *Personality and Individual Differences, 24*(2), 253-266.

Wieser, M. J., Pauli, P. and Mühlberger, A. (2009). Probing the attentional control theory in social anxiety: An emotional saccade task. *Cognitive, Affective, and Behavioral Neuroscience, 9*(3), 314-322.

In: Neuroticism
Editor: Annamaria Di Fabio

ISBN: 978-1-63485-323-1

Chapter 8

THE RELATIONSHIP BETWEEN NEUROTICISM AND EXTRAVERSION IN AN EGYPTIAN CONTEXT

Ahmed M. Abdel-Khalek*
Department of Psychology, Faculty of Arts,
University of Alexandria, Egypt

ABSTRACT

Considerable controversy had surrounded the association between neuroticism (N) and extraversion (E). Eysenck emphasized the independence of N and E, whereas recent investigations revealed their negative correlation. The present research reported four studies to test out the relationship between N and E in many different Egyptian samples. In study I,16 subgroups (*N*=1,704) responded to the N and E scales of Forms A and B of the Eysenck Personality Inventory (EPI), as well as Cycloid disposition (C), and Rhathymia (R) from Guilford's STDCR battery. Results revealed that 47.2% of the correlations (r's) between three N and three E questionnaires were statistically significant. All of them were negative. Some E scales were more "sensitive" to show significant r's with N than others. In study II, a slang Arabic version of the EPI was administered to 642 illiterate subjects (Ss) in 16 subgroups. Thirty seven and half per cent of the r's between N and E scales were significant. Study III indicated significant and positive r's between both the self-ratings of N and introversion, as well as positive r's between the self-rating of introversion and the N scale of the EPI among undergraduates. Study IV showed that 57% of Ss in two samples considered the adjective "introvert" as an indicator of disorder. This adjective "introvert" had sten values = 6.5 and 7.3 in the two samples, among 10 traits referring to disorder. By and large, N and E negative association is significant but small in the third to half of the correlations.

Keywords: neuroticism, extraversion, relations, Egyptians

---

* Corresponding author: Ahmed M. Abdel-Khalek, e-mail: aabdel-khalek@hotmail.com.

INTRODUCTION

Considerable controversy had surrounded N and E relationship. In the early twenties, Jung (1921/1923) pointed out that "it is a mistake to believe that introversion is more or less the same as neurosis. As concepts, the two have not the slightest connection with each other." Therefore, Jung stressed the independence of introversion and neurosis. Contrary to Jung's conception, Freud (1920) considered the association between the two concepts as quite close. According to him: "An introvert is not yet a neurotic, but he finds himself in a labile condition, he must develop symptoms at the next dislocation of forces, if he does not find other outlets for his pent-up libido". Neither Jung nor Freud tried to verify their points of view empirically.

A great deal of investigations have demonstrated that Neuroticism-stability (N) and Extraversion - introversion (E) are basic descriptive dimensions in the study of personality. N and E have been replicated with high accuracy, in spite of varying the parameters of the samples (Eysenck and Eysenck, 1969, 1985). Many cross-cultural studies have verified that N and E can be discovered in non-Western countries as well (Lynn, 1981). In Egypt, Abdel-Khalek (1981) had carried out a series of investigations on a large number of subjects (Ss) (*N* = 2,238), classified into 20 different subgroups. Clear and high-loaded factors of N and E were extracted. In a cross - cultural study using the Eysenck Personality Questionnaire (EPQ) (Eysenck and Eysenck, 1975), in its Arabic version, Abdel-Khalek and Eysenck (1983) extracted identical factors of N and E in Egypt as in England.

It seems true that the agreement on the high degree of universality of N dimension is greater than that of E. However, Morris (1979) stated that invariably analyses of personality test batteries reveal that E emerges as one of a few factors that account for much of the common variance shared by specific items or specific personality dimensions.

There has been much argument about the E factor in comparison to N. To take but a few examples, there are, at least, three main problems as follows: First, the problem of E unidimensionality (see: Eaves and Eysenck, 1975; Eysenck, 1973a, 1977b), versus multidimensionality (see: Cattell, 1972; Guilford, 1975, 1977; Howarth and Browne, 1972). Guilford (1975) and Howarth (1976) were particularly very critical of Eysenck's E. Carrigan (1960) in her review, concluded that the unidimensionality of E has not been conclusively demonstrated. Second, the problem of the relationship between E and sociability, venturesomeness, and impulsiveness (see: Barratt, 1972; Bentler and McClain, 1976; Eaves and Eysenck, 1975; Eysenck, 1977a, 1978; Lorr and Wunderlich, 1985; Plomin, 1976; Wilson, 1978). These two problems are out of the interest of the present paper. Third, the argument about the E dimension and its projection on, or independence from, N. The last point is the focus of the present investigation.

NEUROTICISM (N)

The typical high N scorer may described as being an anxious, worrying individual, moody and frequently depressed. He is likely to sleep badly, and to suffer from various psychosomatic disorders. He is overly emotional, reacting too strongly to all sorts of stimuli, and finds it difficult to get back on an even keel after each emotionally arousing experience.

His strong emotional reactions interfere with his proper adjustment, making him react in irrational, something rigid ways. When combined with extraversion, such an individual is likely to be touchy and restless, to become excitable and even aggressive. If the high N individual has to be described in one word, one might say that he is a worrier; his main characteristic is a constant preoccupation with things that might go wrong, and a strong emotional reaction of anxiety to these thoughts. The stable individual, on the other hand, tends to respond emotionally only slowly and generally weakly, and to return to baseline quickly after emotional arousal; he is usually calm, even-tempered, controlled and unworried (Eysenck and Eysenck, 1975, pp. 4-5). N is characterized as a pervasive sensitivity to negative or punishment cues in the environment. High N scorers are more readily assess situations as threatening.

Extraversion (E)

The typical extravert is sociable, likes parties, has many friends, needs to have people to talk to, and does not like reading or studying by himself. He craves excitement, takes chances, often sticks his neck out, acts on the spur of the moment, and is generally an impulsive individual. He is fond of practical jokes, always has a ready answer, and generally likes change; he is carefree, easygoing, optimistic, and likes to laugh and be merry. He prefers to keep moving and doing things, tends to be aggressive and lose his temper quickly; altogether his feelings are not kept under tight control, and he is not always a reliable person.

The typical introvert is a quiet, retiring sort of person, introspective, fond of books rather than people; he is reserved and distant except to intimate friends. He tends to plan ahead, 'looks before he leaps' and distrusts the impulse of the moment. He does not like excitement, takes matters of everyday life with proper seriousness, and likes a well-ordered mode of life. He keeps his feelings under close control, seldom behaves in an aggressive manner, and does not lose his temper easily. He is reliable, somewhat pessimistic, and places great value on ethical standards. This description of typical extravert and typical introvert may be regarded as idealized extremes on a continuum which real people may approach to a greater or lesser degree (Eysenck and Eysenck, 1975, p. 4). The extraversion introversion dimension captures the social dimension of personality.

The Biological Basis of N and E

There has been a growing interest in identifying patterns of brain activity that are associated with N and E. Eysenck (1990) and Gray (Pickering and Gray 1999), among others, have led the studies on this domain. N and E are of particular interest because their brain bases might contribute to a predisposition toward mood and anxiety disorders (Wright et al., 2006).

Canli (2004) reviewed the E and N correlations with brain activation in specific brain regions, using the functional magnetic resonance imaging (fMRI). Using this technique, Eisenberger, Lieberman, and Satpute (2005) found that N associated with increased dorsal anterior cingulate cortex (dACC) reactivity, whereas E associated with lateral and medial frontoparietal networks.

Wright et al. (2006) studied the neuroanatomical correlates of E and N using the neuroanatomical/neuroimaging measures of the cerebral cortex and amygdala. They found that the thickness of specific prefrontal cortex regions correlates with measures of N and E. Using a positron emission tomography (PET) to study the resting brain metabolic correlates of N and E, Kim, Hwang, Park, and Kim (2008) found that E was related to dopamine transmission in the striatum, whereas N was related to serotonin transmission in the prefrontal cortex.

N, E AND EMOTIONS

E and N are two personality traits that are linked to both emotion and health. They can be viewed as affect dispositional dimensions. Costa and McCrae (1980) found that the N trait strongly correlates with negative affect and that E trait correlates strongly with positive affect. Persons with high N score have a greater tendency to experience negative affect.

Watson, Wiese, Vaidya, and Tellegen (1999) reported a correlation of .58 between N and the Negative Affect Scale of the Positive and Negative Affect Schedule (PANAS), and a correlation of .51 between E and the Positive Affect Scale. This result has shown differences between N and E. Extraverts have been characterized as sensitive to positive or pleasant cues in the environment, and may have a propensity to experience positive affect (Lucas, Diener, Grob, Suh, and Shao, 2000). Jylhä and Isometsä (2006) found that N correlated strongly with symptoms of depression and anxiety, whereas E correlated negatively with symptoms of depression.

Verduyn and Brans (2012) stated that individual differences in the affective components of E and N can be described in terms of three different aspects: frequency, intensity, and duration. Correlational analyses revealed that E is positively related to the frequency, intensity, and duration of positive emotions, whereas N is positively related to the frequency and duration of negative emotions. Further, regression analyses showed that the duration of positive emotions is the strongest predictor of E, whereas the frequency of negative emotions is the strongest predictor of N.

Extraversion and Happiness

Some authors have used the terms: mental health, happiness, and subjective well-being interchangeably. Costa and McCrae (1980) stated that there is evidence to suggest that E is related to subjective well-being, happiness, positive affect, and optimistic traits. Argyle and Lu (1990) found that scores on happiness were correlated with those on E and enjoyment and on participation in social activities. Hills and Argyle (1998) pointed out that E was the best predictor of participation in leisure activities which resulted in happiness. More recently, Abdel-Khalek (2014) found significant associations of E with agreeableness, conscientiousness, and mental health.

Using a probability sample (N = 6,913) in the USA, Diener, Sandvik, Pavot, and Fujita (1992) found that extraverts were happier whether living alone or with others, in urban or rural areas, whether working in social or nonsocial occupations. Furthermore, extraverts were happier across racial, gender, and age groups. In a similar vein, Furnham and Cheng (1999) found E to be a major correlate of happiness ($r = .50$) among participants from China, Japan, and UK. Francis, Brown, Lester, and Philipchalk (1998) recruited students from USA, Australia, UK, and Canada and found that happiness correlated between .41 and .49 with E. They concluded that the findings support the view that happiness could be called stable extraversion.

Wismeijer and Assen (2008) found that E and conscientiousness was associated with subjective well-being in students at a Dutch university. In general, extraverts feel higher level of positive affect than introverts (Lucas and Baird, 2004), so extroverts are happier than introverts in general, over short time frames, and even in the moment (Wilt and Revelle, 2009). However, Vittersø (2001) found that the effect from emotional stability on subjective well-being is stronger than the corresponding effect from extraversion among 264 Norwegian folk high school students.

The N and E Association

A number of psychometric studies have investigated N and E relationship without a clear-cut agreement. On the one hand, a large body of research has conceptualized N and E as orthogonal, and uncorrelated dimensions (Eysenck, 1973a; Farley and Mealiea, 1972; Moore, 1976). On the other hand, different research findings indicate N and E obliqueness and relationship. These findings have stressed N and E correlation in three fold directions as follows: First, negative correlation between N and E, especially among neurotics, mainly in dysthymic cases (Eysenck, White, and Eysenck, 1976; Hallam, 1976; Hedge, 1972; Laungani, 1985; Patterson and Strauss, 1972). These findings were consistent with relevant results indicating the increase of E score following the psychotherapeutic intervention (Cattell and Scheier, 1961; Hallam, 1976; Ingham, 1966; Levinson and Meyer, 1965). Second, positive correlation between N and E, particularly in cases of antisocial behavior, i.e., criminality, delinquency, and psychopathy (Eysenck, 1977a). Other studies presented the evidence against this issue (Black, 1972). Third, curvilinear correlation between N and E, i.e., both extreme scores may be related to specific disorders that were not found in the middle range of the dimension as stated by Morris (1979).

Using Arab participants, the correlation between N and E of the EPQ was –.26 ($p < .01$, $df = 154$) and -.28 ($p < .01$, $df = 244$) in men and women, respectively (Abdel-Khalek, 2013a). In another study, N and E from the EPQ correlated –.117 (n.s., $N = 113$) and –.218 ($p < .05$, $N = 114$) in men and women, respectively (Abdel-Khalek, 2013b). In the same vein, N and E of the big five personality factors correlated -.40 ($p < .01$, $df = 126$) (Abdel-Khalek, 2014).

The Present Study

The aim of the present study was to test out the relationship between N as a unitary factor, and E in many Egyptian samples, using different procedures through four studies as follows.

Study I: presents the correlation between three N and three E questionnaires among 16 different samples.

Study II: indicates the correlation between N and E using a slang version of the EPI, especially compiled for illiterate Ss, i.e., 16 different samples.

Study III: reports the correlation between the self-rating scales of N and introversion, and between the self-rating scale of introversion and an N questionnaire.

Study IV: explores the rank order of selected trait names, mainly adjectives, to test out the rank of "introvert" among names pertaining to disorder.

STUDY I

Method

Participants

A Convenience 16 samples including 1,704 Ss were chosen (see Table 1).

Measures

The Arabic versions of the N and E subscales of the Eysenck Personality Inventory (EPI) Form A and B (Eysenck and Eysenck, 1964), Cycloid disposition (C), and Rhathymia (R) from Guilfordf's STDCR battery (Guilford, Zimmerman, and Guilford, 1976) were used. Test-retest and split half reliabilities of the scales were .70 to .95 (Abdel-Khalek, 1981).

Procedure

The questionnaires were administered to the samples in small group sessions. All participants were volunteers and could decline participation at any time if they desired so.

Data Analysis

Pearson's product-moment correlation coefficients were computed separately between the total score of each three N and three E scales for each of the 16 samples. The total number of correlations was 144.

Results

Inspection of Table 1 reveals that 47.2% of the NE correlations were statistically significant (39.6%, $p < .01$, and 7.6% $p < .05$). All the significant correlations were negative. There was no-direct effect of different variables, such as age, sex, education, occupation, method of questionnaire administration, and anonymity on the relation. NE correlation in neurotics deserved closer scrutiny. They had no specific position. The same finding held true among prisoners and psychotics as well. However, some E scales were more "prone" or "susceptible" to reveal more significant correlations with N than others, namely, E (EPI,

Form B) scale had 72.9%, and Rhathymia had 60.4% significant correlations with N scales. On the other hand, the E (EPI, Form A) scale had only 8.3% significant correlations.

Table 1. Correlations (*r*) between Extraversion (E) scale; Forms (A) and (B) and Rhathymia (R) and: Neuroticism (N) scale; Forms (A) and (B) and Cycloid disposition (C) among 16 samples

Sample	Sex	n	Correlation ++								
			E (A)/ N(A)	E (A)/ N(B)	E (A)/ C	E(B)/N (A)	E(B)/N (B)	E(B)/C	R/N (A)	R/N (B)	R/C
Pupils	M	211	08	-01	12	-28**	-36**	-29**	-30**	-32**	-24**
Pupils	F	210	-15*	-20**	-13	-34**	-37**	-35**	-32**	-35**	-34**
Undergraduates	M	208	-02	03	10	-31**	-28**	-24**	-27**	-21**	-17*
Undergraduates	F	205	-08	-06	-01	-26**	-27**	-26**	-33**	-30**	-27**
Housewives	F	106	-23*	-19	-08	-37**	-34**	-26**	-44**	-36**	-33**
Nurses	F	104	-08	-10	-07	-33**	-36**	-39**	-31**	-31**	-35**
Labourers	M	87	04	-03	08	-41**	-36**	-39**	-40**	-37**	-36**
Doctors+	M+F	82	-11	-08	03	-43**	-33**	-29**	-40**	-35**	-24**
Teachers	M	79	-04	-12	02	-18	-25*	-23*	-17	-25*	-22
Teachers	F	56	17	15	23	10	06	07	-05	02	-05
Clerks+	M+F	73	-09	03	-05	-26*	-16	-16	-10	-12	-17
Social workers	F	18	-19	-15	-37	-21	-27	-43	-24	-17	-34
Demonstrators	F	14	28	23	53	-02	08	32	-09	-02	25
Prisoners	M	101	12	10	13	-26**	-35**	-31**	-09	-17	-22*
Psychotics+	M+F	84	-15	-23*	-14	-36**	-48**	-40**	-21	-33**	-29**
Neurotics+	M+F	66	-12	-24	-22	-24	-33**	-41**	-23	-24	-29*
No. of Significant (*r*)			2	2	-	11	12	12	8	10	11
%			12.5	12.5	00	68.8	75	75	50	62.5	68.5

\+ Males (M) and females (F) were combined where differences in their scores as well as age were N.S.
++ Decimal points omitted.
$*p < .05. **p < .01.$

STUDY II

Method

Participants

A sample of 642 illiterate Ss in 16 subgroups from different rural and urban places in Upper and Lower Egypt took part in the study. Table 2 sets out the sample size, mean, and standard deviation of age for each group as well as the NE correlation.

The Scale

A slang EPI Arabic version was compiled by the present writer. It comprises 57 items (24 N, 24 E, as well as 9 Lie scales). These items had been derived from the 117 items of the A and B Forms of the EPI. The selection of any given item was done on the basis of its appropriateness for Egyptian illiterates. One week test-retest reliabilities were as follows: .63 and .69 (men); .81, and .81, (women) for the N and E, respectively. Split-half reliabilities were as follows: .90, and .77, (men), .88, and .75, (women) for N and E, successively. It was not unexpected to find some low reliabilities among illiterate Ss. However, some reliabilities were high.

Procedure

The slang Arabic EPI was administered in an individual testing session. Testers pronounced, verbatim, each item and recorded the subject's response, i.e., Yes or No. Administrators were post-graduate students, as well as the present writer. Testing was not anonymous.

Data Analysis

Descriptive statistics and Pearson correlation coefficients were used.

Results

Inspection of Table 2 displays that 37.5% of the correlations between N and E scales of the slang EPI in the 16 subsamples were significant (50%,$p < .01$; 50%, $p < .05$). All the correlations were negative.

Table 2. Mean (*M*), standard deviation (*SD*) of age, and correlation between N and E scales of the EPI slang version among 16 different samples

Samples		*N*	*Age*		NE
			M	*SD*	Correlation
1- Villagers	M	52	33.6	13.6	-.46**
2- Villagers	F	95	36.1	15.4	-.21*
3- Housewives	F	54	36.5	12.9	-.17
4- Pregnant	F	73	26.3	5.7	-.45**
5- Unskilled labourers	M	51	39.0	10.9	-.51**
6- Unskilled labourers	F	52	36.4	11.0	-.27
7- Neurotics	M	19	38.8	12.6	-.28
8- Neurotics	F	45	38.7	12.2	-.16
9- Juvenile Delinquents	M	50	17.4	1.4	-.04
10- Juvenile Delinquents	F	37	17.9	2.8	-.16
11- Peptic Ulcerous	M	16	45.0	10.2	-.42
12- Peptic Ulcerous	F	12	35.8	10.5	-.20
13- Rheumatic Heart	M	27	35.2	15.6	.17
14- Rheumatic Heart	F	31	35.4	13.6	-.12
15- Diabetics	M	13	51.7	4.7	-.54*
16- Psoriatics	F	15	32.8	15.1	-.51*
No. of significant (*r*)					6
%					37.5

* $p < .05$.
** $p < .01$.

Study III

Method

Participants

In study III-a, a sample of 107 male and female undergraduates studying psychology took part in the study. In study III-b, another sample of 95 students was recruited.

Measures

In study IIIa, the self-rating scales of introversion and neuroticism were used. The scores could range from 0 - 10. In study IIIb, the self-rating scale of introversion and the N scale of the EPI (Form A) were administered. It is worth mentioning that in rating scales, the term "introversion" was used and not "extraversion," inasmuch as the former had, in Arabic, more definitive connotation than the latter.

Procedure

Participants were requested to rate themselves and responded in small group sessions.

Data Analysis

Pearson correlation coefficient was used.

Results

Table 3 sets out the results. Reference to this table revealed that both correlations between N and introversion were statistically significant and positive.

Table 3. Pearson correlation (*r*) coefficients between the self-rating scales of N and introversion

Study-samples	*N*	Age		*r*	*p*
		M	*SD*		
III-a	107	22.8	3.1	0.22	.05
III-b	95	20.7	2.4	0.24	.02

Note: The correlation was positive because it was computed between N and introversion and not E.

STUDY IV

Rationale

This study depended upon the following simple postulate: the subject has a preconceived idea about the NE association. This conception may affect his or her response to relevant questionnaire. The transparency nature of its items requires no comment. Thus, if any given subject considered introversion (inverse of E) as a kind of disorder, they will respond in a manner revealing NE interference, so the N E correlation would be negative. Then, the association between N and E could be partially interpreted.

Participants

IV-a: A sample of 30 female undergraduates studying psychology was recruited. IV-b: A sample of 28 (19 men; 9 women) undergraduates studying computer sciences took part in the study.

Measures and Procedure

Twenty Arabic trait names, mainly adjectives, were chosen by the present writer, for example, impulsive, pessimistic, sociable, aggressive, hysterical, introvert, sad, despairing, shy, neurotic, etc. In the first stage, Ss were instructed to check the adjectives indicating disorder. Afterwards, the adjectives which were chosen by >50% of Ss as referring to disorder were isolated, and drafted in a new checklist. The same Ss, in the second stage of this study, were requested to define rank order for each item. Rank one pertaining to the more severe disorder, then, the less severe, and so on.

Data Analysis

Percentage and ranking were computed.

Results

Table 4 shows that more than half of the participants reported that the adjective "introvert" indicated disorder. None of them said that "sociable" refered to disorder. The second stage of this study revealed that the mean of the rank order of "introvert" among the adjectives referring to disorder is 6.5/10 in sample 1, and 7.3/10 in sample 2.

Table 4. The percentage of participants reported that the adjective "introvert" indicates disorder and the mean score of "introvert" between the adjectives referring to disorder

College students	*N*	Age		Introvert indicates disorder	Mean rank order*
		M	*SD*		
Psychology	30	24.2	4.5	57.0%	6.5
Computer Sciences	28	23.4	3.7	57.1%	7.3

* The ranks ranged from 1 (severe disorder) to 10 (mild disorder).

Discussion

The relationship between N and E is more complex, and it has multiphasic psychometric and clinical aspects in personality psychology and psychopathology. Therefore, it has to be thoroughly scrutinized by different procedures, and rigorously conceptualized in different ways. The present research aimed to investigate this relationship through four varied studies.

When three N and three E questionnaires were administered to different 16 subgroups (total N = 1,704 Ss; the number of correlations = 144), about half of the correlations between N and E were statistically significant. The significant correlations were inclusively negative as shown in study I. This result is consistent with the majority of previous work. Eysenck and Eysenck (1964) pointed out that small negative correlations between N and E have been found with the Maudsley Personality Inventory (MPI), between –.1 and –.2 for normal groups, ranging up to –.4 with neurotic groups. Nevertheless, the present study revealed that neurotics had no specific position as regards NE correlation. Using the EPQ, Eysenck and Eysenck (1975) reported low but significant correlations between N and E in British Ss. The same conclusion has been reached with the EPQ among samples tested in different countries, e.g., Nigeria (Eysenck, Adelaja, and Eysenck, 1977), Yugoslavia (Lojk, Eysenck, and Eysenck, 1979), Brazil (Tarrier, Eysenck, and Eysenck, 1980), Egypt (Abdel-Khalek and Eysenck, 1983), India (Laungani, 1985), Iran (Shapurian and Hojat, 1985), and Israel (Eysenck and Yanai, 1985).

However, Eysenck and Eysenck (1964) reported near zero correlation between N and E in normal, neurotic, and psychotic groups with the EPI, the predecessor of the EPQ. Orpen (1972) reached the same conclusion in Afrikaans-speaking school pupils with Afrikaans EPI version. In a similar vein, Eysenck, Eysenck, and Barrett (1985) found near zero correlation between N and E in a revised EPQ version. The last finding in the above mentioned studies (near zero correlation) was less frequent.

By and large, the significant negative N E correlation was only found in half of the studies. It is particularly noteworthy that some E scales were more liable or subject to reveal such a relationship, namely the E (EPI, Form B), Rhathymia (R), and E (EPI, Form A) scales, respectively. Thus, the items of these scales deserve closer scrutiny.

Study II confirmed the main finding in study I, but at a different level, i.e., 37.5% of the N E correlations were statistically significant in study II, versus 47.2% in study I. The importance of study II (16 subgroup, $N = 642$) was based on the quite different educational level, and accordingly occupation and socio-economic status of Ss. All of them were inclusively illiterate. Nevertheless, no good explanation was noted for the different percentages of NE correlations.

Different points of view were introduced to explain the negative low but significant correlation between N and E. One of these explanations was reported by Jones (1960). He pointed out that extreme introverts, by reason of unrealistic ambitions and standards, may create for themselves life-stresses which increase the risk of neurotic breakdown, whereas extreme extraverts, with lower standards and a tendency to ignore or avoid difficulties, may reduce the stress to which they are subjected. On the other hand, Eysenck and Claridge (1962) stated that the hypothesis of genuine interaction effects between introversion and neuroticism should not be disregarded. There may be a point in the conditionability, which according to theory characterizes the introvert, where fear responses are acquired at a rate and at a strength which exceeds the strength of the normal extinction processes; this point may delimit a region of positive feedback which could be responsible for the interaction.

At the physiological level, Eysenck (1973b) linked N and E with the arousal-activation mechanism. He postulated that two such mechanisms, linked respectively with the reticular formation and visceral brain; the former produces cortical arousal, and is, in turn, basic to individual differences in E, while the latter produces autonomic activation, and is, in turn, basic to individual differences in N. According to this hypothesis introverts are characterized by higher cortical arousal levels than extraverts. High N scorers are characterized by high levels of limbic activation, whereas low N scorers are characterized by low levels of activation. These two systems are postulated to be independent for most of the time, except on occasions when strong emotions are produced in the individual concerned; such strong emotions produce strong arousal in the cortex, either directly or through the reticular formation. Therefore, Eysenck hypothesized that the possible dependence between the arousal of the visceral brain and the arousal of the reticular activating system, may explain the negative correlation between N and E, as stated by Brody (1972).

On the other hand, Morris (1979) pointed out that it may be inferred from the multidimensionality of the E concept, that there are subcomponents of both introversion and extraversion that represent better adjustment and subcomponents of each relating to specific types of maladjustment.

Therefore, there are different explanations of the negative NE correlation, whether they are social, psychometric, pertaining to conditionability, and/or physiological. Apart from, and in addition to, these reasonable interpretations, the present researcher introduces a different point of view, depending on less sophisticated procedures as follows: based on the transparency characteristic of the questionnaire items, the subjects' preconceived idea concerning the NE relation may affect his or her response. Study IV indicated that 57% of Ss in two different subgroups considered the adjective “introvert” as an indicator to disorder, and this adjective had sten values = 6.5 and 7.3 in the two samples, i.e., its rank order among ten traits referring to disorder. It is predictable, therefore, from such Ss that their response tended to show negative correlation between N and E inventories. Study III confirmed the finding of study IV. The former revealed that both the correlations between self-rating scales of introversion and neuroticism, and the association between the self-rating scale of introversion and a questionnaire of N, were significant.

The aforementioned finding did not contradict the early ideas on the subject. As stated by Diamond (1957), Downey found that psychologists who characterized themselves as introvert also tended to characterize themselves as emotionally less stable than those who characterized themselves as extravert. Heidbreder showed that introverts quite generally agreed that extravert traits were more desirable. The Thurstones found that the less serious forms of neurotic maladjustments have the characteristics ordinarily known as introversion.

Nevertheless, the relationship between N and E questionnaires and objective behaviour tests purporting to measure E, e.g., sedation threshold level, the Archemedes spiral after-effect (Eysenck and Claridge, 1962), and the lemon test (Eysenck and Eysenck, 1969) were claimed to be correlated with E (and not N) verbal scales. According to Eysenck's theory, a distinction between constitutional and behavioral extraversion was held. While questionnaires were sensitive measures to the latter, objective tests were probably sensitive measures to the former (Eysenck and Claridge, 1962).

This may explain the discrepancy of significance in N and E correlations between two levels, i.e., the verbal scales and the objective behavior personality tests. Cattell and Scheier's (1961) finding, however, contradicted this explanation. They stated that the objective test battery agrees in a moderate but significant relation of invia (introversion) with neuroticism.

CONCLUSION

The present study was based on several Egyptian samples, with large number of participants and they were different in many demographic variables. Different questionnaires and rating scales were used. It could be concluded that N and E correlation is statistically significant and negative in the third to half of the correlations. To quote yet again from Eysenck and Eysenck (1975), they stated: We had aimed at complete independence of N and E factors; but the scales based on these factors, clearly depart slightly from orthogonality. These departures are not serious from an applied point of view, but they should be noted.

Meanwhile we can consider this slight sort of obliqueness as a manifestation of an unavoidable interaction between N and E, especially in the verbal scales. This interaction is similar to that between E and 'g'; the general factor of intelligence, and in the case of N and 'g' as well.

REFERENCES

Abdel-Khalek, A.M. (1981). Extraversion and neuroticism as basic personality dimensions in Egyptian samples. *Personality and Individual Differences*, *2*, 91-97.

Abdel-Khalek, A. M. (2013a). Constructions of anxiety and dimensional personality model among college students. *Psychological Reports, 112*, 992-1004.

Abdel-Khalek, A. M. (2013b). Love of life and its associations with personality dimensions in college students. In F. Sarracino (Ed.), *The happiness compass: Theories, actions, and perspectives for well-being* (pp. 53-65). New York: Nova Science Publishers.

Abdel-Khalek, A. M. (2014). Extraversion, personality, mental health, and religiosity: Significant associations. In A. D. Haddock and A. P. Rutkowski (Eds), *Psychology of extraversion* (pp. 55-73). New York: Nova Science Publishers.

Abdel-Khalek, A. M. and Eysenck, S. B. G. (1983). A cross-cultural study of personality: Egypt and England. In A. M. Abdel-Khalek (Ed.*)*, *Research in Behavior and Personality* (Vol. 3; pp. 215-226). Alexandria, Egypt: DarAl-Maaref.

Argyle, M. and Lu, L. (1990).The happiness of extraverts. *Personality and Individual Differences*, *11*, 1011-1017.

Barratt, E. S. (1972). Anxiety and impulsiveness. In C. D. Spielberger (Ed.), *Anxiety: Current trends in theory and research* (Vol. I; pp. 195-222). New York: Academic Press.

Bentler, P. M. and McClain, J. (1976).A multitrait-multimethod analysis of reflection-impulsivity. *Child Development*, *47*, 218-226.

Black, W. A. M. (1972). Extraversion, neuroticism, and criminality. *Australian and New Zealand Journal of Criminology*, *5*, 99-106.

Brody, N. (1972). *Personality: Research and theory*. New York: Academic Press.

Canli, T. (2004). Functional brain mapping of extraversion and neuroticism: Learning from individual differences in emotion processing. *Journal of Personality*, *72*, 1105-1132.

Carrigan, P. M. (1960). Extraversion-introversion as a dimension of personality: A reappraisal. *Psychological Bulletin*, *57*, 329-360.

Cattell, R. B. (1972). The 16 PF and basic personality structure: A reply to Eysenck. *Journal of Behavioral Science*, *1*, 169-187.

Cattell, R. B. and Scheier, I. H. (1961). *The meaning and measurement of neuroticism and anxiety*. New York: Ronald.

Costa, P. T. and McCrae, R. R. (1980). Influence of extraversion and neuroticism on subjective well-being: Happy and unhappy people. *Journal of Personality and Social Psychology*, *38*, 668-678.

Diamond, S. (1957). *Personality and temperament*. New York: Harper.

Diener, Ed., Sandvik, Ed., Pavot, W. and Fujita, F. (1992). Extraversion and subjective well-being in a US national probability sample. *Journal of Research in Personality*, *26*, 205-215.

Eaves, L. and Eysenck, H. J. (1975). The nature of extraversion: A genetical analysis. *Journal of Personality and Social Psychology*, *32*,102-112.

Eisenberger, N. I., Lieberman, M. D. and Satpute, A. B. (2005). Personality from a controlled processing perspective: An fMRI study of neuroticism, extraversion, and self-consciousness. *Cognitive, Affective, and Behavioral Neuroscience*, *5*, 169-181.

Eysenck, H. J. (1973a). *Eysenck on extraversion*. London: Crosby Lockwood Staples.

Eysenck, H. J. (1973b). Personality, learning and anxiety.In H. J. Eysenck (Ed.), *Handbook of abnormal psychology*, (2nd Ed.; pp. 390-419). London: Pitman Medical.

Eysenck, H. J. (1977a). *Crime and personality*. London: Routledge and Kegan Paul.

Eysenck, H. J. (1977b). Personality and factor analysis: A reply to Guilford. *Psychological Bulletin*, *84*, 405-411.

Eysenck, H. J. (1990). Biological dimensions of personality. In L. A. Pervin (Ed.), *Handbook of personality: Theory and research* (pp. 244-276). New York: Guilford Press.

Eysenck, H. J. and Claridge, G. (1962).The position of hysterics and dysthymics in a two-dimensional framework of personality description. *Journal of Abnormal and Social Psychology*, *64*, 46-55.

Eysenck, H. J. and Eysenck, M. W. (1985).*Personality and individual differences: A natural science approach*. New York: Plenum Press.

Eysenck, H. J. and Eysenck, S. B. G. (1964). *Manual of the Eysenck Personality Inventory*. Kent: Hodder and Stoughton.

Eysenck, H. J. and Eysenck, S. B. G. (1969). *Personality structure and measurement*. London: Routledge and Kegan Paul.

Eysenck, H. J. and Eysenck, S. B. G. (1975). *Manual of the Eysenck Personality Questionnaire*. Kent: Hodder and Stoughton.

Eysenck, S. B. G., Adelaja, O. and Eysenck, H. J. (1977). A comparative study of personality in Nigerian and English subjects. *Journal of Social Psychology*, *102*, 171-178.

Eysenck, S. B. G. and Eysenck, H. J. (1978). Impulsiveness and venture- someness: Their position in a dimensional system of personality description. *Psychological Reports*, *43*, 1247-1255.

Eysenck, S. B. G., Eysenck, H. J. and Barrett, P. (1985).A revised version of the psychoticism scale. *Personality and Individual Differences*, *6*, 21-29.

Eysenck, S. B. G., White, O. and Eysenck, H. J. (1976). Personality and mental illness. *Psychological Reports*, *39*, 1011-1022.

Eysenck, S. B. G. and Yanai, O. (1985). A cross-cultural study of personality: Israel and England. *Psychological Reports*, *57*, 111-116.

Farley, F. H. and Mealiea, W. L. (1972). Personality and fears. *Journal of Personality Assessment*, *36*, 451-453.

Francis, L. J., Brown, L.B., Lester, D. and Philipchalk, R. (1998). Happiness as stable extraversion: A cross-cultural examination of the reliability and validity of the Oxford Happiness Inventory among students in the U. K., U. S. A., Australia, and Canada. *Personality and Individual Differences*, *24*, 167-171.

Freud, S. (1920). *A general introduction to psycho-analysis*. New York: Liver Wright.

Furnham, A. and Cheng, H. (1999) .Personality as predictor of mental health and happiness in the East and West. *Personality and Individual Differences*, *27*, 395-403.

Guilford, J. P. (1975). Factors and factors of personality. *Psychological Bulletin*, *82*, 802-814.

Guilford, J. P. (1977). Will there all factor of extraversion introversion please stand up? A reply to Eysenck. *Psychological Bulletin*, *84*, 412-416.

Guilford, J. S., Zimmerman, W. S. and Guilford, J. P. (1976).*The Guilford-Zimmerman Temperament Survey handbook: Twenty-five years of research and application.* San Diego, CA: EdITS.

Hallam, R. S. (1976). Eysenck personality scales: Stability and change after therapy. *Behavior Research and Therapy*, *14*, 369-372.

Hedge, M. N. (1972). Stuttering, neuroticism and extraversion. *Behavior Research and Therapy*, *10*, 395-397.

Hills, P. and Argyle, M. (1998). Positive moods derived from leisure and their relation to happiness and personality. *Personality and Individual Differences*, *25*, 523-535.

Howarth, E. (1976). A psychometric investigation of Eysenck's Personality Inventory. *Journal of Personality Assessment*, *40*, 173-185.

Howarth, E. and Browne, J. A. (1972).An item-factor-analysis of the Eysenck Personality Inventory. *British Journal of Social and Clinical Psychology, 11*,162-174.

Ingham, J. C. (1966). Changes in MPI scores in neurotic patients: A three year follow-up. *British Journal of Psychiatry*, *112*, 931-939.

Jones, H. G. (1960). Learning and abnormal behaviour.In H. J. Eysenck (Ed.), *Handbook of abnormal psychology* (pp. 488-528). New York: Basic Books.

Jung, C. G. (1923). *Psychological types* (H. G. Baynes, Trans.). London: Routledge and Kegan Paul. (Original work published in 1921).

Jylhä, P. and Isometsä, E. (2006).The relationship of neuroticism and extraversion to symptoms of anxiety and depression in the general population. *Depression and Anxiety*, *23*, 281-289.

Kim, S. H., Hwang, J. H., Park, H. S. and Kim, S. E. (2008). Resting brain metabolic correlates of neuroticism and extraversion in young men. *Neuro Report*, *19*, 883-886.

Laungani, P. (1985). National differences in personality: India and England. *Personality and Individual Differences*, *6*, 217-221.

Levinson, F. and Meyer, V. (1965). Personality changes in relation to psychiatric status following orbital cortex undercutting. *British Journal of Psychiatry*, *111*, 207-218.

Lojk, L., Eysenck, S. B. G. and Eysenck, H. J. (1979). National differences in personality: Yugoslavia and England. *British Journal of Psychology*, *70*, 381-387.

Lorr, M. and Wunderlich, R. A. (1985).A measure of impulsiveness and its relation to extraversion. *Educational and Psychological Measurement*, *45*, 251-257.

Lucas, R. E. and Baird, B. M. (2004). Extraversion and emotional reactivity. *Journal of Persoanlity and Social Psychology*, *86*, 473-485.

Lucas, R. E. and Diener, E., Grob, A., Suh, E. M. and Shao, L. (2000).Cross-cultural evidence for the fundamental features of extraversion. *Journal of Personality and Social Psychology*, *79*, 452-468.

Lynn, R. (1981). Cross-cultural differences in neuroticism, extraversion and psychoticism.In R. Lynn (Ed.), *Dimensions of personality* (pp. 263-286). Oxford: Pergamon Press.

Moore, N. C. (1976). The personality and mental health of flat dwellers. *British Journal of Psychiatry*, *128*, 259-261.

Morris, L. W. (1979). *Extraversion and introversion: An interactional perspective*. New York: John Wiley.

Orpen, C. (1972). The cross-cultural validity of the Eysenck Personality Inventory: A test in Afrikaans-speaking South Africa. *British Journal of Social and Clinical Psychology, 11*, 244-247.

Patterson, M. L. and Strauss, M. E. (1972). An examination of the discriminant validity of the Social Avoidance and Distress Scale. *Journal of Consulting and Clinical Psychology, 39*, 169.

Pickering, A. D. and Gray, J. A. (1999).The neuroscience of personality.In L. A. Pervin and O. P. John (Eds.), *Handbook of personality* (2nd ed.; pp. 277-299). New York: Guilford Press.

Plomin, R. A. (1976). Extraversion: Sociability and impulsivity? *Journal of Personality Assessment, 40*, 24-30.

Shapurian, R. and Hojat, M. (1985). Psychometric characteristics of a Persian version of the Eysenk Personality Questionnaire. *Psychological Reports, 57*, 631-639.

Tarrier, N., Eysenck, S. B. G. and Eysench, H. J. (1980). National differences in personality: Brazil and England. *Personality and Individual Differences, 1*, 164-171.

Verduyn, P. and Brans, K. (2012).The relationship between extraversion, neuroticism and aspects of trait affect. *Personality and Individual Differences, 52*, 664-669.

Vittersø, J. (2001). Personality traits and subjective well-being: Emotional stability, not extraversion, is probably the important predictor. *Personality and Individual Differences, 31*, 903-914.

Watson, D., Wiese, D., Vaidya, J. and Tellegen, A. (1999). The two general activation system of affect: Structural findings, evolutionary considerations, and psychobiological evidence. *Journal of Personality and Social Psychology, 76*, 820-838.

Wilson, G. (1978). Introversion/Extroversion. In H. London and J. E. Exner (Ed.), *Dimensions of personality* (pp. 217-261). New York: John Wiley.

Wilt, J. and Revelle, W. (2009). Extraversion. In M. Leary and R. Hoyle (Eds.), *Handbook of individual differences in social behavior* (pp. 27-45). New York: Guilford Press.

Wismeijer, A. and Assen, M. N. (2008). Do neuroticism and extraversion explain the negative association between self-concealment and subjective well-being? *Personality and Individual Differences, 45*, 345-349.

Wright, C. I., Williams, D., Feczko, E., Barrett, L. F., Dickerson, B. C., Schwartz, C. E. and Wedig, M. M. (2006). Neuroanatomical correlates of extraversion and neuroticism. *Cerebral Cortex*.doi: 10.1093/Cercor/bhj 118.

In: Neuroticism
Editor: Annamaria Di Fabio

ISBN: 978-1-63485-323-1

Chapter 9

NEUROTICISM AND FLOURISHING IN WHITE COLLAR WORKERS: FROM SELF-ESTEEM TO INTRAPRENEURIAL SELF-CAPITAL FOR ADAPTIVE OUTCOMES

Annamaria Di Fabio* and Alessio Gori
Department of Education and Psychology (Psychology Section), University of Florence, Florence, Italy

ABSTRACT

Several researchers have documented the role of personality traits in predicting health outcomes. This study aims to investigate the role of Emotional Stability (low Neuroticism), Self-Esteem and Intrapreneurial Self-Capital in contributing to adaptive outcomes. The current investigation utilized a sample of 141 white collar workers to examine whether Emotional Stability (low Neuroticism) and Self-Esteem predict the Flourishing dimension as an adaptive outcome. Furthermore, in the same sample, the role of Intrapreneurial Self-Capital was analyzed in relation to Emotional Stability (low Neuroticism) and Flourishing. The first hypothesized model, with Emotional Stability (low Neuroticism) and Self-Esteem as independent variables and Flourishing as predicted variable, indicated a poor mediation role of Self-Esteem. The second hypothesized model showed the strong role of Intrapreneurial Self-Capital as a mediator between Emotional Stability (low Neuroticism) and Flourishing. Findings demonstrated that a full understanding of the link between personality traits, in this case Emotional Stability (low Neuroticism), psychological resources and health, requires the consideration of different models, and that the new construct of Intrapreneurial Self-Capital showed an important role in contributing to adaptive outcomes.

* Corresponding author: Annamaria Di Fabio, e-mail: adifabio@psico.unifi.it.

INTRODUCTION

Well-being (WB) is an important research topic which is highly relevant in many fields of psychology (Lucas, Diener, and Suh, 1996; Wu and Yao, 2006), and is predictive of a range of important life outcomes. In general terms, having a strong sense of WB has been associated in prospective studies with greater success in work and relationships (Luhmann, Lucas, Eid, and Diener, 2013; Lyubomirsky, King, and Diener, 2005), lower mortality (Chida and Steptoe, 2008), healthier ageing (Ostir, Markides, and Goodwin, 2000) and lower cognitive decline (Gerstorf, Lovden, Rocke, Smith, and Lindenberger, 2007) and resilience (Di Fabio and Palazzeschi, 2015).

According to the positive psychology perspective, the multi-dimensional construct of WB (Diener, 2003) has distinguished between hedonic well-being and eudaimonic well-being (Ryan and Deci, 2001; Ryff and Singer, 2008; Waterman et al., 2010). The former is defined in terms of satisfaction with life, pleasure attainment, and pain avoidance (Andrews and Withey, 1976; Di Fabio and Gori, 2015; Kahneman, Diener, and Schwarz, 1999), while the latter considers well-being as relative to optimal functioning and self-realization, focusing on resources and strengths (Ryff and Singer, 2008; Vázquez, Hervás, and Ho, 2006; Waterman et al., 2010). Kashdan, Biswas-Diener, and King (2008) suggested that these two ways of thinking about WB are not entirely different from each other, while Henderson and Knight (2012) proposed that these conceptions "should not be treated categorically, nor considered mutually exclusive, but rather that hedonia and eudemonia operate in tandem, in a synergistic fashion" (p. 201). Thus, Seligman (2011) combined several components derived from both aspects and designated a new Flourishing theory of well-being, which tries to integrate these two conceptions. Therefore, the term 'Flourishing' was proposed to describe the desirable state whereby both hedonist and eudaemonist components of well-being are simultaneously present within an individual (Huppert and So, 2013). According to these authors, Flourishing "is the combination of feeling good and functioning effectively" (2013, p. 838).

In order to understand what factors influence WB, this study aims to investigate the role of a number of different variables in contributing to psychological Flourishing, in particular, Emotional Stability (low Neuroticism), Self-Esteem, and Intrapreneurial Self-Capital (Di Fabio, 2014), a novel construct encompassing a set of internal resources with which to better cope with the challenges of the twenty-first century.

Psychological Flourishing

Flourishing, a construct which assesses of overall life of well-being, is receiving a great deal of attention from researchers in various different fields all over the world (Dunn and Dougherty, 2008; Fredrickson and Losada, 2005). Flourishing is defined as having high levels of both hedonic well-being and eudaimonic well-being (Huppert, 2009; Huppert and So 2013; Keyes 2002) although the literature points to various different ways in which Flourishing is operationalized (Hone, Jarden, Schofield, and Duncan, 2014).

According to Keyes (2002, 2005), to be a flourishing individual, the presence of hedonic symptoms and positive functioning are necessary. This model of flourishing is derived from three theoretical points of view: 1) Diener's studies on emotional well-being (Diener, Suh,

Lucas, and Smith, 1999), 2) Ryff's distinction between hedonic (subjective or emotional) well-being and eudaimonic (psychological) well-being (Ryff, 1989), and 3) his own studies on social well-being (Keyes, 1998; e.g., Hone et al., 2014). Keyes (2005) developed a 14-item scale with items representing emotional well-being, psychological well-being, and social well-being (Hone et al., 2014).

Other authors have defined Flourishing differently. Fredrickson and Losada (2005), for example, define it as a concept related to living "within an optimal range of human functioning, connoted by goodness, generativity, growth, and resilience" (Fredrickson and Losada, 2005, p. 678).

Diener and colleagues (2009), following the earlier humanistic psychology theories, created the Flourishing Scale, a brief, eight-item measure designed to assess a number of different areas, such as relationships, self-esteem, purpose, and optimism (Diener et al., 2009; Diener et al., 2010). Specifically, this scale combines dimensions of wellbeing that Ryff (1989), and Ryan and Deci (2001) suggest are important for positive functioning (e.g., competence, self-acceptance, meaning, and connectedness) with optimism, giving, and engagement, which have also been shown to contribute to well-being (Brown, Nesse, Vinokur, and Smith, 2003; Csikszentmihalyi, 1990; Hone et al., 2014; Putnam, 1995; Scheier, Carver, and Bridges, 2001; Seligman, 2006).

In his book, *Flourish*, Seligman (2011) theorizes that wellbeing has five components which can be defined and measured as separate but correlated constructs (Positive emotions, Engagement, Relationships, Meaning in life, and Accomplishments; PERMA, Seligman, 2011), based on the theoretical point of view that these dimensions are generally what individuals choose freely, "for their own sake" (2011, p., 97). The heart of this theoretical framework of flourishing is the belief, as outlined by Seligman in his book, that "the topic of positive psychology is well-being, that the gold-standard for measuring well-being is flourishing, and that the goal of positive psychology is to increase flourishing" (Seligman, 2011, p. 13).

Huppert and So (2013) proposed a categorical diagnosis for flourishing and, through the means of Exploratory factor analysis (EFA), identified three factors: positive characteristics (comprising emotional stability, vitality, optimism, resilience, and self-esteem), positive functioning (comprising engagement, competence, meaning, and positive relationships), and positive appraisal (comprising life satisfaction and positive emotion). This solution covers both the eudaimonic and hedonic aspects of wellbeing (Hone et al., 2014).

Several studies have suggested that both hedonic and eudaimonic activities should be pursued for the most optimal and diverse well-being (Huta and Ryan, 2010). Individuals with a high level of Flourishing seem to have good mental and physical health, and to be more resilient to vulnerabilities and challenges in life than non-flourishers (Bergsma, Veenhoven, ten Have, and de Graaf, 2011; Diener and Seligman 2002; Huppert, 2009; Kobau et al., 2011; Lyubomirsky et al., 2005; Ryff and Singer, 1998, 2008; Schotanus-Dijkstra et al., 2015; Veenhoven, 2008). There is also an apparent link between Flourishing and longevity (Fredrickson and Losada, 2005).

Flourishing individuals thus have higher levels of motivation to work actively to pursue new goals, to improve their own skills and resources, and to have more support and assistance from coworkers and supervisors in their workplace (Lyubomirsky et al., 2005). Despite the central focus of Flourishing in positive psychology research (Huppert, 2009; Rose, 2008;

Seligman, 2011), only a few studies have investigated the variables which are strictly related to this construct.

Neuroticism as Predictor of Well-Being

Personality traits have recently been studied as predictors of important health outcomes (Hampson and Friedman, 2008). Attention has been paid in particular to the contribution of Neuroticism (low Emotional stability) to health and well-being. Neuroticism is a personality trait that refers to individual differences in negative emotional response to threat, frustration, or loss (Costa and McCrae, 1992; Goldberg, 1993) measured by items related to anxiety, fear, worry, irritability, anger, sadness, frustration, hostility, envy, vulnerability, and loneliness (Costa and McCrae, 1992; Goldberg, 1993; Lahey, 2009; Thompson, 2008). Individuals with high scores on neuroticism are generally self-critical, can feel inadequate, and are sensitive to the criticism of others (Watson, Clark, and Harkness, 1994). The dimension of neuroticism – also referred to as negative emotionality or negative affectivity – is included in nearly all major models of personality traits (Matthews, Deary, and Whiteman, 2003), including three-factor (Eysenck, 1947; Tellegen, 1982) and five-factor models (Costa and McCrae, 1992; Goldberg, 1993; Zuckerman, Kuhlman, Teta, Joireman, and Kraft, 1993). Individuals with low scores on neuroticism are generally defined as emotionally stable and less reactive to stress. In other words, people with a good level of Emotional stability tend to be calm, even-tempered, patient, undemanding, optimistic, and imperturbable: thus, Emotional stability is the opposite of neuroticism.

Several studies have found that neuroticism is associated with mental and physical health independently of its correlation with demographic factors (Kendler, Kuhn, and Prescott, 2004; Neeleman, Ormel, and Bijl, 2001; Roberts et al., 2007; Stronks, van de Mheen, Looman, and Mackenback, 1997). A considerable number of studies have documented a link between personality trait level and health (Hampson and Friedman, 2008; Smith, 2006), and this association is strongest for conscientiousness and neuroticism. For example, high neuroticism and low conscientiousness are each associated with earlier mortality (Friedman et al., 1993; Wilson, Mendes de Leon, Bienas, Evans, and Bennett, 2004). A clear association between Neuroticism and both health behaviors and health outcomes has also been demonstrated: Neuroticism is related to the exposure people have to stressors, but also to their reaction (or overreaction) to stress (Bolger and Schilling, 1991; Kling, Ryff, Love, and Essex, 2003; Mroczek and Almeida, 2004). The majority of existing studies on personality have assessed the associations between Neuroticism and various measures of well-being (Bardi and Ryff, 2007; Deneve and Cooper, 1998; Schmutte and Ryff, 1997), and documented that individuals with a low level of Neuroticism (high Emotional stability) and a high level of Extraversion tend to experience a greater level of well-being. The present study aims to verify the association of Emotional Stability (low Neuroticism) and well-being, assessing the effect of two other variables: Self-esteem and Intrapreneurial Self-Capital.

Self-Esteem, Mental Health and Well-Being

Self-Esteem (SE) can be described as person's sense of self-worth or personal value. Self-esteem (SE) is the evaluative and affective dimension of the self-concept (Harter, 1999), and generally refers to a person's global appraisal of his/her positive or negative value (Rogers, 1981; Mann, Hosman, Schaalma, and de Vries, 2003; Markus and Nurius, 1986).

SE seems to be crucial for psychological and social well-being. Several studies have documented the protective role of SE as a protective factor in physical and mental health (Mann et al., 2004; Orth, Robins, and Meier, 2009) and its association to mental well-being, adjustment, happiness, productivity, coping, success, and satisfaction (Baumeister, Campbell, Krueger, and Vohs, 2003; Boden, Fergusson, and Horwood, 2008; Mann et al., 2004). Several studies indicate that SE is an important psychological factor contributing to health and quality of life (Evans, 1997), and one of the most important predictors of happiness (Furnham and Cheng, 2000). The literature also suggests that low self-esteem is related to depressed moods (Beck, Steer, Epstein, and Brown 1990; Patterson and Capaldi, 1992) and depressive disorders (Dori and Overholser, 1999; Rice, Ashby, and Slaney, 1998). This impact of SE in depressive disorders can be reduced by teaching people to challenge their pessimistic thoughts, and by increasing positive subjective thinking (Seligman, 1995; Seligman, Reivich, Jaycox, and Gillham, 1995; Seligman and Csikszentmihalyi, 2000). Furthermore high self-esteem seems associated with high self-fulfillment (Di Fabio and Bucci, 2015).

In sum, positive self-esteem seems to be associated with mental well-being, adjustment, happiness, success and satisfaction (Mann et al., 2004), but its role with regard to Flourishing has not yet been fully explored.

Intrapreneurial Self-Capital

Intrapreneurial self-capital is defined as the positive self-evaluation of the self-concept, the hardiness exhibited by individuals as commitment, control and challenge, the self-efficacy to find creative solutions to problems, the strengths to transform constraints into resources, the quest to develop one's own skills, the perceived ability to apply decision-making skills to every aspect of life, and to make decisions carefully and adaptively (Di Fabio, 2014a, p. 100). Intrapreneurial self-capital provides the personal resources to deal with the constant changes and transitions of life (Di Fabio, 2014a). The higher order construct of intrapreneurial self-capital consists of seven specific sub-constructs (Core Self-Evaluation, Hardiness, Creative Self-Efficacy, Resilience, Goal Mastery, Decisiveness, and Vigilance) (Di Fabio, 2014a). Core Self-Evaluation (Judge, Erez, Bono, and Thorensen, 2003) is related to a positive self-concept in terms of self-esteem, self-efficacy, locus of control, and the absence of pessimism (Di Fabio, 2014a). The second sub-construct, Hardiness, refers to the individual's beliefs about the self and the world and about how to remain connected with this world; it includes three dimensions: commitment, control and challenge (Maddi, 1990). Creative Self-Efficacy refers to one's perception of one's own ability to creatively solve problems, including perception of one's own problem-solving skills and ability to generate new ideas (Tierney and Farmer, 2002). Resilience is the perceived ability to cope with adversity in an adaptive way and to use adaptive strategies to deal with discomfort and adversity (Tugade and Fredrickson, 2004). Goal Mastery refers to continually developing skills and attainment of the highest possible level of performance (Midgley et al., 2000). Decisiveness is defined as the perceived ability to make decisions in a timely manner in any life context (Frost and Shows, 1993). Vigilance refers to an adaptive decision-making style defined as a careful and adaptive search for relevant information to evaluate options before making a choice (Mann, Burnett, Radford, and Ford, 1997; Di Fabio, 2014a). Given the importance and the potential of this new construct in the sphere of positive psychology, this study aims to verify its role in contributing to Well-being and, in particular, to Flourishing.

The Present Research

Analyzing the literature previously presented, we initially hypothesized that: (1) Emotional Stability (low Neuroticism) can influence Well-being (assessed by Flourishing); (2) Emotional Stability (low Neuroticism) is correlated to Self-Esteem (SE); and (3) Self-Esteem can be associated to Well-being (assessed by Flourishing). In other words, we hypothesized that:

- Step 1: Emotional Stability (low Neuroticism) is correlated with Flourishing (estimating the path *c* in Figure 1) for establishing whether there is the possibility of a mediated effect;
- Step 2: Emotional Stability (low Neuroticism) is correlated with Self-Esteem, the mediator variable (estimating and testing the path *a* in the Figure 1);
- Step 3: Self-Esteem affects Flourishing. This hypothesis is evaluated using Emotional Stability (low Neuroticism) and Self-Esteem as predictors to analyse whether Self-Esteem mediates the relationship between Emotional Stability (low Neuroticism) and Flourishing. This hypothesis can be verified by analyzing the effect of Emotional Stability (low Neuroticism) on Flourishing, controlling for Self-Esteem (path *c*' in Figure 1).

Then, in a second mediation model with the same structure, we hypothesized that: (1) Emotional Stability (low Neuroticism) can influence Well-being (assessed by Flourishing); (2) Emotional Stability (low Neuroticism) is related to Intrapreneurial Self-Capital (ISC); and (3) Intrapreneurial Self-Capital can be associated to Well-being (assessed by Flourishing). In other words, we hypothesized that Intrapreneurial Self-Capital (ISC) mediates the relationship between Emotional Stability (low Neuroticism) and Flourishing. This hypothesis can be verified by analyzing the effect of Emotional Stability (low Neuroticism) on Flourishing, controlling for Intrapreneurial Self-Capital (ISC) (path *c*' in Figure 2).

METHOD

Participants and Procedure

Participants in this study were 141 (124 men) white collar workers with a mean age of 42.26 years (*SD* = 11.16). All participants completed the instruments described in the 'measures' section, and gave informed consent after receiving a complete description of the study. With regard to ethical standards for research, the study adhered to the latest version of the Declaration of Helsinki revised in Fortaleza (World Medical Association [WMA], 2013). Participants did not receive any form of payment, and were free to leave the study any time.

Measures

Ten Item Personality Inventory (TIPI; Gosling, Rentfrow, and Swann, 2003). The Ten Item Personality Inventory (TIPI) was developed using descriptors related to other Big Five measures. Each consists of two adjectives, separated by a comma, rated on a 7-point Likert scale from 1 (*strongly disagree*) to 7 (*strongly agree*). The TIPI enables assessment of the Big Five personality traits: Extraversion (E) (e.g., "I see myself as extraverted, enthusiastic"), Agreeableness (A) (e.g., "I see myself as sympathetic, warm"), Conscientiousness (C) (e.g., "I see myself as dependable, self-disciplined"), Neuroticism (N) (e.g., "I see myself as calm, emotionally stable"), Openness (O) (e.g., "I see myself as open to new experiences, complex"). In this study, we used an Italian version of this brief measure that had shown a good level of internal reliability (E = .82; A = .78; C = .79; N = .71; O = .74) (Di Fabio, Gori, and Giannini, 2016).

Rosenberg Self-Esteem Scale (RSES; Rosenberg, 1965). The Rosenberg Self-Esteem Scale (RSES) is a 10-item Likert scale for assessing global self-esteem, with responses given on a four point scale ranging from *strongly agree* to *strongly disagree* (e.g., "On the whole, I am satisfied with myself", "I take a positive attitude towards myself"). Multiple studies have demonstrated the psychometric properties of the RSES to be good (Corwyn, 2000). In this study, we used the Italian version of the RSES (α =.84) (Prezza, Trombaccia, and Armento, 1997).

Intrapreneurial Self-Capital Scale (ISCS; Di Fabio, 2014a). Intrapreneurial self-capital is defined as a core of individual intrapreneurial resources used to cope with career and life challenges. It includes dimensions of core self-evaluation, hardiness, creative self-efficacy, resilience, goal mastery, decisiveness, and vigilance (Di Fabio, 2014a). The Intrapreneurial Self-Capital Scale was developed by Di Fabio (2014a) to measure this new construct. The ISCS uses a 5-point Likert-type scale (1 = *strongly disagree*, 2 = *disagree*, 3 = *neither agree nor disagree*, 4 = *agree*, 5 = *strongly agree*) and is composed of 28 items (e.g., "I am able to deal with most of my problems", "I am able to improve the ideas produced by others", "I am able to achieve objectives despite obstacles", "One of my goals in training is to learn as much as I can"). In this study, we used the Italian version of this measure that had shown a good internal consistency (α = .86) (Di Fabio, 2014a).

Flourishing Scale (FS; Diener et al., 2010). The Flourishing Scale is a self-report composed of eight items on a 7-point Likert scale ranging from 1 (strongly disagree) to 7 (strongly agree) that assesses the respondent's self-perceived success in important areas of his or her life, such as relationships, self-esteem, purpose, and optimism. Examples of items are: "My social relationships are supportive and rewarding", "I lead a purposeful and meaningful life", and "I am optimistic about my future". This scale provides a single total score. Its psychometric properties have been analyzed (Diener et al., 2010). In this study we used the Italian version of this scale (α = .88) (Di Fabio, 2016).

Data Analysis

Descriptive statistics and correlation among variables were calculated, with the additional aim of testing the possibility of performing a mediation analysis. In line with the purpose of the study – to determine the effects of Emotional Stability (low Neuroticism) and Self-esteem, and subsequently Intrapreneurial Self-Capital, on levels of Flourishing – we carried out two mediation analyses. In a second mediation analysis, the variable Self-Esteem was replaced with the Intrapreneurial Self-Capital variable. Following the Baron and Kenny approach (1986), the dependent variable was Flourishing, with Emotional Stability (low Neuroticism) as the predictor at the first step, followed by Emotional Stability (low Neuroticism) and Self-Esteem (Intrapreneurial Self-Capital in the second mediation analysis) at the second, and evaluation of the interaction term at the third. After each mediation analysis had been performed, we tested the significance of the indirect effect using bootstrapping procedures. Unstandardized indirect effects were computed for each of 5,000 bootstrapped samples, and the 95% confidence interval was computed by determining the indirect effects at the 2.5th and 97.5th percentiles. In addition, a Sobel test was performed in order to obtain another indication of the indirect effects for both mediations.

RESULTS

As described above, mediation analyses were conducted following the Baron and Kenny (1986) procedure. Results showed strong correlations among the variables under investigation (see Table 1).

Table 1. Descriptive statistics and correlations among variables under investigation

	M	*SD*	Min.	Max.	Skewness	Kurtosis	1	2	3
Emotional Stability (low Neuro-ticism)	5.61	1.16	2	7	-.82	.05	1		
Self-Esteem	35.35	4.73	25	40	-.64	-.75	.38**	1	
Intra-preneurial Self-Capital	111.95	12.95	84	140	.09	-.39	.50**	.47**	1
Flourishing	45.32	7.88	14	56	-1.14	2.82	.42**	.30**	.68**

(**$p < .01$).

In respect of the first mediation, we hypothesized that Emotional Stability (low Neuroticism) would be correlated with Flourishing (estimating the path *c* in Figure 1) for establishing whether there is the possibility of a mediated effect; results supported this first hypothesis ($\beta = .424$, $p < .001$).

The second step showed that Emotional Stability (low Neuroticism) was positively related to Self-Esteem, supporting the second hypothesis (β = .379, p < .001). The third step of this simple mediation indicated that the effect of Emotional Stability (low Neuroticism) on Flourishing was reduced after controlling Self-Esteem (path c' in Figure 1) but still significant (β = .361, p < .001) (see Figure 1). However, the indirect effect proved not to be significant in both the bootstrapping procedure (*Boot* LLCI = .0127 – *Boot* ULCI = 1.15) and the Sobel test (z = 1.827, p = .068).

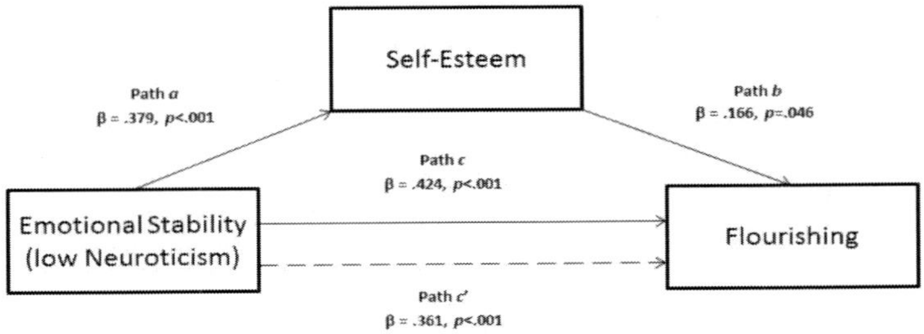

Figure 1. Standardized regression coefficients for the relationship between Emotional Stability (low Neuroticism) and Flourishing as mediated by Self-Esteem.

With regard to the second mediation, we hypothesized that Emotional Stability (low Neuroticism) would be correlated with Flourishing (estimating the path c in the Figure 1) for establishing whether or not there is the possibility of a mediated effect; results supported this first hypothesis (β = .424, p < .001).

The second step showed that Emotional Stability (low Neuroticism) was positively related to Intrapreneurial Self-Capital, supporting the second hypothesis (β = .498, p < .001). The third step of this simple mediation indicated that Intrapreneurial Self-Capital mediates the relationship between Emotional Stability (low Neuroticism) and Flourishing, because the effect of Emotional Stability (low Neuroticism) on Flourishing was reduced after controlling Intrapreneurial Self-Capital (path c' in Figure 2). In this case, given that Emotional Stability (low Neuroticism) is no longer significant in predicting Flourishing, as it was before in path c, and the Flourishing variable is predicted by Intrapreneurial Self-Capital, we can observe a total mediation (see Figure 2): the relationship between Emotional Stability (low Neuroticism) and Flourishing passed from an observed effect of β = .424, p < .001 in the path c to an insignificant effect (β = .115, p = .110) in the path c'. With regard to this mediation, the indirect effect was significant with both the bootstrapping procedure (*Boot* LLCI =1.28 – *Boot* ULCI = 3.08) and Sobel test (z = 5.31, p < .001).

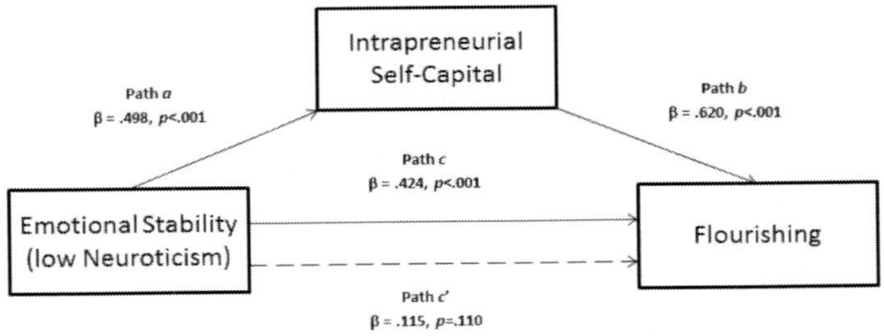

Figure 2. Standardized regression coefficients for the relationship between Emotional Stability (low Neuroticism) and Flourishing as mediated by Intrapreneurial Self-Capital.

DISCUSSION

In recent years, a great deal of research has focused on well-being in order to investigate the causes of overall satisfaction (Oishi, 2012). As previously mentioned, the notion of well-being refers to subjective (or hedonic) well-being and psychological (or eudaimonic) well-being (Riff and Singer, 2000; Ryan and Deci, 2001). Furthermore, researchers have advanced various theoretical models of well-being, incorporating a broad range of constructs (Gale et al., 2013; Kashdan et al., 2008). Certain authors have combined components derived from both aspects and arrived at a new theory of well-being centering on the notion of Flourishing, which attempts to integrate these two conceptions (hedonic and eudaimonic) (Diener et al., 2010; Huppert and So, 2013; Seligman, 2011). Flourishing should therefore be understood as "the combination of feeling good and functioning effectively" (Huppert and So, 2013, p. 838). Thus, we have identified the variable 'Flourishing' as an adaptive outcome capable of incorporating a global concept of well-being. Indeed, the other important variable of this study was Emotional Stability (low Neuroticism), since most existing studies on personality have assessed the associations between this construct and well-being (Deneve and Cooper, 1998; Schmutte and Ryff, 1997). In line with these studies, the present research documented an association between Emotional Stability (low Neuroticism) and general well-being (measured by Flourishing) as attested to by the results of mediation analyses.

Having confirmed these results, this study aimed to investigate the role of two important variables, Self-Esteem and Intrapreneurial Self-Capital, in contributing to adaptive outcomes. The first of these two constructs seems to be important for psychological and social well-being; several studies have documented the association of Self-Esteem, mental well-being, happiness, productivity, success, and satisfaction (Baumeister et al., 2003; Mann et al., 2004). In line with these studies, this work partially confirmed the role of Self-Esteem in contributing to adaptive outcomes (in terms of Flourishing), and also, albeit with a small effect, in respect of other variables under investigation. Although this construct seems directly connected to Flourishing, its role as a mediator between Emotional Stability (low Neuroticism) and Flourishing seems to be only partial, since it produces (only) a little reduction in the relationship between the other two variables mentioned above (Baron and Kenny, 1986). In any case, the mediation effect of Self-Esteem seems not to be significant with both the bootstrapping procedure and Sobel test. This model therefore highlights the strong association between Emotional Stability (low Neuroticism) and Flourishing. From this perspective emerges the possibility that there could be other relevant mediators for this model.

The other new construct under investigation, however – Intrapreneurial Self-Capital (ISC) – seems to have a preponderant role in contributing to adaptive outcomes. In fact, the second mediation analyses indicated that ISC mediates the relationship between Emotional Stability (low Neuroticism) and Flourishing, producing a significant reduction in the relationship between these two constructs. Indeed, both of the procedures for assessing the mediation effect indicate the presence of a significant effect. These results suggest that the new construct of Intrapreneurial Self-Capital, defined as a core of personal resources (Di Fabio, 2014a), can strongly impact upon adaptive outcomes.

This study also has some limitations that need to be addressed. The first relates to the number of participants, which is somewhat restricted due to the difficulty of recruiting subjects with these characteristics. Further studies should better investigate this novel construct of Intrapreneurial Self-Capital with a larger sample, and also in different international contexts. It could also be useful to replicate this study using a measure that more precisely assesses Neuroticism, such as the Revised Eysenck Personality Questionnaire (EPQ-R; Eysenck and Eysenck, 1991) or the Revised NEO Personality Inventory (NEO PI-R; Costa and McCrae, 1992). A further limitation relates to cross-sectional measurement, which complicates testing of the causal relationships between variables of the hypothesized models. Indeed, Emotional Stability was assessed using a short-measure, and these personality traits usually require a larger number of items so as to cover all facets of the characteristics under investigation.

However, notwithstanding these limitations, these results suggest that Intrapreneurial Self-Capital plays a substantial role in promoting effective well-being across the myriad personal and professional transitions and complex challenges of twenty-first century life (Blustein, 2011; Di Fabio, 2014a, 2014b; Di Fabio and Kenny, 2015; Di Fabio and Bernaud, 2014; Di Fabio and Maree, 2013). Research results and theoretical models of this study illustrate the fact that Emotional Stability (low Neuroticism) remains an important contributor to well-being, and that Intrapreneurial Self-Capital is a good mediator between Emotional Stability (low Neuroticism) and Flourishing. Indeed, focusing on aspects of Intrapreneurial Self-Capital places renewed emphasis on the importance of the preventive perspective (Kenny and Hage, 2009; Hage et al., 2007), and specifically on the importance of combining the efforts to increase resources with those ones to decrease risk. Working to increase this core of resources, attitudes, competencies, and skills is essential for promoting various aspects of well-being, both hedonic and eudaimonic, including career success.

CONCLUSION

This study confirmed the positive and significant relationship between Emotional Stability (low Neuroticism) and general well-being (assessed via measurement of Flourishing) (Bardi and Ryff, 2007; Deneve and Cooper, 1998; Schmutte and Ryff, 1997). According to these results, individuals with a good Emotional Stability (low Neuroticism), who are usually even-tempered, patient and optimistic, tend to experience high levels of life satisfaction and general well-being. Moreover, these results highlighted the direct relationship of two other variables – Self-Esteem and Intrapreneurial Self-Capital – with Flourishing. On the one hand, these results partially support the association between Self-Esteem and mental well-being, confirming the results of previous studies (Baumeister, Campbell, Krueger, and Vohs, 2003; Boden, Fergusson, and Horwood, 2008; Mann et al., 2004), while on the other hand showing the poor ability of this variable to be a mediator between Emotional Stability (low Neuroticism) and Flourishing.

Although Self-Esteem still remains a crucial variable in contributing to well-being, an emerging construct – Intrapreneurial Self-Capital – which incorporates a number of different aspects of resourcefulness, emerges as a powerful mediator variable between Emotional Stability (low Neuroticism) and Flourishing. These results may doubly impact on well-being: first because the various aspects of this new construct are directly related to Flourishing, and secondly because Intrapreneurial Self-Capital is a core of attitudes and resourcefulness that can be improved through a training program aimed at strengthening human potential. To be a flourishing individual, the presence of hedonic components and positive functioning is necessary (Keyes, 2002, 2005), as is resilience to vulnerabilities and challenges (Bergsma, Veenhoven, ten Have, and de Graaf, 2011; Diener and Seligman 2002; Huppert, 2009; Kobau et al., 2011; Lyubomirsky et al., 2005; Ryff and Singer, 1998, 2008; Schotanus-Dijkstra et al., 2015; Veenhoven, 2008).

References

Andrews, F. M. and Withey, S. B. (1976). *Social indicators of well-being: America's perception of life quality*. New York: Plenum Press.

Bardi, A. and Ryff, C. D. (2007). Interactive effects of traits on adjustment to a life transition. *Journal of Personality*, *75*, 955-984.

Baron, R. M. and Kenny, D. A. (1986). The moderator-mediator variable distinction in social psychological research: Conceptual, strategic, and statistical considerations. *Journal of Personality and Social Psychology*, *51*(6), 1173-1182.

Baumeister, R. F., Campbell, J. D., Krueger, J. I. and Vohs, K. E. (2003). Does high self-esteem cause better performance, interpersonal success, happiness, or healthier lifestyles? *Psychological Science in the Public Interest*, *4*, 1-44.

Beck, A., Steer, R. A., Epstein, N. and Brown, G. (1990). Beck Self Concept Test. *Psychological Assessment*, *2*, 191-197.

Bergsma, A., Veenhoven, R., ten Have, M. and de Graaf, R. (2011). Do they know how happy they are? On the value of self-rated happiness of people with a mental disorder. *Journal of Happiness Studies*, *12*, 793-806.

Blustein, D. L. (2011). A relational theory of working. *Journal of Vocational Behavior*, *79*(1), 1-17.

Boden, J. M., Fergusson, D. M. and Horwood, L. J. (2008). Does adolescent self-esteem predict later life outcomes? A test of the causal role of self-esteem. *Development and Psychopathology*, *20*, 319 -339.

Bolger, N. and Schilling, E. A. (1991). Personality and the problems of everyday life: The role of Neuroticism in Exposure and reactivity to daily stressors. *Journal of Personality*, *59*, 355-386.

Brown, S. L., Nesse, R. M., Vinokur, A. D. and Smith, D. M. (2003). Providing social support may be more beneficial than receiving it: Results from a prospective study of mortality. *Psychological Science*, *14*(4), 320-327.

Chida, Y. and Steptoe, A. (2008). Positive psychological well-being and mortality: A quantitative review of prospective observational studies. *Psychosomatic Medicine*, *70*(7), 741-756.

Corwyn, R. F. (2000). The factor structure of global self-esteem among adolescents and adults. *Journal of Research in Personality*, *34*, 357-379.

Costa, P. T. and McCrae, R. R. (1992). Four ways five factors are basic. *Personality and Individual Differences*, *13*, 653-665.

Costa, P. T. and McCrae, R. R. (1992). *NEO PI-R professional manual*. Odessa., FL: Psychological Assessment Resources.

Csikszentmihalyi, M. (1990). *Flow: The psychology of optimal experience*. New York: Harper Collins.

DeNeve, K. M. and Cooper, H. (1998). The happy personality: A meta-analysis of 137 personality traits and well-being. *Psychological Bulletin, 124*, 197-229.

Di Fabio, A. (2014a). Intrapreneurial Self-Capital: A new construct for the 21st century. *Journal of Employment Counseling, 51*, 98-111.

Di Fabio, A. (2014b). Career counseling and positive psychology in the 21st century: New constructs and measures for evaluating the effectiveness of intervention. *Journal of Counsellogy, 1*, 193-213.

Di Fabio, A. (2016). Flourishing Scale: Primo contributo alla validazione della versione italiana. [Flourishing Scale: First contribution to the validation of the Italian version]. *Counseling. Giornale Italiano di Ricerca e Applicazioni, 9*(1).

Di Fabio, A. and Bucci, O. (2015). Affective profiles in Italian high school students: Life satisfaction, psychological well-being, self-esteem, and optimism. *Frontiers in Psychology, 6*, 1310. doi: 10.3389/fpsyg.2015.01310

Di Fabio, A. and Kenny, M. E. (2015). The contributions of emotional intelligence and social support for adaptive career progress among Italian youth. *Journal of Career Development, 42*, 48-49.

Di Fabio, A. and Gori, A. (2015). Measuring adolescent life satisfaction: Psychometric properties of the Satisfaction With Life Scale in a sample of Italian adolescents and young adults. *Journal of Psychoeducational Assessment*. Advance online publication. doi: 10.1177/0734282915621223.

Di Fabio, A., Gori, A., and Giannini, M. (2016). Analizzare le proprietà psicometriche di una misura dei Big Five con un metodo alternativo: L'esempio del Ten Item Personality Inventory (TIPI) [Analysing the psychometric properties of a Big Five measurement tool with an alternative method: the example of the Ten Item Personality Inventory (TIPI)]. Counseling. Giornale Italiano di Ricerca e Applicazioni, 9(2).

Di Fabio, A. and Bernaud, J.-L. (Eds.). (2014). *The Construction of the Identity in 21st Century: A Festschrift for Jean Guichard*. New York: Nova Science Publishers.

Di Fabio, A. and Maree, J. G. (Eds.). (2013). *Psychology of Career Counseling: New challenges for a new era. Festschrift in honour of Prof. Mark Savickas*. New York: Nova Science Publishers.

Di Fabio, A. and Palazzeschi, L. (2015). Hedonic and eudaimonic well-being: The role of resilience beyond fluid intelligence and personality traits. *Frontiers in Psychology, 6*, 1367.

Diener, E. (2003). What is positive about positive psychology: The curmudgeon and Pollyanna. *Psychological Inquiry, 14*, 115-120.

Diener, E. and Seligman, M. E. P. (2002). Very happy people. Psychological Science, *13*(1), 81-84.

Diener, E., Suh, E. M., Lucas, R. E. and Smith, H. E. (1999). Subjective well-being: Three decades of progress. *Psychological Bulletin, 125*, 276-302.

Diener, E., Wirtz, D., Biswas-Diener, R., Tov, W., Kim-Prieto, C., Choi, D., et al. (2009). *New measures of well-being*. The Netherlands: Springer. The collected works of Ed Diener.

Diener, E., Wirtz, D., Tov, W., Kim-Prieto, C., Choi, D. W., Oishi, S. and Biswas-Diener, R. (2010). New well-being measures: Short scales to assess flourishing and positive and negative feelings. *Social Indicators* Research, *97*(2), 143-156.

Dori, G. A. and Overholser, J. C. (1999). Depression, hopelessness and self-esteem: accounting for suicidality in adolescent psychiatric inpatients. *Suicide and Life Threatening Behavior*, *29*, 309-318.

Dunn, D. S. and Dougherty, S. B. (2008). Flourishing: Mental health as living life well. *Journal of Social and Clinical Psychology*, *27*, 314-316.

Evans, D. R. (1997) Health promotion, wellness programs, quality of life and the marketing of psychology. *Canadian Psychology*, *38*, 1-12.

Eysenck, H. J. (1947). *Dimensions of personality*. Oxford, England: Kegan Paul.

Fredrickson, B. L. and Losada, M. F. (2005). Positive affect and complex dynamics of human flourishing. *American Psychologist*, *60*, 678-686.

Friedman, H. S., Tucker, J. S., Tomlinson-Keasey, C., Schwartz, J.E., Wingard, D. L., Criqui, M. H. (1993). Does childhood personality predict longevity? *Journal of Personality and Social Psychology*, *65*, 176-185.

Frost, R. O. and Shows, D. L. (1993). The nature and measurement of compulsive indecisiveness. *Behavior Research Therapy*, *31*, 683-692.

Furnham, A. and Cheng, H. (2000). Lay theories of happiness. *Journal of Happiness Studies*, *1*, 227-246.

Gerstorf, D., Lovden, M., Rocke, C., Smith, J. and Lindenberger, U. (2007). Well-being affects changes in perceptual speed in advanced old age: Longitudinal evidence for a dynamic link. *Developmental Psychology*, *43*(3), 705-718.

Goldberg, L. R. (1993). The structure of phenotypic personality traits. *American Psychologist*, *48*, 26-34.

Gosling, S. D., Rentfrow, P. J. and Swann, W. B., Jr. (2003). A very brief measure of the Big Five personality domains. *Journal of Research in Personality*, *37*, 504-528.

Hage, S. M., Romano, J. L., Conyne, R. K., Kenny, M., Matthews, C., Schwartz, J. P. and Waldo, M. (2007). Best practice guidelines on prevention practice, research, training, and social advocacy for psychologists. *The Counseling Psychologist*, *35*, 493-566.

Hampson, S. E. and Friedman, H. S. (2008). Personality and health: A life span perspective. In: O. P. John, R. Robins, and L. Pervin (Eds.). *The handbook of personality (3rd ed.)*. New York: Guilford Press.

Harter, S. (1999). *The Construction of the self. A developmental perspective*. Guilford Press, New York.

Eysenck, H. J. and Eysenck, S. B. G. (1991). *Manual of the Eysenck Personality Scales*. London: Hodder and Stoughton.

Henderson, L. W. and Knight, T. (2012). Integrating the hedonic and eudaimonic perspectives to more comprehensively understand wellbeing and pathways to well-being. *International Journal of Wellbeing*, *2*, 196-221.

Hone, L., Jarden, A., Schofield, G. M. and Duncan, S. (2014). Measuring flourishing: The impact of operational definitions on the prevalence of high levels of wellbeing. *International Journal of Wellbeing*, *4*(1), 62-90.

Huppert, F. A. (2009). Psychological well-being: Evidence regarding its causes and consequences. *Applied Psychology: Health and Well-being*, *1*(2), 137-164.

Huppert, F. A. and So, T. C. (2013). Flourishing across Europe: Application of a new conceptual framework for defining well-being. *Social Indicators Research*, *110*(3), 837-861.

Huta, V. and Ryan, R. M. (2010). Pursuing pleasure or virtue: The differential and overlapping well-being benefits of hedonic and eudaimonic motives. *Journal of Happiness Studies*, *11*, 735-762.

Judge, T. A., Erez, A., Bono, J. E. and Thoresen, C. J. (2003). The core self evaluations scale: Development of a measure. *Personnel Psychology*, *56*(2), 303-331.

Kahneman, D., Diener, E. and Schwarz, N. (Eds.). (1999). *Well-being: The foundations of hedonic psychology*. New York: Russel Sage Foundation.

Kashdan, T. B., Biswas-Diener, R. and King, L. A. (2008). Reconsidering happiness: The costs of distinguishing between hedonics and eudaimonia. *The Journal of Positive Psychology*, *3*(4), 219-233.

Kendler, K. S., Kuhn, J., Prescott, C. A. (2004). The interrelationship of neuroticism, sex, and stressful life events in the prediction of episodes of major depression. *American Journal of Psychiatry*, *161*, 631-636.

Kenny, M. E. and Hage, S. M. (2009). The next frontier: Prevention as an instrument of social justice. *The Journal of Primary Prevention*, *30*, 1-10.

Keyes, C. L. M. (1998). Social well-being. *Social Psychology Quarterly*, *61*, 121-140.

Keyes, C. L. M. (2002). The Mental Health Continuum: From languishing to flourishing in life. *Journal of Health and Social Behavior*, *43*(2), 207-222.

Keyes, C. L. M. (2005). Mental illness and/or mental health? Investigating axioms of the complete state model of health [Research Support, Non-U.S. Gov't]. *Journal of Consulting and Clinical Psychology*, *73*(3), 539-548.

Keyes, C. L. M. (2005). Mental illness and/or mental health? Investigating axioms of the complete state model of health. *Journal of Consulting and Clinical Psychology*, *73*, 539-548.

Kling, K. C., Ryff, C. D., Love, G. and Essex, M. (2003). Exploring the influence of personality on depressive symptoms and self-esteem across a significant life transition. *Journal of Personality and Social Psychology*, *85*, 922-932.

Kobau, R., Seligman, M. E., Peterson, C., Diener, E., Zack, M. M., Chapman, D. and Thompson, W. (2011). Mental health promotion in public health: Perspectives and strategies from positive psychology. *American Journal of Public Health*, *101*(8), e1-e9.

Lahey, B. B. (2009). Public health significance of neuroticism. *American Psychologist*, *64*, 241-256.

Lucas, R. E., Diener, E. and Suh, E. (1996). Discriminant validity of well-being measures. *Journal of Personality and Social Psychology*, *71*(3), 616-628.

Luhmann, M., Lucas, R. E., Eid, M. and Diener, E. (2013). The prospective effect of life satisfaction on life events. *Social Psychological and Personality Science*, *4*(1), 39-45.

Lyubomirsky, S., King, L. and Diener, E. (2005). The benefits of frequent positive affect: Does happiness lead to success? *Psychological Bulletin*, *131*(6), 803-855.

Maddi, S. R. (1990). Issues and interventions in stress mastery. In H. S. Friedman (Ed.), *Personality and disease* (pp. 121-154). New York: Wiley.

Mann, L., Burnett, P., Radford, M. and Ford, S. (1997). The Melbourne Decision Making Inventory: An instrument for measuring patterns for coping with decisional conflict. *Journal of Behavioral Decision Making*, *10*, 1-19.

Mann, M., Hosman, C. M. H., Schaalma, H. P. and de Vries, N. K. (2004). Self-esteem in a broad-spectrum approach for mental health promotion. *Health Education research, 19,* 357-372.

Markus, H. and Nurius, P. (1986). Possible selves. *American Psychologist, 41*, 954-969.

Matthews, G., Deary, I. J. and Whiteman, M. C. (2003). *Personality traits (2nd ed.).* Cambridge, England: Cambridge University Press.

Midgley, C., Maehr, M. L., Hruda, L. Z., Anderman, E., Anderman, L., Freeman, K. E., and Urdan, T. (2000). Manual for the patterns of adaptive learning scales. *Ann Arbor, 1001,* 48109-1259.

Mroczek, D. K. and Almeida, D. M. (2004). The effect of daily stress, personality, and age on daily negative affect. *Journal of Personality, 72*, 355-378.

Neeleman, J., Ormel, J., Bijl, R. V. (2001). The distribution of psychiatric and somatic ill health: Associations with personality and socioeconomic status. *Psychosomatic Medicine, 63*, 239-247.

Orth, U., Robins, R. W. and Meier, L. L. (2009). Disentangling the effects of low self-esteem and stressful events on depression: Findings from three longitudinal studies. *Journal of Personality and Social Psychology, 97*, 307-321.

Ostir, G. V., Markides, K. S., Peek, M. K. and Goodwin, J. S (2001). The association between emotional well-being and the incidence of stroke in older adults. *Psychosomatic Medicine, 63*(2), 210-215.

Patterson, G. R. and Capaldi, D. M. (1992). Mediational model for boys' depressed mood. In J. Rolf, A. S. Masten, D. Cicchetti, K. H. Nuechterlein, and S. Weintraub (Eds.), *Risk and protective factors in development of psychopathology* (pp. 141-163). Cambridge University Press, Cambridge.

Prezza, M., Trombaccia, F. R. and Armento, L. (1997). The Rosenberg Self-Esteem Scale: Italian translation and validation [La scala dell'Autostima di Rosenberg: traduzione e validazione Italiana]. *Applied Psychology Bulletin, 223*, 34-44.

Putnam, R. D. (1995). Bowling alone: America's declining social capital. *Journal of Democracy, 6*(1), 65-78.

Rice, K. G., Ashby, J. S. and Slaney, R. B. (1998). Self-esteem as a mediator between perfectionism and depression: A structural equations analysis. *Journal of Counseling Psychology, 45*, 304-314.

Roberts, B. W., N. R. Kuncel, R. L. Shiner, A. Caspi, and L. R. Goldberg (2007). The power of personality: The comparative validity of personality traits, socioeconomic status, and cognitive ability for predicting important life outcomes. *Perspectives in Psychological Science, 2*(4), 313-345.

Rogers, T. B. (1981). A model of the self as an aspect of the human information processing system. In N. Canton and J. F. Kihlstrom (Eds.), *Personality, cognition and social interaction* (pp. 193-214). Erlbaum, Hillsdale, NJ.

Rose, G. (2008). *Rose's strategy of preventive medicine*. Oxford: Oxford University Press.

Rosenberg, M. (1965). *Society and the adolescent self-image*. Princeton: Princeton University Press.

Ryan, R. M. and Deci, E. L. (2001). To be happy or to be self-fulfilled: A review of research on hedonic and eudaimonic well-being. In S. Fiske (Ed.), *Annual Review of Psychology* (Vol. 52, pp. 141-166). Palo Alto, CA: Annual Reviews.

Ryff, C. D. (1989). Happiness is everything, or is it? Explorations on the meaning of psychological well-being. *Journal of Personality and Social Psychology, 57*, 1069-108.

Ryff, C. D. and Singer, B. (1998). The contours of positive human health. *Psychological Inquiry, 9*(1), 1-28.

Ryff, C. D. and Singer, B. H. (2008). Know thyself and become what you are: A eudaimonic approach to psychological well-being. *Journal of Happiness Studies, 9*, 13-39.

Scheier, M. F., Carver, C. S. and Bridges, M. W. (2001). Optimism, pessimism, and psychological wellbeing. In E. C. Chang (Ed.), *Optimism and pessimism: Implications for theory, research, and practice* (pp. 189-216). Washington, DC: American Psychological Association.

Schmutte, P. S. and Ryff, C. D. (1997). Personality and well-being: Reexamining methods and meanings. *Journal of Personality and Social Psychology, 73*, 549-559.

Schotanus-Dijkstra, M., Pieterse, M. E., Drossaert, C. H. C., Westerhof, G. J., de Graaf, R., ten Have, M., ... and Bohlmeijer, E. T. (2015). What factors are associated with flourishing? Results from a large representative national sample. *Journal of Happiness Studies*, 1-20.

Seligman, M. E. (2006). *Learned optimism: How to change your mind and your life* (1st Vintage Books ed.). New York: Vintage Books.

Seligman, M. E. (2011). *Flourish: A visionary new understanding of happiness and well-being* (1st Free Press hardcover ed.). New York, NY: Free Press.

Seligman, M. E. P. and Csikszentmihalyi, M. (2000). Positive psychology: An introduction. *American Psychologist, 55*, 5-14.

Seligman, M. E. P. (1995). *What you can change and what you can't*. Knopf, New York.

Seligman, M.E.P., Reivich, K., Jaycox, L. and Gillham, J. (1995). *The optimistic child*. Houghton Mifflin: Boston, MA.

Smith, T. W. (2006). Personality as risk and resilience in physical health. *Current Directions in Psychological Science, 15*, 227-231.

Stronks, K., van de Mheen, H. D., Looman, C. W. N., Mackenbach, J. P. (1997). Cultural, material, and psychosocial correlates of the socioeconomic gradient in smoking behavior among adults. *Preventive Medicine, 26*, 754-766.

Tellegen, A. (1982). *Multidimensional Personality Questionnaire Manual*. Minnesota: University of Minnesota Press.

Thompson, E. R. (October, 2008). Development and validation of an international English Big-Five mini-makers. *Personality and Individual Differences, 45*(6), 542-548.

Tierney, P. and Farmer, S. M. (2002). Creative Self-Efficacy: Its potential antecedents and relationship to creative performance. *Academy of Management Journal, 45*(6), 1137-1148.

Vázquez, C., Hervás, G. and Ho, S. (2006). Intervenciones clinicas basadas en la psicologia positiva: Fundamentos y aplicaciones [Clinical interventions based on positive psychology: Foundations and applications]. *Psicología Conductual, 14*, 401-432.

Veenhoven, R. (2008). Healthy happiness: Effects of happiness on physical health and the consequences for preventive health care. *Journal of Happiness Studies, 9*, 449-469.

Waterman, A. S., Schwartz, S. J., Zamboanga, B. L., Ravert, R. D., Williams, M. K., Bede Agocha, V., … and Donnellan, M. B. (2010). The Questionnaire for Eudaimonic Well-Being: Psychometric properties, demographic comparisons, and evidence of validity. *The Journal of Positive Psychology, 5*, 41-61.

Watson, D., Clark, L. A. and Harkness, A. R. (1994). Structures of personality and their relevance to psychopathology. *Journal of Abnormal Psychology*, *103*, 18-31.

Wilson, R. S., Mendes de Leon, C. F., Bienas, J. L., Evans, D. A., Bennett, D. A. (2004). Personality and mortality in old age. The Journals of Gerontology, *Series B: Psychological Sciences and Social Sciences*, *59*, 110-116.

World Medical Association [WMA]. (2013). World Medical Association Declaration of Helsinki ethical principles for medical research involving human subjects. *Journal American Medical Association*, *310*, 2191-2194. doi: 10.1001/jama.2013.281053.

Wu, C. H. and Yao, G. (2006). Analysis of factorial invariance across gender in the Taiwan version of the Satisfaction With Life Scale. *Personality and Individual Differences*, *40*, 1259-1268.

Zuckerman, M., Kuhlman, D. M., Joireman, J., Teta, P. and Kraft, M. (1993). A comparison of three structural models for personality: The Big Three, the Big Five, and the Alternative Five. *Journal of Personality and Social Psychology*, *65*(4), 757-768.

In: Neuroticism
Editor: Annamaria Di Fabio

ISBN: 978-1-63485-323-1

Chapter 10

Neuroticism and Career Outcomes: An Empirical Study from a Preventive Perspective

Annamaria Di Fabio* and Ornella Bucci
Department of Education and Psychology (Psychology Section), University of Florence, Florence, Italy

Abstract

Career outcomes (career decision-making self-efficacy, career decision, employability) in previous studies have emerged relating to personality traits, particularly to neuroticism, but rarely were they simultaneously analyzed confronting different groups of participants in the same study to compare results. In the present paper, the association between career outcomes and the Big Five personality factors were investigated among 219 Italian high school students and 234 Italian university students. The participants filled out the Big Five Questionnaire (BFQ), the Career Decision Self-Efficacy Scale (CDSES), the Career Decision-making Difficulties Questionnaire (CDDQ), and the Self Perceived Employability Scale (SPES) for students. The results of the present study showed that, in particular, neuroticism consistently explained a significantly larger percentage of variance in all career outcomes variables. The results of the present study contribute to the in-depth exploration of career outcomes (career decision-making self-efficacy, career decision, employability), broadening knowledge of its associations with personality traits and particularly with neuroticism in young people. In a preventive perspective on the basis of the relation between neuroticism and career outcomes, it could be possible to individuate young people at risk of high neuroticism with early intervention with specific trainings for promoting career outcomes.

* Corresponding author: Annamaria Di Fabio, email: adifabio@psico.unifi.it.

INTRODUCTION

The role of personality traits in vocational choice was recognized (Borges and Savickas, 2002; Holland, 1997; Tokar, Fischer, and Subich, 1998) and the analysis of personality in career decision-making received great attention (Gati et al., 2011; Nilsson et al., 2007). In the literature, studies examined the relations between career outcomes (career decision-making self-efficacy, career decision, employability) and personality traits with a particular focus on neuroticism.

Career decision-making self-efficacy can be defined as an individual's belief to be able to successfully perform tasks related to career decision-making (Betz, Klein, and Taylor, 1996). It is important in the process of choosing a profession and in career construction (Betz et al., 1996) especially in the post-modern era characterized by economic uncertainty and complex contexts (Arnoux-Nicolas, Sovet, Lhotellier, Di Fabio, and Bernaud, 2016; Di Fabio and Bucci, 2015a, 2016; Di Fabio and Kenny, 2015; Di Fabio and Maree, 2016; Di Fabio and Palazzeschi, 2015; Di Fabio and Saklofske, 2014a; Guichard, 2013; Savickas, 2011, 2013). Regarding career decision-making self-efficacy in previous studies relations revealed personality traits, particularly inverse with neuroticism (i.e., Bullock-Yowell, Andrews, and Buzzetta, 2011; Di Fabio and Saklofske, 2014a; Hartman and Betz, 2007).

Hartman and Betz (2007), examining the associations between twenty-four distinct domains of career-related self-efficacy and the Five Factors model (McCrae and Costa, 1987) in university students, underlined that neuroticism showed significant negative relationships with nearly all forms of career decision-making self-efficacy. In a subsequent study conducted in university students (Bullock-Yowell et al., 2011), a relation emerged between career decision-making self-efficacy and neuroticism, but relations also appeared between conscientiousness and openness of the Five Factors model (McCrae and Costa, 1987). In the study by Di Fabio and Saklofske (2014a) carried out in Italian high school students, the strongest relation emerged between career decision-making self-efficacy and neuroticism investigated in terms of its contrary (emotional stability), and secondarily with Extraversion according to the Five Factors model (McCrae and Costa, 1987). The analysis of the literature thus showed that the inverse relation between career decision-making self-efficacy and neuroticism emerged. Individuals with less neuroticism seem to perceive themselves as more able to face career tasks (Betz et al., 1996).

Career decision was studied in the literature particularly through its opposite pole of career indecision (Osipow, 1999) and career decision-making difficulties (Gati, Krausz, and Osipow, 1996).

Analyzing difficulties regarding career decisions allowed detection of individual differences in career indecision (Gati et al., 1996), distinguishing three kinds of difficulties according to the stage in the career decision-making process. It is possible to differentiate between the career decision-making difficulties that could be encountered before the career decision-making process begins and the difficulties that could be encountered during the career decision-making process itself, once that has been undertaken. The career decision-making difficulties before starting the career decision-making process are related to lack of readiness; instead the career decision-making difficulties in the course of the career decision-making process are of two different kinds: difficulties relative to lack of information and difficulties relative to inconsistent information.

Career decision difficulties have traditionally been investigated and emerged with personality traits according to the Five Factors model (McCrae and Costa, 1987). In particular, positive relations with neuroticism and inverse relations with extraversion emerged in previous studies (Albion and Fogarty, 2002; Di Fabio and Palazzeschi, 2009; Di Fabio, Palazzeschi, Asulin-Peretz, and Gati, 2013; Di Fabio, Palazzeschi, and Bar-On, 2012; Di Fabio, Palazzeschi, Levin, and Gati, 2015; Feldman, 2003). Instead the other three factors, Agreeableness, Conscientiousness, and Openness to Experience, have not been found to be associated with career decision-making difficulties (Feldman, 2003; Kanfer, Wanberg, and Kantrowitz, 2001). In the Italian context, some studies regarding the relations between career decision-making difficulties and personality traits according to the Five Factors model (McCrae and Costa, 1987) were carried out. Results of these studies showed positive relations of career decision-making difficulties, particularly with neuroticism in term of its contrary (emotional stability), and to a lesser extent inverse relations with Extraversion in young workers engaged in a paid training (Di Fabio and Palazzeschi, 2012; Di Fabio et al., 2015), in university students (Di Fabio et al., 2012, 2011) and in high school students (Di Fabio et al., 2015). Individuals with more neuroticism seem to have more difficulties in career decision-making processes (Gati et al., 1996), because neuroticism seems to be associated with underperformance due to the emotional components involved in the career decision-making process (Boudreau et al., 2001; Di Fabio et al., 2012, 2015). Furthermore individuals with high neuroticism seem to be less vigilant in job searching and more impulsive in their decision making, increasing their perceived stress level (Boudreau et al., 2001; Di Fabio et al., 2012, 2015).

Regarding employability, it's important to consider on one hand that it is not a synonym for employment, on the other hand that it is configured as a key feature for workers in the twenty-first century. Employability expresses the importance of the personal aspects that do not refer only to the possession of up to date professional skills but also to the ability of individuals to adapt, increasing their possibilities of employment (Fugate, Kinicki, and Ashforth, 2004). Employability implies the importance of taking into account which possibilities of employment people perceive to have and what factors influence this perception (Rothwell and Arnold, 2007). In relation to employability in the literature, multiple definitions emerged (Di Fabio and Palazzeschi, 2013b), underlining different aspects: maintenance of work (Hillage and Pollard, 1998); personal resources (Fugate et al., 2004); professional expertise, anticipation (be able to understand before what factors can promote one's own employability), optimization (be able to invest in a focused manner on actions for development of one's own employability), balance between personal and professional needs (Van der Heijde and Van der Heijden, 2006); sustainability, qualification, future-oriented perspective (Rothwell and Arnold, 2007); satisfaction and success (Dacre Pool and Sewell, 2007); meta-competences (behavioral adaptability, self-knowledge, career orientation awareness, sense of purpose, self-esteem) (Coetzee, 2008); internal and external factors (De Cuyper and De Witte, 2011).

Regarding employability, the previous studies showed relations with personality traits, particularly inverse relations with neuroticism (Di Fabio, 2014; Di Fabio and Bucci, 2013; Di Fabio and Kenny, 2015; Wille, De Fruyt, and Feys, 2013). In the Italian context, we have some studies regarding the relations between perceived employability and personality traits according to the Five Factors model (McCrae and Costa, 1987): above all inverse relations with neuroticism in terms of its contrary (emotional stability) emerged but also to a lesser extent, positive relations with Extraversion in university students and high school students (Di Fabio, 2014; Di Fabio and Bucci, 2013; Di Fabio and Kenny, 2015). The results of these studies showed particularly the inverse relation between perceived employability and neuroticism in terms of emotional stability as its contrary. Individuals with low neuroticism seem to perceive more possibilities to be employable (Di Fabio, 2014; Di Fabio and Bucci, 2013; Di Fabio and Kenny, 2015).

In the literature, career outcomes (career decision-making self-efficacy, career decision, employability) in previous studies emerged related to personality traits, particularly to neuroticism, but rarely were these career variables simultaneously analyzed confronting groups of participants in the same study to compare results (Di Fabio et al., 2015).

Aim and Hypotheses

Previous research has shown associations between personality and career outcomes underling the relations with neuroticism particularly, but rarely they analyzed different career variables simultaneously and they studied different groups of participants in the same study to compare results. According to this framework and the literature, the aim of the present study was to investigate neuroticism among personality traits as it relates to career decision-making self-efficacy, career decision, perceived employability in two different groups of students: high school students and university students.

Specifically, the Following Hypotheses Were Formulated

H1. In the two groups of students (high school students and university students), among personality traits the stronger association will emerge between career decision-making self-efficacy and neuroticism (Bullock-Yowell et al., 2011; Di Fabio and Saklofske, 2014a; Hartman and Betz, 2007).

H2. In the two groups of students (high school students and university students), among personality traits the stronger association will emerge between career decision (in terms of its opposite pole of career decision-making difficulties) and neuroticism (Albion and Fogarty, 2002; Di Fabio and Palazzeschi, 2009; Di Fabio et al., 2013, 2015).

H3. In the two groups of students (high school students and university students), among personality traits the stronger association will emerge between perceived employability and neuroticism (Di Fabio, 2014; Di Fabio and Bucci, 2013; Di Fabio and Kenny, 2015; Wille et al., 2013).

Material and Methods

Participants

The first group was composed of 219 Italian high school students attending the last two years of a school system in Tuscany, Italy (93 men, 42.47%; 126 women, 57.53%) with an age ranged from 17 and 19 years (M = 18.13, SD = 0.56). The second group comprised 234 students of the University of Florence (Italy) from different majors (113 men, 48.29%; 121 women, 51.71%) with an age ranged from 23 to 27 (M = 25.67, SD = 1.83).

Measures

Big Five Questionnaire (BFQ)

To evaluate personality traits, the Italian version of the Big Five Questionnaire (BFQ, Caprara, Barbaranelli, and Borgogni, 1993) was used. The questionnaire comprises 132 items with response options on a 5-point Likert scale ranging from 1 = *Absolutely false* to 5 = *Absolutely true*. The questionnaire measures five personality traits. The Cronbach's alpha coefficients were: .82 for Extraversion, .76 for Agreeableness, .83 for Conscientiousness, .91 for Emotional Stability, and .77 for Openness.

Career Decision Self-Efficacy Scale - Short Form (CDSES-SF)

To evaluate career decision-making self-efficacy, the Career Decision Self-Efficacy Scale - Short Form (CDSES-SF, Betz and Taylor, 2000) in the Italian version by Nota, Pace and Ferrari (2008) was used. The questionnaire is composed of 20 items with response options on a 5-point Likert scale ranging from 1 = *I have no confidence* to 5 = *I have complete confidence*. The Cronbach's alpha coefficient for the total score used in the present study is .79.

Career Decision-Making Difficulties Questionnaire (CDDQ)

To evaluate career decision-making difficulties, the Career Decision-making Difficulties Questionnaire (CDDQ, Gati et al., 1996) in the Italian version by Di Fabio and Palazzeschi (2013a) was used. The questionnaire comprises 34 items with response options on a 9-point Likert scale ranging from 1 = *Does not describe me* to 9 = *Describes me well*. The CDDQ permits detection of three dimensions (Lack of readiness, Lack of information, and Inconsistent information) and ten subdimensions. The Cronbach's alpha coefficient for the total score used in the present study is .93.

Self-Perceived Employability Scale (SPES)

To evaluate perceived employability, the Self-Perceived Employability Scale (Rothwell, Herbert, and Rothwell, 2007) in the Italian version for high school students (Di Fabio and Bucci, 2015b) and in the Italian version for university students (Di Fabio and Palazzeschi, 2013b) were used. The scale is composed of 16 items with response options on a 5-point Likert scale ranging from 1 = *Strongly disagree* to 5 = *Strongly agree*. The Cronbach's alpha coefficients are: .80 for the Italian version for high school students and .81 for the Italian version for high school students.

Procedure and Data Analysis

The questionnaires were administered in groups by trained psychologists. The order of the questionnaires was counterbalanced during administration to control the possible effects of presentation. The administration followed the requirements of privacy and informed consent of the Italian law (Law Decree DL-196/2003). Pearson's *r* correlations and stepwise regressions were effected.

RESULTS

Correlations between BFQ, CDSES-SF, CDDQ, and SPES for the two groups (high school students and university students) are reported in Table 1.

To further assess the associations of BFQ with CDSES-SF, CDDQ, and SPES, we carried out a stepwise multiple regression analysis using CDSES-SF, CDDQ, and SPES as the dependent variables and the Big Five factors that are correlated (neuroticism in terms of its contrary emotional stability and extraversion) as the independent variables, separately for each of the two groups. A summary of these analyses is presented in Table 2.

Career Decision-making Self-Efficacy. Similar results emerged for the explanation of career decision-making self-efficacy in the two groups of participants with only two out of the five BFQ factors explaining career decision-making self-efficacy (*Adjusted* R^2= .37 for high school students; *Adjusted* R^2= .35 for university students). These factors were Neuroticism (in terms of emotional stability as its contrary) and Extraversion: for high school students (β = -.39, ΔR^2 = .25; β = .34, ΔR^2 = .12; for Neuroticism and Extraversion, respectively), for university students (β = -.38, ΔR^2 = .24; β = .32, ΔR^2 = .24; for Neuroticism and Extraversion, respectively).

Table 1. Correlations between CDSES-SF, CDDQ, SPES and BFQ in high school students (*N* = 219, above diagonal) and university students (*N* = 123, below diagonal)

	1	2	3	4	5	6	7	8
1. CDSES-SF	-	.35**	.45**	.46**	.20	.16	-.53**	.10
2. CDDQ	.35**	-	.48**	-.42**	.18	.15	.48**	.18
3. SPES	.34**	.38**	-	.42**	.20	.17	.50**	.16
4. BFQ E	.48**	-.42**	.44**	-	.14	.11	-.33**	.23*
5. BFQ A	.12	.17	.24*	.24**	-	.11	-.27**	.10
6. BFQ C	.19	.12	.22*	.21**	.22*	-	-.28**	.24*
7. BFQ N	-.50**	.45**	-.47**	-.34**	-.33**	-.31**	-	-.39**
8. BFQ O	.13	.19	.22*	.28**	.38**	.32**	-.38**	-

Note: * p < .05. ** p < .01.
CDSES-SF = Career decision-making self-efficacy; CDDQ = Career decision-making difficulties; SPES = perceived employability; BFQ E = Extraversion; BFQ A = Agreeableness; BFQ C = Conscientiousness; BFQ N = Neuroticism; BFQ O = Openness to Experience.

Career decision (in terms of its opposite pole of career decision-making difficulties). Similar results emerged for the explanation of career decision (in terms of its opposite pole of career decision-making difficulties) in the two groups of participants with only two out of the five BFQ factors explaining career decision-making difficulties (*Adjusted* R^2= .36 for high school students; *Adjusted* R^2= .34 for university students). These factors were Neuroticism (in terms of emotional stability as its contrary) and Extraversion: for high school students (β = .34, ΔR^2 = .26; β = -.30, ΔR^2 = .10; for Neuroticism and Extraversion, respectively), for university students (β = .37, ΔR^2 = .24; β = -.29, ΔR^2 = .10; for Neuroticism and Extraversion, respectively).

Employability. Similar results emerged for the explanation of perceived employability in the two groups of participants with only two out of the five BFQ factors explaining employability (*Adjusted* R^2= .34 for high school students; *Adjusted* R^2= .31 for university students). These factors were Neuroticism (in terms of emotional stability as its contrary) and Extraversion: for high school students (β = -.36, ΔR^2 = .24; β = .29, ΔR^2 = .10; for Neuroticism and Extraversion, respectively), for university students (β = -.30, ΔR^2 = .21; β = .28, ΔR^2 = .10; for Neuroticism and Extraversion, respectively).

Table 2. Results of Multiple Regression Analysis

	High school students N = 219			University students N = 234		
	CDSES-SF	CDDQ	SPES	CDSES-SF	CDDQ	SPES
BFQ	β ΔR^2	β ΔR^2	β ΔR^2	β ΔR^2	β ΔR^2	β ΔR^2
BFQ E	.34*** .12	-.30*** .10	.29*** .10	.32*** . .11	-.29** .10	.28*** .10
BFQ N	-.39*** .25	.34*** .26	-.36*** .24	.-.38*** .24	.37** .24	-.30*** .21
Adjusted R^2	.37***	.36***	.34***	.35***	.34***	.31***

** p< .01. *** p< .001.

Discussion

The present study aimed to examine the particular contribution of neuroticism among personality traits as it relates to career outcomes (career decision-making self-efficacy, career decision, employability) analyzed simultaneously in two different groups of students (Italian high school students and Italian university students). The results of the present study confirmed

the first hypothesis since in both of the two groups of students, the stronger association emerged between career decision-making self-efficacy and neuroticism in terms of its contrary (emotional stability) among personality traits in line with the literature (Bullock-Yowell et al., 2011; Di Fabio and Saklofske, 2014a; Hartman and Betz, 2007). Individuals with low neuroticism who are more able to control their emotions and their impulses possess a greater belief about their own ability to successfully perform career decision-making tasks (Betz et al., 1996). Furthermore, an association emerged between career decision-making self-efficacy and Extraversion: dynamic individuals were more open towards interpersonal relationships and perceived to have a greater self-efficacy in career decision-making in line with the literature (Di Fabio and Saklofske, 2014a).

The results of the present study also confirmed the second hypothesis, since in both the two groups of students (high school students and university students), the stronger association emerged between career decision (in terms of its opposite pole of career decision-making difficulties) and neuroticism in terms of its contrary (emotional stability) among personality traits, in line with the literature (Albion and Fogarty, 2002; Di Fabio and Palazzeschi, 2009; Di Fabio et al., 2013, 2015). Individuals with low neuroticism who perceived themselves as more able to control their emotions and impulses perceived fewer difficulties in career decision-making process (Gati et al., 1996). Furthermore, an association emerged between career decision (in terms of its opposite pole of career decision-making difficulties) and Extraversion, underlining that individuals who perceived themselves as more energetic, desiring to be with others and have a tendency to look for social situations, perceive to encounter less difficulties in career decision-making, also in line with the previous studies (Albion and Fogarty, 2002; Di Fabio and Palazzeschi, 2009; Di Fabio et al., 2013, 2015).

Finally, the results of the present study confirmed the third hypothesis since in both of the two groups of students, the stronger association emerged between perceived employability and neuroticism in terms of its contrary (emotional stability) among personality traits, in line with the literature (Di Fabio, 2014; Di Fabio and Bucci, 2013; Di Fabio and Kenny, 2015; Wille et al., 2013). Individuals with low neuroticism who are more able to control their emotions and their impulses perceive more possibilities to be employable (Rothwell and Arnold, 2007). Furthermore, an association emerged between perceived employability and Extraversion, underlining those individuals who perceived themselves as more active and open towards social situations seem to have a greater perceived employability, in line with the literature (Di Fabio, 2014; Di Fabio and Bucci, 2013; Di Fabio and Kenny, 2015).

The results of the present study confirmed the stronger contribution of neuroticism in career outcomes (career decision-making self-efficacy, career decision, employability) on the one side, on the other side permitted to analyze the relation between personality traits and career outcomes by studying simultaneously different groups of participants (high school students and university students). In particular, the present study emerged that personality traits, especially neuroticism, were more inversely related to career outcomes (career decision-making self-efficacy, career decision, employability) in high school students than in university students. With the passage from high school to university, young people faced an important transition, inevitably dealing with career decision-making and career choice processes (Di Fabio et al., 2015). For some of these young people this could produce an increase in individual resources that could reduce the influence of personality traits. Anyway the fact that the relations between neuroticism and career outcomes persist with a lesser extent also in university students (Di Fabio et al., 2015), suggests that individuals with high levels of this personality trait continue to experience less career decision-making self-efficacy, career decision, and perceived employability also in the university period. This could suggest that these critical career outcomes may be more persistent for individuals with high neuroticism, recalling the importance of early care for this personality trait in individuals to promote positive career outcomes.

Notwithstanding the results of the present study underline the relations between personality traits, particularly neuroticism and career outcomes, it is necessary to highlight limitations relative to the generalizability of the results obtained in specific Italian groups of high school students and university students. Future research should include participants who are more representative of the Italian context and also verify the results in other international contexts. Future research should also use a longitudinal approach to investigate the causality underlying the associations between personality traits and career outcomes.

Despite these limitations, the results of the present study contribute to the in-depth exploration of career outcomes (career decision-making self-efficacy, career decision, employability), underlining their associations with personality traits and in particular with neuroticism in two different stages of young people (high school students and university students) simultaneously examined in this study.

CONCLUSION

On the basis of the results obtained in the present study, it is possible to underline the relations between career outcomes and personality traits, particularly with neuroticism. This relation is very important because it could also be useful in a preventive perspective (Di Fabio et al., 2015; Di Fabio and Kenny, 2015). In a preventive framework, the relevance of preventive programs focus on reducing risk factors and increasing protective factors that can decrease the probability of negative outcomes is stressed (Di Fabio and Bucci, 2015a; 2016; Di Fabio and Palazzeschi, 2015; Hage et al., 2007; Kenny and Hage, 2009). In fact, preventive perspective is more fruitful when efforts to remove risks are combined with efforts to increase resources (Hage et al., 2007; Kenny and Hage, 2009) with the focus of building individual strengths (Di Fabio, 2015; Di Fabio and Kenny, 2012a, 2012b, 2015; Di Fabio, Kenny, and Claudius, in press; Di Fabio and Saklofske, 2014a, 2014b). In this preventive perspective on the basis of the relation between neuroticism and career outcomes, it is possible to individuate young people at risk with high neuroticism and to intervene early, both paying attention to this trait of personality and also providing specific trainings on these career outcomes to increase them (Pečjak and Košir, 2007), promoting the enhancement of individual resources and favouring a positive youth development (Kenny et al., 2014; Lerner et al., 2005). That means to take care of building strength in individuals (Di Fabio, 2015; Di Fabio and Kenny, 2015; considering that these career outcomes (career decision-making self-efficacy, career decision, perceived employability) constitute essential resources to face challenges in early transitions and early careers in the 21st century. According to a preventive framework (Hage et al., 2007; Kenny, Di Fabio, and Minor, 2014; Kenny and Hage, 2009), promoting the enhancement of these essential resources could favor both job placement and the well-being of individuals (Di Fabio and Kenny, 2015; Di Fabio and Saklofske, 2014a; Di Fabio and Palazzeschi, 2015).

REFERENCES

Albion, M. J. and Fogarty, G. J. (2002). Factors influencing career decision making in adolescents and adults. *Journal of Career Assessment*, *10*(1), 91-126.

Arnoux-Nicolas, C., Sovet, L., Lhotellier, L., Di Fabio, A., Bernaud, J.-L. (2016). Adverse work conditions and turnover intentions: The mediating role of meaning of life and meaning of work. In A. Di Fabio and D. L. Blustein (Eds.), "From meaning of working to meaningful lives: The challenges of expanding decent work". Research topic in *Frontiers in Psychology. Section Organizational Psychology.*

Betz, N. E., Klein, K. L. and Taylor, K. M. (1996). Evaluation of a short form of the career decision-making self-efficacy scale. *Journal of Career Assessment, 4*(1), 47-57.

Betz, N. E. and Taylor, K. M. (2000). *Manual for the Career Decision Making Self-Efficacy scale (CDMSES) and CDMSES-Short Form.* Unpublished manuscript, The Ohio State University, Columbus, OH.

Borges, N. J. and Savickas, M. L. (2002). Personality and medical specialty choice: a literature review and integration. *Journal of Career Assessment, 10*(3), 362-380.

Boudreau, J. W., Boswell, W. R. and Judge, T. A. (2001). Effects of personality on executive career success in the United States and Europe. *Journal of Vocational Behavior, 58*(1), 53-81.

Bullock-Yowell, E., Andrews, L. and Buzzetta, M. E. (2011). Explaining career decision-making self-efficacy: Personality, cognitions, and cultural mistrust. *The Career Development Quarterly, 59*(5), 400-411.

Caprara, G. V., Barbaranelli, C. and Borgogni, L. (1993). *BFQ: Big Five Questionnaire* (2nd ed.). Firenze, Italy: Giunti O.S.

Coetzee, M. (2008). Psychological career resources of working adults: A South African survey. *South African Journal of Industrial Psychology 34*(2), 32-41.

Dacre Pool, L. and Sewell, P. (2007). The key to employability: Developing a practical model of graduate employability. *Education + Training, 49*(4), 277-289.

De Cuyper, N. and De Witte, H. (2011). The management paradox: Self-rated employability and organizational commitment and performance, *Personnel Review, 40*, 152-172.

Di Fabio, A. (2015). Beyond fluid intelligence and personality traits in social support: The role of ability based emotional intelligence. *Frontiers in Psychology, 6*, 395. doi: 10.3389/fpsyg.2015.00395.

Di Fabio, A. (2014, February). *In light of the changing work scene: New challenges for research and intervention.* Invited Keynote at the Symposium sponsored by Linch School of Education of Boston College, in D. L. Blustein (Chair). Career Development and the Psychology of Working. Boston College, Boston.

Di Fabio, A. and Bucci, O. (2013). Tratti di personalità o intelligenza emotiva per l'occupabilità di studenti universitari? [Personality traits and emotional intelligence for employability of university students?]. *Counseling. Giornale Italiano di Ricerca e Applicazioni, 6*, 195-204.

Di Fabio, A. and Bucci, O. (2015a). Affective profiles in Italian high school students: Life satisfaction, psychological well-being, self-esteem, and optimism. *Frontiers in Psychology, 6*, 1310. doi: 10.3389/fpsyg.2015.01310

Di Fabio, A. and Bucci, O. (2015b). Self-Perceived Employability Scale for students: Contributo alla validazione italiana con studenti di scuola secondaria di secondo grado. *Counseling. Giornale Italiano di Ricerca e Applicazioni, 8*(2).

Di Fabio, A. and Bucci, O. (2016). Green positive guidance and green positive life counseling for decent work and decent lives: Some empirical results. In A. Di Fabio and D. L. Blustein (Eds.), "From meaning of working to meaningful lives: The challenges of expanding decent work". Research topic in *Frontiers in Psychology. Section Organizational Psychology.*

Di Fabio, A. and Kenny, M. E. (2012a). The contribution of emotional intelligence to decisional styles among Italian high school students. *Journal of Career Assessment, 20*, 404-414.

Di Fabio, A. and Kenny, M. E. (2012b). Emotional intelligence and perceived social support among Italian high school students. *Journal of Career Development, 39*, 461-475.

Di Fabio, A. and Kenny, M. E. (2015). The contributions of emotional intelligence and social support for adaptive career progress among Italian youth. *Journal of Career Development, 42*, 48-49.

Di Fabio, A. and Kenny, E. M. (2016). From decent work to decent lives: Positive Self and Relational Management (PS&RM) in the 21st century. In A. Di Fabio and D. L. Blustein (Eds.), "From meaning of working to meaningful lives: The challenges of expanding decent work". Research topic in *Frontiers in Psychology. Section Organizational Psychology.*

Di Fabio, A., Kenny, M. E. and Claudius, M. (in press). Fostering adaptive career management and psychological well-being in uncertain times. In M. Israelashvili and J. L. Romano (Eds.), *Cambridge handbook of international prevention science.* Cambridge: Cambridge University Press.

Di Fabio, A. and Maree, J. G. (2016). Using a transdisciplinary interpretive lens to broaden reflections on alleviating poverty and promoting decent work. In A. Di Fabio and D. L. Blustein (Eds.), "From meaning of working to meaningful lives: The challenges of expanding decent work". Research topic in *Frontiers in Psychology. Section Organizational Psychology.*

Di Fabio, A. and Palazzeschi, L. (2009). Emotional intelligence, personality traits and career decision difficulties. *International Journal for Educational and Vocational Guidance, 9*(2), 135-146.

Di Fabio, A. and Palazzeschi, L. (Eds.). (2013a). *Adattamento italiano del CDDQ - Career Decision-making Difficulties Questionnaire* [*Italian adaptation of the CDDQ - Career Decision-making Difficulties Questionnaire*]. Firenze: Giunti O.S.

Di Fabio, A. and Palazzeschi, L. (2013b). Self-perceived Employability for students: Un primo contributo alla validazione italiana [Self-perceived Employability for students: A first contribution to Italian validation]. *Counseling. Giornale Italiano di Ricerca e Applicazioni, 6*, 97-105.

Di Fabio, A. and Palazzeschi, L. (2015). Hedonic and eudaimonic well-being: The role of resilience beyond fluid intelligence and personality traits. *Frontiers in Psychology, 6*, 1367.

Di Fabio, A. and Palazzeschi, L. (2016). Marginalization and precariat: The challenge of intensifying life construction intervention. In A. Di Fabio and D. L. Blustein (Eds.), "From meaning of working to meaningful lives: The challenges of expanding decent work". Research topic in *Frontiers in Psychology. Section Organizational Psychology.*

Di Fabio, A., Palazzeschi, L., Asulin-Peretz, L. and Gati, I. (2013). Career indecision versus indecisiveness: Associations with personality traits and emotional intelligence. *Journal of Career Assessment, 21*, 42-56.

Di Fabio, A., Palazzeschi, L. and Bar-On, R. (2012). The role of personality traits, core self-evaluation and emotional intelligence in career decision-making difficulties. *Journal of Employment Counseling, 49*, 118-129.

Di Fabio, A., Palazzeschi, L., Levin, N. and Gati, I. (2015). The role of personality in the career decision-making difficulties of Italian young adults. *Journal of Career Assessment, 23*, 281-293.

Di Fabio, A. and Saklofske, D. H. (2014a). Comparing ability and self-report trait emotional intelligence, fluid intelligence, and personality traits in career decision. *Personality and Individual Differences, 64*, 174-178.

Di Fabio, A. and Saklofske, D. H. (2014b). Promoting individual resources: The challenge of trait emotional intelligence. *Personality and Individual Differences, 65*, 19-23.

Feldman, D. C. (2003). The antecedents and consequences of early career indecision among young adults. *Human Resource Management Review, 13*, 499-531.

Fugate, M., Kinicki, A. J. and Ashforth, B. E. (2004). Employability: A psycho-social construct, its dimensions, and applications. *Journal of Vocational Behavior, 65*(1), 14-38.

Gati, I., Gadassi, R., Saka, N., Hadadi, Y., Ansenberg, N., Friedman, R. and Asulin-Peretz, L. (2011). Emotional and personality-related aspects of career decision-making difficulties: Facets of career indecisiveness. *Journal of Career Assessment*, 19, 3-20.

Gati, I., Krausz, M. and Osipow, S. H. (1996). A taxonomy of difficulties in career decision making. *Journal of Counseling Psychology, 43*, 510-526.

Guichard, J. (2013a, November). *Career guidance, education, and dialogues for a fair and sustainable human development.* Inaugural conference of the UNESCO chair of Lifelong guidance and counselling, University of Wroclaw, Poland.

Hage, S. M., Romano, J. L., Conyne, R. K., Kenny, M., Matthews, C., Schwartz, J. P. and Waldo, M. (2007). Best practice guidelines on prevention practice, research, training, and social advocacy for psychologists. *The Counseling Psychologist, 35*, 493-566.

Hartman, R. O. and Betz, N. E. (2007). The five-factor model and career self-efficacy general and domain-specific relationships. *Journal of Career Assessment, 15*(2), 145-161.

Hillage, J. and Pollard, E. (1998). *Employability: Developing a framework for policy analysis*. London: DfEE.

Holland, J. L. (1997). *Making vocational choices: A theory of vocational personalities and work environments.* Odessa, FL: Psychological Assessment Resources.

Kanfer, R., Wanberg, C. R. and Kantrowitz, T. M. (2001). Job search and employment: A personality-motivational analysis and meta-analytic review. *Journal of Applied Psychology, 86*(5), 837-855.

Kenny, M. E., Di Fabio, A. and Minor, K. (2014). School-based research and practice in Italy. In M. J. Furlong, R. Gilman, and E. S. Huebner (Eds.), *Handbook of positive psychology in the schools* (2nd ed., pp. 450-464). New York, NY: Routledge, Taylor and Francis.

Kenny, M. E. and Hage, S. M. (2009). The next frontier: Prevention as an instrument of social justice. *The Journal of Primary Prevention, 30*, 1-10.

Lerner, R. M., Lerner, J. V., Almerigi, J. B., Theokas, C., Phelps, E., Gestsdottir, S. and von Eye, A. (2005). Positive Youth Development, Participation in community youth development programs, and community contributions of fifth-grade adolescents findings from the first wave of the 4-H study of Positive Youth Development. *The Journal of Early Adolescence, 25*(1), 17-71.

McCrae, R. R. and Costa, P. T. (1987). Validation of the five-factor model of personality across instruments and observers. *Journal of Personality And Social Psychology, 52*(1), 81-90.

Nilsson, J. E., Flores, L. Y., Berkel, L. V., Schale, C. L., Linnemeyer, R. M. and Summer, I. (2007). International career articles: A content analysis of four journals across 34 years. *Journal of Vocational Behavior*, *70*, 602-613.

Nota, L., Pace, F. and Ferrari, L. (2008). Career Decision Self-Efficacy Scale–Short Form: Uno studio per l'adattamento italiano [Career Decision Self-Efficacy Scale–Short Form: A study for Italian adaptation]. *GIPO: Giornale Italiano di Psicologia dell'Orientamento*, *9*, 23-35.

Osipow, S. H. (1999). Assessing career indecision. *Journal of Vocational Behavior*, *55*(1), 147-154.

Pečjak, S. and Košir, K. (2007). Personality, motivational factors and difficulties in career decision-making in secondary school students. *Psihologijske Teme*, *16*(1), 141-158.

Rothwell, A. and Arnold, J. (2007). Self-perceived employability: Development and validation of a scale. *Personnel Review*, *36*(1), 23-41.

Rothwell, A., Herbert, I. and Rothwell, F. (2007). Self-perceived employability: Construction and initial validation of a scale for university students. *Journal of Vocational Behavior*, *73*, 1-12.

Savickas, M. L. (2011). *Career counseling*. Washington, DC: American Psychological Association.

Savickas, M. L. (2013, September). *Life Designing. What is it?* Invited Keynote at IAEVG International Conference, Montpellier, France.

Tokar, D., Fischer, A. and Subich, L. M. (1998). Personality and vocational behavior: A selective review of the literature, 1993-1997. *Journal of Vocational Behavior*, *53*, 147-179.

Van Der Heijde, C. M. and Van Der Heijden, B. I. (2006). A competence-based and multidimensional operationalization and measurement of employability. *Human resource management*, *45*(3), 449-476.

Wille, B., De Fruyt, F. and Feys, M. (2013). Big five traits and intrinsic success in the new career era: A 15-year longitudinal study on employability and work-family conflict. *Applied Psychology*, *62*(1), 124-156.

In: Neuroticism
Editor: Annamaria Di Fabio

ISBN: 978-1-63485-323-1

Chapter 11

NEUROTICISM ACROSS CULTURES: MACRO-LEVEL INSIGHTS INTO THE WORLDWIDE DISTRIBUTION OF NEUROTICISM

Radek Trnka* and Inna Čábelková
[1]Faculty of Humanities, Charles University in Prague, Praha, Czech Republic
Prague College of Psychosocial Studies, Praha, Czech Republic
[2]Faculty of Humanities, Charles University in Prague, Praha, Czech Republic

ABSTRACT

The chapter reviews the main explanations and interpretations for differences between cultures in mean levels of neuroticism. The relationships between neuroticism and *cultural dimensions* are also presented to provide a complex overview of current *cross-cultural* investigation in neuroticism. Three paradigmatic questions of current cross-cultural research in neuroticism were identified in the present study: the question of a) the *heritability* of neuroticism; b) *randomness*, i.e., if worldwide distribution of neuroticism is systematic or random; and c) independence of neuroticism in terms of the independence of its measurement with measurement of cultural dimensions. The present review distinguished six different interpretations for differences between cultures in mean levels of neuroticism that has emerged in current cross-cultural research: 1) *intercultural differences* in neuroticism reflect slight differences in culture-specific components of neuroticism, all cultures share a similar personality dimension of neuroticism, but this trait does not mean completely the same thing in various cultures; 2) the mainstream religion in a given *culture* influences the level of neuroticism in that culture; 3) geographically close cultures also show similar levels of neuroticism in comparison with geographically distant cultures; 4) intercultural differences in neuroticism are caused by culturally endorsed response styles; 5) intercultural differences in neuroticism reflect

* Correponding author: Radek Trnka, email: trnkar@volny.cz.

genetic differences between cultural groups; 6) intercultural differences in neuroticism may be caused by adaptations of psychometric personality questionnaires to other languages. Taking these interpretations together provides an intriguing theoretical background for further theoretical developments in this field. Various implications for both theory and empirical research are discussed in the Discussion subsection of this chapter. For example, we discussed the role of acquiescence response bias, differential item functioning in factor loadings, the Euclidean similarities of personality profiles across cultures, or various methodological problems of comparing neuroticism in different cultures.

INTRODUCTION

Researchers working on neuroticism in the field of personality psychology are traditionally focused on the individual level of analysis and inter-individual differences. Whereas inter-individual differences reflect the distribution of neuroticism inside a particular population, cross-cultural psychology investigates the patterns of distribution of temperamental traits across different populations and groups. Cross-cultural investigation provides us with a broader, macro-level look at neuroticism and culture-personality links. Both the individual and cultural levels of analysis are interrelated, and their contrasting and mutual relationships are essential for an in-depth understanding of this issue. For these reasons, this chapter provides a macro-level overview exploring the distribution of neuroticism across cultures and possible explanations for differences in the mean levels of neuroticism in different cultures. In other words, the main goal is to provide an overview of current approaches for interpreting intercultural differences in neuroticism.

Psychologists suggest neuroticism to be a high-order personality trait (Schmitt, Allik, McCrae, and Benet-Martínez, 2007) and a component of temperamental qualities. Temperament refers to individual differences in behavioral styles, i.e., differences between people that appear early in life, show substantial stability over time, represent predictable modes of response and possibly have fairly direct neurobiological correlates (Ormel, Rosmalen, and Farmer, 2004). Neuroticism is defined as an individual's propensity to experience negative emotions, i.e., to be anxious, nervous, sad and tense (John, Naumann, and Soto, 2008). It represents a contrast to emotional stability. Neuroticism, or Negative Affectivity, belongs along with Extraversion, Agreeableness, Conscientiousness and Openness to the basic components of the Big Five model of personality (McCrae and Costa, 1997). Neuroticism is a temperamental trait of emotionality, i.e., the tendency to arouse quickly when stimulated and inhibit slowly; a tendency to have unrealistic ideas; an inability to control urges; a disposition to complain; inefficient ways of coping with stress, a tendency to appraise events as stressful and a tendency to appraise emotions more negatively (John et al., 2008; Trnka, Balcar, Kuška, and Hnilica, 2012). Typical facets of neuroticism are Anxiety, Angry Hostility, Depression, Self-Consciousness, Vulnerability, Impulsiveness (Costa and McCrae, 1992), Irritability, Depression, Rumination–Compulsiveness (Soto, John, Gosling, and Potter, 2008) and Insecurity (Saucier AND Ostendorf, 1999).

Currently, extensive cross-cultural comparisons of basic temperamental traits have attracted the attention of researchers. Cross-cultural researchers compared cultures with the use of mean-level trait scores, also called mean levels of personality traits, national levels of personality traits or national trait scores. Intercultural differences are thought to be detectable based on such mean levels of personality traits. For example, Table 1 shows the intercultural differences in neuroticism based on the study of Schmitt et al. (2007). This research group applied the Big Five Inventory to map the *geographical distribution* of high-order personality traits (Benet-Martínez and John, 1998). Data from 56 different cultures were included in this large cross-cultural study (Figure 1). The Big Five Inventory and the Revised NEO Personality Inventory (NEO–PI–R) are members of the Big Five family of questionnaires that belongs to the most frequently used personality inventories in current cross-cultural research (Costa and McCrae, 1992). It is very important to note that the Neuroticism scale of the NEO–PI–R also showed significant correlation with the Neuroticism scale of Eysenck's Personality Questionnaire (EPQ, Eysenck and Eysenck, 1975), which was widely used by cross-cultural studies in the 1980s and 1990s (see Allik, 2005, for an overview of this period of cross-cultural research). As is apparent in Table 1, some cultures differ in mean levels of neuroticism. For example, Japan, Argentina, Spain, or South Korea had relatively high mean levels of neuroticism in comparison with Congo, Slovenia or Ethiopia. These differences may elicit various explanations and ideas. The main aim of this chapter is to summarize such explanations for intercultural differences in neuroticism.

Table 1. Mean levels of neuroticism based on responses to the Big Five Inventory across 56 Nations

	nation	Neuroticism (M)	SD
1.QUARTIL	Congo	44.58	8.32
	Slovenia	45.28	7.65
	Ethiopia	46.12	6.90
	Croatia	46.16	7.49
	Estonia	46.99	8.79
	Tanzania	47.73	6.55
	Finland	47.84	9.75
	Mexico	48.00	9.52
	Ukraine	48.02	5.88
	Fiji	48.03	7.39
	Romania	48.03	8.44
	Malaysia	48.14	6.31
	Zimbabwe	48.26	9.14
	Botswana	48.61	9.32
2.QUARTIL	Netherlands	48.61	9.71
	Switzerland	48.72	6.02
	South Africa	49.01	8.69
	Israel	49.27	9.63
	New Zealand	49.59	9.92
	Austria	49.69	8.94
	Indonesia	49.73	9.66
	Jordan	49.86	8.76
	Turkey	49.88	10.18
	India	50.00	10.80
	United States	50.00	10.00
	Germany	50.17	8.33
	Bolivia	50.21	9.62

Table 1. (Continued)

	nation	Neuroticism (M)	SD
3.QUARTIL	Australia	50.29	7.74
	Marocco	50.29	8.44
	Czech Republic	50.58	9.66
	Serbia	50.82	10.41
	Portugal	50.87	9.08
	Canada	51.02	9.11
	Latvia	51.11	9.49
	Bangladesh	51.20	8.58
	United Kingdom	51.39	8.48
	Chile	51.39	9.87
	Philippines	51.41	8.42
	Cyprus	51.44	10.11
	Slovakia	51.57	8.65
	Italy	51.66	9.72
	Poland	51.80	9.65
4.QUARTIL	Lithuania	51.87	8.74
	France	52.29	9.34
	Malta	52.35	10.07
	Hong Kong	52.41	8.65
	Taiwan	53.13	8.89
	Brazil	53.14	9.07
	Greece	53.19	9.80
	Lebanon	53.35	9.14
	Peru	53.39	8.29
	Belgium	53.60	9.81
	South Korea	53.99	6.62
	Spain	54.03	9.20
	Argentina	55.05	9.21
	Japan	57.87	7.38

Extracted from data published in Schmitt et al., 2007.

Neuroticism may have serious impacts on depression, anxiety disorders, distress, negative emotional outcomes, poor coping with stress, anger-motivated aggression, physical tension-related symptoms and a negative link to subjective well-being. Due to these negative health outcomes, more and more scholars are interested in comparing different cultures from the viewpoint of distribution of neuroticism across different populations.

Such cross-cultural comparisons are fundamental for an effective public health policy and planning intervention programs on both international and national levels, because they are able to estimate the vulnerability of a population toward some negative health outcome related to neuroticism. Health interventions and campaigns are suggested to be more effective when adapted to a specific cultural environment. For example, our previous study focused on the function of cultural factors influencing the course of the therapeutic treatments (Kuška et al., 2015). Cultural context and cultural knowledge represented very important factors that may either facilitate or block the treatment process. We concluded (ibid) that psychotherapy should favor the development of interventions that originate from the characteristics of each

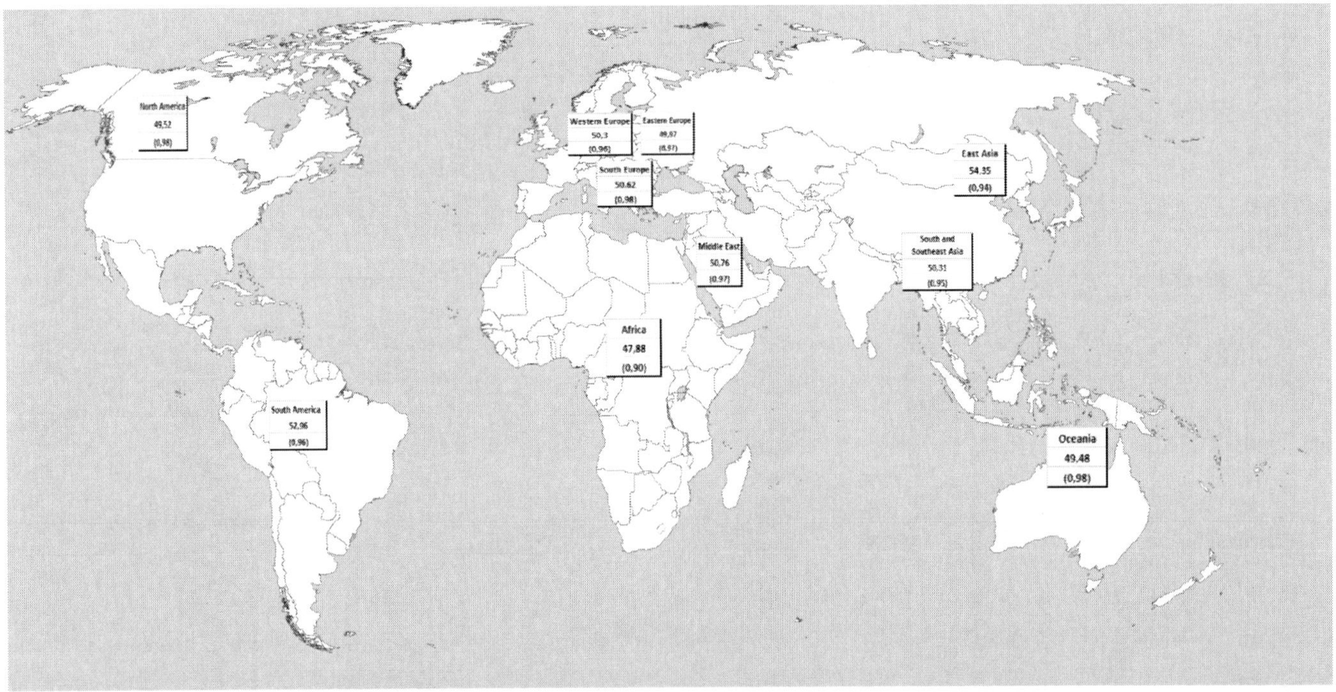

Figure 1. Distribution of mean levels of neuroticism across 10 world regions. The numbers in brackets are congruence coefficients of the Big Five neuroticism scales between the North America and other world regions. (extracted from data published in Schmitt et al., 2007)

cultural group. Similarly, intervention programs are assumed to be more effective when adapted to the character of a particular population.

As seen above, it is exceptionally important to gather in-depth knowledge about today's cross-cultural differences in neuroticism for effective public health policy and planning. However, to our knowledge, no review including systematic presentation of explanations and interpretations of these cross-cultural differences has thus far been published. This chapter aims to fill this gap and provide the readers with an interpretative overview of ways in which cross-cultural researchers explain the empirical findings supporting various differences and similarities between cultures in neuroticism. Therefore, the main focus of this review is to put together various cross-cultural interpretations, explanatory models and explanations. This focus will provide researchers in this field with a broad and comprehensive interpretative theoretical background that may be used for interpreting cross-cultural differences in future empirical studies. The summarizing of interpretations from current cross-cultural research has a very significant potential for the theory development, because it enables the whole spectrum of interpretative approaches for intercultural differences in neuroticism emerging in current cross-cultural psychology to be seen.

Culture and Cultural Dimensions

When entering the field of cross-cultural psychology, we should first posit an important question: "What is culture?" However, the answer is not very easy. There are many definitions of culture (see Baldwin, Faulkner, Hecht, and Sheryl, 2006, for an overview) and it is above the scope of the current review to introduce all of the main approaches in this field. Culture may be understood, for example, as a structure or as a pattern, i.e., as a system of ideas, behavior and symbols (Baldwin et al., 2006). When going into a more detailed description, Baldwin et al. distinguished cognitive structure, structure of behavior, structure of signification, relational structure and the social organization of a given culture. Cognitive structure includes shared thoughts, beliefs, assumptions, meanings, attitudes, preferences, values, standards and interpretations. Structure of behavior is related to shared behavioral rules, norms, social scripts, prototypical actions, normative patterns of behavior, customs, habits, practices, ceremonies and rituals. Symbol systems, language, and communication processes together constitute the structure of signification. Relational structure means the patterns of relationships to others and it partly overlaps with the structure of behavior, because behavioral norms, such as feeling rules and display rules, also influence functioning in a shared relational environment. Social organization includes political institutions, legal institutions, religion and any other organizational forms. This structural definition of culture covers plenty of different cultural dimensions and provides a suitable theoretical rationale for the present study.

To make a statistical cross-cultural comparison possible, several more empirically-focused definitions of culture have been developed. The above-mentioned structural definition of culture, though all-encompassing, does not allow for the sufficient degree of operationalization for statistical cross-cultural comparison of cultural patterns and their effects. An important work in this direction was conducted by Geert Hofstede, who suggested comparing cultures according to a set of cultural dimensions on the country level (Hofstede,

Hofstede, and Minkov, 2010). This model required more narrow definition of culture, namely "culture is the collective programming of the mind that distinguishes the members of one group or category of people from the other" (Ibid, p. 6). This mental programming starts in families, continues in schools and affects the behavior of individuals throughout their lifetime. The cultural programs make the behavior of individuals within a culture understandable for other members of the culture and diminish the number of possible conflicts and misunderstandings. Conflicting mental programs of members of different cultures may cause intercultural conflicts and misinterpretations. The actual behavior of individuals is defined both by the culture and by unique individual personal characteristics, for example, temperamental traits.

Research studying the dimensions of culture and personality traits required explanations about how cultures and personalities interact. Given the wide variety of individual traits and possible biological nature of these (McCrae and Costa, 2003), research on cultural differences no longer maps how culture shapes personality but rather suggests how culture and personalities interact in human behavior (Hofstede and McCrae, 2004; Triandis and Suh, 2002). Besides that, a number of studies map the specific traits of character which are consistently more frequent in some cultures than others, suggesting that some dimensions of culture and personalities are more in harmony with each other and may offer an explanation of cultural differences in personality traits. Let us provide a short outline of the theory relating to cultural dimensions here.

Quantitative research on the interrelation of personality and culture required a definition of "national character," which is "relatively enduring personality characteristics and patterns that are modal among the adult members of the society" (Inkeles and Levinson, 1954/1969, p. 17; Hofstede and McCrae, 2004, p. 54). Though easy to understand and apply, the concept was extensively criticized, as it led to stereotyping on the basis of nationality or cultural background. On the other hand, the concept enabled cross-cultural statistical comparisons, and for this reason it was resurrected at the beginning of 1990 as more quantitative data became available. However, though frequently applied, the concept has still not been accepted by many cultural anthropologists today, supposedly because they rarely use statistical methods of analysis and mostly rely on traditional techniques while studying segments of modern societies (Inkeles and Levinson, 1954/1969).

Hofstede's original classification of cultures included four dimensions: power distance, individualism versus collectivism, masculinity versus femininity and uncertainty avoidance. Later the author added long-term orientation and indulgence versus restraint dimensions. The power distance dimension maps how societies handle inequality and expresses the degree to which the less powerful members of a society accept and expect that power is distributed unequally. The individualist side of the individualism-collectivism dimension reflects preferences for a social framework in which individuals are expected to care only for themselves and their nuclear families. The opposite side, collectivism, expresses a preference for a framework in society in which individuals are expected to care and be cared for by their widely defined relatives or members of widely defined in-group in exchange for unquestioning loyalty. The third dimension of masculinity-femininity reflects the dichotomy between tough and tender. Masculine societies prefer values like assertiveness, activeness and heroism. Feminine societies care more about modesty, cooperation, caring for the weak and quality of life. The uncertainty avoidance dimension deals with the fact that the future can never be known and the extent to which societies tend to control the future. It expresses the degree to which the members of a society feel uncomfortable with uncertainty and ambiguity, and therefore tend to create rules and practices to minimize ambiguity in the future. The next dimension – long-term orientation – reflects the relative role of the past and the future in decision-making. Societies which score low on the long-term orientation dimension prefer to comply with traditions and norms at the expense of modern social changes. Societies scoring high on this dimension encourage modern approaches in order to be prepared for the future. The last but not least dimension is indulgence versus restraint. In indulgent societies members are allowed to gratify their needs related to enjoying life and having fun relatively freely. In societies on the restraint end the gratification of needs is regulated by strict social norms (Hofstede et al., 2010).

After the early conceptualization of cultural differences by Geert Hofstede in the late 1980s, other authors continued this line of analysis. One of the most widely known conceptualizations was conducted by psychologist Shalom H. Schwarz (Schwartz, 2006). Schwartz studied the differences in values of college students and elementary school teachers in more than 60 countries. His value dimensions were defined as embeddedness versus autonomy (both intellectual and affective), hierarchy versus egalitarianism, and mastery versus harmony. Embeddedness in collectivity reflects a situation when individuals identify with a group and find their meaning through social relationships. Autonomy suggests that individuals identify with themselves and find their meaning in their own uniqueness. Autonomy is then broken down to intellectual autonomy that reflects the pursuit of independent ideas, and affective autonomy that suggests independent pursuit of positive experiences. The hierarchy versus egalitarianism dimension reflects the way resources are organized and distributed in society. In a hierarchical society resources are distributed hierarchically, and individuals comply with the roles designated for them in the hierarchy. In an egalitarian society individuals are seen as equals, and there is a desire that resources be distributed more equally. The mastery versus harmony dimension reflects the desire to direct and change the social world to enhance one's interests on one hand or to seek to live in harmony with, preserve and understand the social and natural world as they are on the other hand (Schwartz, 2006).

The other widely used concept of cultural dimensions belongs to Inglehart and Welzel, who distinguished two main dimensions: survival values versus self-expression values and traditional values versus secular-rational values (Inglehart and Welzel, 2005). On the self-expression pole of the first dimension the authors reported values such as subjective well-being, tolerance, trust, civic activism and self-expression. These values are more characteristic for post-industrial societies where economic survival is not an issue for the majority of population. On the survival pole the behavior of population is shaped by existential insecurity and intellectual and social constraints. Traditional values then emphasize traditional values, such as the importance of family, religion and respect for authority. The secular-rational pole expresses values opposite to the list above (ibid. p. 52).

Cross-cultural research also covers further areas and topics, but we omit them because they are far from the main aim of the present study. Let us turn our attention to the method of retrieving manuscripts and the search procedure. Our study has the character of a review focusing on interpretations, explanatory models and explanations. At the first stage, the main goal was to find and sort all available scientific evidence in this field between years 2004 and 2015. The review methodology was inspired by the Cochrane handbook for systematic reviews (Higgins and Green, 2011) but modified for the purpose of the present study. Given the objectives of our review, peer-reviewed literature providing empirical evidence from 2004 to 2014 was retrieved using a search strategy based on the search terms: neuroticism, cross-cultural and personality. Criteria for considering studies were: cross-cultural focus or design, inclusion of an interpretation (or several interpretations) for the intercultural differences in neuroticism, and the year of publication between 2004 and 2015. Manuscripts published between 2004 and 2014 were accessed via the Web of Science, Google Scholar, Econlit and Ebsco electronic databases. A series of individual searches was conducted using various combinations of the key words list with the logic operator "AND." There were no restrictions regarding language or types of participants. The retrieved manuscripts were then scanned from the viewpoint of relevance for the main focus of this chapter. The manuscripts included either any kind of explanation for intercultural differences in neuroticism, or cross-cultural papers that revealed an overlap of neuroticism with any cultural dimensions were chosen for inclusion in the current review. Both theoretical and empirical studies were included when they included interpretation (or several interpretations) for the intercultural differences in neuroticism. On the other hand, studies that were specialized, for example, on cross-cultural gender or age differences in personality without any explanation for differences or similarities in neuroticism between cultures, were not included for the present review.

Some of retrieved studies provided interpretations derived from personality and cross-cultural theory; others provided interpretations of findings from empirical cross-cultural research. Interpretations for intercultural differences in neuroticism from 10 empirical studies and 2 theoretical studies were summarized and sorted. Both interpretations based on theory and empirical research are presented in the subsequent section in order to provide readers with a comprehensive list of possible answers to the question of why various cultures have reported different levels of neuroticism.

Why Do Cultures Differ in Levels of Neuroticism?

This question illustrates well the main focus of this subsection. During the past decade, many explanations for intercultural differences in personality traits have been proposed by cross-cultural researchers. Some of the explanations are based on real differences reflecting cultural disparity, and others are rather methodological, focusing on problems with data gathering or research designs. All of the main groups of arguments are briefly introduced in the following text. The goal of this study is not to determine what kinds of interpretations are more common or to systematically determine which interpretations have yielded more empirical support thus far. We would like rather to provide readers with a broad range of various interpretations to map the main streams of ideas in current cross-cultural research. The authors of this chapter are sympathizers of a pluralistic interpretative approach in the social sciences. Scientific thinking changes over time, and therefore we do not want to discriminate against some interpretations that currently belong among the marginal ones. The dominant interpretation today might not be a dominant interpretation after a few years. The results of future empirical studies or developments in theory cannot be anticipated. The following interpretative overview provides readers with a basic orientation in this field and summarizes the main arguments for intercultural differences in levels of neuroticism.

We start at a general theory explaining the relationship between personality and cultural factors. Benet-Martínez and Oishi introduced the basic features of the cross-cultural approach to personality (Benet-Martínez and Oishi, 2008). They described the cross-cultural approach as relating implicitly with the ecocultural model that posits causal links between the physical environment, culture, socialization and personality. Each culture exists in a particular physical and social environment. This environment shapes the culture. Each culture has its own special characteristics, cultural norms and standards, and members of these cultures acquire these patterns during the process of socialization. Shared language, customs, and beliefs are suggested to be the most important factors systematically shaping personality traits (Allik and McCrae, 2004). Thus, the personality might be shaped by the socialization within the particular cultural environment.

Neuroticism as a temperamental trait is not likely to be a product of socialization without any influence of genetic predispositions, but the national levels of neuroticism may be moderated, at least to some extent, by cultural influences. The largest cross-cultural study conducted, that of Schmitt et al. (2007), revealed a small to moderate main effect of nation on neuroticism when comparing national levels of neuroticism from 56 different cultures. These results show partial cultural disparity in this personality trait, but there are more possible interpretations of it.

For example, one of the theory-derived explanations suggests cultural variations in the components of traits captured from the Five-Factor Model. This kind of explanation of cross-cultural differences works with the assumption that most cultures share similar personality dimensions, for example, extraversion, neuroticism, agreeableness and conscientiousness (Benet-Martínez and Oishi, 2008), but these dimensions do not reflect 100% of universal personality traits. On the other hand, both universal and culture-specific components of temperamental traits are thought to exist. We may speak about cultural variants of extraversion, neuroticism, agreeableness and conscientiousness. So:

Interpretation # 1

Intercultural differences in neuroticism reflect slight differences in culture-specific components of neuroticism. All cultures share similar personality dimension of neuroticism, but this trait does not mean completely the same thing in various cultures.

Church et al. revealed that about 40%-50% of the items from the Revised NEO Personality Inventory exhibited some form of differential item functioning in factor loadings and intercepts when comparing samples from the United States, Philippines and Mexico (Church et al., 2011). The differential item functioning refers to the lack of measurement invariance at the item level. Some of the intercultural differences yielded were reduced or eliminated after deleting the differential functioning items. This effect and the differential item functioning in the scales from the Revised NEO Personality Inventory support the idea about the existence of culture-specific components within the basic dimensions of the Big Five model of personality.

Further, some empirical results indicated that the different levels of mean scores for neuroticism may be related to mainstream religion in a given culture. Allik and McCrae compared 36 different cultures using the five-factor model of personality (Allik and McCrae, 2004). Multidimensional scaling projected these cultures into four quadrants based on the mean levels of neuroticism and extraversion, where the horizontal axis was associated with extraversion and the vertical axis with neuroticism (see Figure 2 in Allik and McCrae, 2004).

Interestingly, the upper right quadrant included mostly Catholic cultures, the lower right, Protestant, the lower left, Muslim, and the upper left, Confucian cultures. It implies that members of Catholic and Confucian cultures were high in neuroticism and, on the other hand, members of Protestant and Muslim cultures reported lower levels of neuroticism. Further, a meta-analysis of Saroglou compared mostly Protestant participants from the United States with mostly Catholic participants from Europe (Saroglou, 2010). The Protestant participants were lower in neuroticism than the Catholic participants, similarly as in the study of Allik and McCrae (2004). From these insights we may formulate the following interpretation:

Interpretation # 2

The mainstream religion influences the level of neuroticism in a given culture.

The results of the study by Allik and McCrae (2004) also indicated that cultures with adjacent positions based on mean scores of neuroticism and extraversion were also geographically close. Therefore, it is reasonable to interpret these findings that psychological distance may parallel physical distance. Such similarities may be related to mutual cultural influences between neighboring or geographically close cultures. Thus, this large cross-cultural study supports the idea that distribution of personality traits like neuroticism and extraversion is organized geographically:

Interpretation # 3

Geographically close cultures show similar levels of neuroticism in comparison with geographically distant cultures.

The effect of geographical proximity was also tested in the cross-cultural study of Schmitt et al. (2007). The authors used the Euclidean similarity of the personality profiles of different cultures, that is the sum of the squared differences among the five corresponding scores for each pair of two nations in the sample. The empirical results did not show a clear trend between the similarity of geographical region and the mean personality profiles of cultures. Some pairs of cultures with high Euclidean similarity also shared the same geographical region, history, culture and ancestry, for example, Germany and Austria, Greece and Cyprus, Latvia and Lithuania, Congo and Tanzania, Botswana and South Africa, or Malaysia and the Fiji Islands. On the other hand, some of the closest pairs had little in common that could explain the similarity of their personality profiles. This is the example of Estonia and Mexico, Indonesia and the United Kingdom, or Israel and Finland.

Similarly, Ladwig, Richter, Ringle, and Heitger (2012) compared the mean personality profiles of 14 different cultures with hierarchical cluster analyses using a squared Euclidean distance measure. Some clusters with similar personality profiles included cultures from the same geographical region, for example, Taiwan and Korea (cluster 3), but there were also clusters including geographically distant cultures, such as Israel and Mexico (cluster 4) or Germany, the United States and New Zealand (cluster 1). These cultures were similar in the Euclidean distance between their personality profiles, but it is rather not likely to expect some geographical, cultural or historical relatedness.

Another explanation for different levels of neuroticism in various cultures is related to the way in which members of different cultures respond to questions in psychological questionnaires. The people in different cultures may not differ in personality dimensions itself, but in their response styles. The culturally endorsed response styles may also be a possible source of intercultural differences in neuroticism. The Big Five personality traits are measured by psychological psychometric personality questionnaires like the Revised NEO Personality Inventory (NEO–PI–R, Costa and McCrae, 1992). Allik (2005) pointed out that the differences between cultures in the levels of neuroticism may be due to the non-identical response styles of people from different cultures. The response style means the manner in which people respond to questions in psychometric personality questionnaires. Response styles may be shared in a given culture, and most members of a culture may then respond in a similar manner. Thus, the measurement may show good internal reliability of the scale in a particular population sample, but the response style may influence the mean level for neuroticism for a particular culture:

Interpretation # 4

Intercultural differences in neuroticism are caused by the non-identical response styles of people from different cultures.

One of the possibilities is that members of different cultures may have a culturally endorsed response style in terms of the manner in which they respond to positively or negatively phrased statements. Therefore, the formulations of statements in psychometric personality questionnaires may influence the responding of participants. This kind of intercultural difference in response styles is called acquiescence or acquiescence bias (Schmitt et al., 2007; Terracciano et al., 2005). It is possible that in some cultures people have a stronger tendency to agree with test items regardless of their content. In this case, positively phrased statements are suggested to reach higher scores than negatively phrased statements.

Some authors are against the possibility that response styles may cause intercultural differences in the levels of neuroticism. For example, Schmitt et al. (2007) argued that culturally endorsed styles of responding to personality questionnaires are not likely to distort the cross-cultural trait measures. Their previous study (McCrae, 2001) showed that personality trait measures possessed five major dimensions, and that these are not only based on individual responses but also from group data, where each culture was represented as a single subject by their mean scores. This argument stands against the above-mentioned interpretation.

Besides approaches highlighting cultural influences on personality, there are also more biologically based approaches. For example, the genotypic view (Benet-Martínez and Oishi, 2008) understands temperamental traits as inherited basic tendencies that are largely independent from culture. Such personality traits may be, for example, biologically-based traits captured from the Five-Factor Model. Some authors call them the high-order personality traits (Schmitt et al., 2007). These basic personality tendencies are supposed to be universal and are suggested to be a result of variation in the distribution of alleles of trait-related genes (Allik and McCrae, 2004):

Interpretation # 5

Intercultural differences in neuroticism reflect genetic differences between cultural groups. Neuroticism is thus a universal personality trait and is fully comparable between members of different cultures.

This interpretation was supported by the large cross-cultural study of Church and Terracciano (2005). This research group compared 50 different cultures using the 3rd-person version of the Revised NEO Personality Inventory. The authors concluded that the personality traits captured from the Five-Factor Model are common to all human groups. The "Psychic unity of mankind" supports the assumption that all human beings share all basic cognitive and psychological characteristics. This study also rejected the critique focusing on the self-reported character of most previous cross-cultural comparisons. Due to the use of the 3rd-person version of the Revised NEO Personality Inventory, self-reporting bias was not likely to be expected.

Some scholars (Allik, 2005; Terracciano et al., 2005) pointed out that adapting psychometric personality questionnaires to another linguistic group may be an important source of bias for cross-cultural comparisons. This methodological shortcoming is suggested to be a serious problem for achieving the true metric comparability of scores on the same test in different languages. When true metric comparability of mean-level trait scores would be questionable, the yielded intercultural differences may be distorted by such translation bias. So:

Interpretation # 6

Intercultural differences in neuroticism may be caused by adaptations of psychometric personality questionnaires to other languages.

Are Neuroticism and Cultural Dimensions Interrelated?

When exploring neuroticism across cultures, one important question arises: is neuroticism correlated with any other cultural dimensions? Some cross-cultural studies have revealed very interesting results in this field. Hofstede and McCrae conducted simple zero order correlations between the neuroticism measured by the Revised NEO Personality Inventory and Hofstede's cultural dimensions for a sample of 33 countries (Hofstede and McCrae, 2004). The correlation coefficients were 0.57 for masculinity (significant at the 1% level) and 0.58 for uncertainty avoidance (significant at the 1% level). In other words, countries with higher scores on neuroticism scored higher in both uncertainty avoidance and masculinity. Further, Hofstede and McCrae (2004) also conducted stepwise multiple regression analysis to study the relationship between neuroticism and cultural dimensions, where neuroticism was used as the dependent variable and cultural dimensions as the explanatory ones. In this regression the variance in national scores for neuroticism was explained by uncertainty avoidance at 31% and masculinity accounted for another 24% (stepwise regression analysis). All together these two variables explain 55% of the variability in neuroticism.

Allik and McCrae (2004) studied the relative distances between countries in personality characteristics, employing multidimensional scaling (MDS) where the orientation of axes followed the two most significant personality dimensions: neuroticism and extraversion. They computed the correlations of country scores on vertical (neuroticism) and horizontal (extraversion) axes with various personal and cultural characteristics. Their results suggest, similarly to (Hofstede and McCrae, 2004) that neuroticism is significantly related to Hofstede's dimension of uncertainty avoidance (significant at the 0.01% level) and masculinity (significant at the 5% level). In addition, countries with higher mean levels of neuroticism were lower in the interpersonal trust dimension coming from Inglehart's model (significant at 5% levels).

Somewhat different correlations between neuroticism and cultural dimensions were reported by Özkan and Lajunen (2007). The purpose of Özkan and Lajunen (2007) was to study unintentional injuries and fatalities internationally and explain them with the differences in cultural and personality characteristics. Before doing so, Özkan and Lajunen computed correlation coefficients for all the variables in the analysis. The results suggest that neuroticism correlated positively with power distance and masculinity (significant at the 5% level) and with the harmony value of the Schwartz scale (significant at the 1% level). Interestingly, the correlation of neuroticism with power distance was not statistically significant in the above-mentioned studies (Özkan and Lajunen, 2007).

Further, Migliore (2011) studied the relationship between neuroticism, as one of the Big Five personality traits, and Hofstede's cultural dimensions in the US and India. The sample criteria included: minimum two years of work experience, living and working in the US and India, a minimum education of a four-year bachelor's degree from a college or university in business or in a technical specialty. The methods included the Pearson correlation analysis (zero-order and partial-order) and multiple analyses of variance. The results showed statistically significant correlations between neuroticism and masculinity for academically trained professionals, but not for managers (Migliore, 2011). This study showed that the relation between neuroticism and culture may work well for some categories of people but not for others in terms of different occupational, economic or social characteristics.

At this point, we have to define Hofstede's dimensions of uncertainty avoidance and masculinity in more detail to better understand these constructs strongly correlated with neuroticism in the above-mentioned studies. Uncertainty avoidance means the ability to tolerate the fact that the future is uncertain or the tendency to avoid uncertainty (Hofstede et al., 2010). It is "the extent to which the members of a culture feel threatened by ambiguous or unknown situations" (Ibid, p. 191). Hofstede et al. suggested that all people understand that the future is uncertain and that they need to cope with this awareness (Hofstede et al., 2010). Individuals who scored lower in coping with unpredictability also reported higher levels of neuroticism (Hofstede and McCrae, 2004). Hofstede et al. suggested that extreme uncertainty may cause intolerable anxiety, fear and worry (Hofstede et al., 2010). These unpleasant feelings may be partially caused by potential situations that have yet to occur, but they are also driven by our reactions to certain situations. Similarly to Hofstede's other dimensions, the ability to tolerate the future being uncertain varies on individual and cultural levels and needs to be dealt with.

On the national level we are able to diminish uncertainty caused by nature via technological progress. Uncertainty caused by behavior of other people can be reduced by the system of laws. Religion helps to accept uncertainties we cannot eliminate by our own effort. As a result, a low ability to tolerate uncertainty may lead to a disproportionate development of laws and rules and the rise of religious practices and technological progress in certain cultures (Hofstede et al., 2010).

We need to separate uncertainty avoidance and risk avoidance. The essence of uncertainty avoidance is the feeling of being threatened by ambiguous or unknown situations, where certain probabilities of occurrence are not evident. On the other hand, risk avoidance is focused on an event with a certain probability of occurrence. For example diving fast or practicing certain sports may be a source of fear, but they rarely produce anxiety feelings and cannot be classified in terms of uncertainty avoidance (Ibid, p. 197). Therefore, uncertainty avoidance, as the factor producing anxiety, is likely to be correlated with neuroticism.

Further, Hofstede et al. define the masculinity dimension as follows: "A society is called masculine when emotional gender roles are clearly distinct: men are supposed to be assertive, tough, and focused on material success, whereas women are supposed to be modest, tender, and concerned with the quality of life. A society is called feminine when emotional gender roles overlap: both men and women are supposed to be modest, tender, and concerned with the quality of life" (Ibid, p. 120). In general we can call the assertive, tough pole "masculine" and the modest, caring pole "feminine," though the gender differences described above also play an important role. Table 2 describes both the masculine and feminine poles of this dimension using Hofstede's original questions employed for the measurement of masculinity-femininity.

Hofstede and McCrae (2004) interpreted their findings by three possible causes of systematic differences in mean levels of personality traits across cultures:

a) The distribution of genetically determined traits of personality factors differs systematically across nations
b) Common personality characteristics are acquired in children during the process of their development in a given culture
c) National cultures influence the ways respondents answer personality tests. (Hofstede and McCrae, 2004, p. 70)

Explanations a) and c) are in line with the above-mentioned Interpretation # 5 and Interpretation # 4. However, for the case of neuroticism as a temperamental trait, it is rather unlikely to suppose that it would be fully acquired during the process of socialization in childhood without any inherent predisposition (Ormel et al., 2004). In contrast, masculinity-femininity on the individual level is suggested to be influenced more by socialization within a particular culture than neuroticism.

Table 2. Masculine and feminine poles of Hofstede's masculinity dimension

Masculine pole	Feminine pole
Earnings: have an opportunity for high earnings	Manager: have good working relationship with your direct superior
Recognition: get the recognition you deserve when you do a good job	Cooperation: work with people who cooperate well with one another
Advancement: have an opportunity for advancement to higher-level jobs	Living area: live in an area desirable to you and your family
Challenge: have challenging work to do – work from which you can get a personal sense of accomplishment	Employment security: have the security that you will be able to work for your company as long as you want to.

Source: Hofstede et al., 2010.

Discussion

The main aim of this chapter was to search for various interpretations, explanatory models and explanations that have been applied to explain differences or similarities between cultures in neuroticism in previous research. Discussions of intercultural differences in neuroticism have oscillated along three general key issues or paradigmatic questions. First, the "heritability of neuroticism" is a dilemma that has attracted the attention of researchers. This dilemma is not new (Church et al., 2006, 2011) and may be seen as a classical dilemma in cross-cultural psychology focusing on personality traits. The essential questions are "to what extent is neuroticism the result of genetic predispositions?," or "to what extent is neuroticism the result of socialization practices of parents?," or "to what extent is neuroticism the result of socialization within a particular culture?"

A second key issue is the randomness or regularity in distribution of mean personality profiles across different cultures. Two different cultures may have similar or different mean levels of neuroticism, but are these similarities or differences the results of systematic distribution patterns or rather a random coincidence? We call this dilemma "randomness."

Third, the interrelation of neuroticism with some cultural characteristics is questioned. Does the measurement of neuroticism map a unique personality trait that is not correlated with any other cultural variable? Or, is neuroticism correlated with some cultural dimensions? This question is one of the "independence of neuroticism."

Genetic Predispositions or Cultural Influences?

The three above-stated questions reflect several basic dilemmas of current cross-cultural research in neuroticism and other temperamental traits. When starting with the question of heritability, one of possible views regarding how to sort out the interpretations of intercultural differences in neuroticism is the hypothesized degree of cultural or biological determinism. For example, Interpretation # 5 represents the extreme biologically deterministic explanation, suggesting that the level of neuroticism depends exclusively on the genetic information of the individual, i.e., on specific alleles of trait-related genes. This perspective has its roots in biology, and it posits that intercultural differences in neuroticism can be explained from a genetic point of view (Church and Terracciano, 2005; McCrae, 2004; McCrae et al., 2010; Hofstede and McCrae, 2004; Triandis and Suh, 2002). Adherents of this explanation suggest that biology interacts with culture in the process of adaptation and forms specific skills, habits and values. Culture then shapes the manifestations of traits but does not influence the traits per se. In the extreme form of these theories, cultures do not have any influence on genetically given personality traits (Hofstede and McCrae, 2004; McCrae, 2004). From this view, the different world populations have different mean levels of neuroticism (see Table 1) as a result of the distribution of trait-related genes within these populations.

At this point, the simple question "how did it happen?" may be posited. In other words, the dynamic and evolutionary aspects should be taken into account here. If different populations differ in mean levels of neuroticism today, it implies that 1) these populations might have different genetic origins in their ancestry and that the genetic pool of these populations remains relatively stable over time, i.e., were not significantly changed by migrations, or that 2) different levels of neuroticism are the results of different selection processes during the course of cultural *evolution*, or that 3) different levels of neuroticism are the results of a random coincidence of two independent pathways of cultural development. These hypothetical alternatives are highly speculative, because we do not have evidence about the levels of neuroticism in different cultures from the past available. Information about the levels of neuroticism and other temperamental traits in our ancestors is lacking. However, such questions might be stimulating and thought-provoking for the researchers in the field of evolutionary psychology and for this reason are briefly outlined here.

In a similar vein, Hofstede and McCrae (2004) posited two hypothetical processes that may cause the current geographical distribution of temperamental traits across countries: selective migration and reverse causation. Selective migration suggests that people move to and from a certain social group and to and from a certain country on the basis of the availability of positions comfortable given their personality traits. So, if genetically determined personality traits are not in harmony with culture of the country, the person immigrates to another country with a more favorable culture. The reverse causation hypothesis suggests that culture is shaped by the genetically determined personalities of its members. From this point of view, it is possible that cultures are the effect of the genetically given personality structures (Hofstede and McCrae, 2004).

Some empirical studies have brought evidence that does not support the assumption of 100% genetic determination of neuroticism. Ormel et al. (2004) took together the results of various twin and adoption studies and concluded that genetic influences account for 40-50% of the individual differences in neuroticism. They pointed out that about 50-60% of such differences is due to environmental influences, measurement error and random processes. The general term, environmental influences, covers both the physical environment and cultural influences. The authors distinguished "the immutable component of neuroticism" involving the effects of genes, intrauterine and perinatal influences, and environmental exposures and experiences during childhood. On the other hand, "the changing component of neuroticism" covers the effects of cumulative environmental exposures and experiences during adult life. The purely genetic predisposition of a person is called the pre-behavioral phenotype or endophenotype. The pre-behavioral phenotype for neuroticism is suggested to be linked with neural systems subserving emotional processes (Ormel et al., 2004).

When turning back to the interpretations provided in this chapter, some of them posit the idea that cultural influences really do play an important role in differentiating mean levels of neuroticism on the cultural level of analyses. More specifically, Interpretation # 1 supposes slight differences in the culture-specific components of neuroticism; Interpretation # 2 highlights the influence of mainstream religion; and Interpretation # 4 is based on the assumption that different cultures vary in the response styles of their members. All of these interpretations share the assumption of cultural influence on mean levels of neuroticism in different cultures, but each represents a different explanatory model.

Interpretation # 1 suggests that different cultures have slightly differentiated ideas about what the neuroticism is, or what it means to be neurotic. Each culture has its own history, which means the development of ideas, meanings, behavior and symbols over time. Therefore, the dominant shared meaning about the semantic content of the words neuroticism/neurotic is a part of the cognitive structure of each culture. For this reason, it is reasonable to think about the cultural origin of the research tool that is used for cross-cultural comparison.

Western psychologists constructed the trait of neuroticism based on the items that were most frequently reported by respondents from these cultures to characterize the neuroticism. The scales in psychometric personality questionnaires consist of groups of these items representing shared meanings about what the neuroticism is, or what it means to be neurotic. These meanings are shared in the culture where the psychometric personality questionnaire was originally developed and standardized. These scales have also shown quite good internal reliability when applied on samples from the same culture. The neuroticism scales from the Big Five family of questionnaires has also shown relatively high congruence coefficients even across various cultures (Schmitt, et al., 2007; Church and Terracciano, 2005), which means that most of the studied cultures share the basic meaning of neuroticism as a personality construct. On the other hand, Church et al. (2011) revealed that about 40%–50% of the items from the Revised NEO Personality Inventory exhibited some form of differential item functioning in factor loadings and intercepts when comparing samples from the United States, Philippines and Mexico. Some of the intercultural differences were reduced or eliminated after deleting the differential functioning items. These results are very thought-provoking, because the differential functioning items that alone showed the lack of measurement invariance may be seen as culture-specific components in the meanings of these high-order personality traits.

Aside from the hypothesis about culture-specific components of neuroticism, some explanations highlight the role of language and response style. Both Interpretation # 4 and Interpretation # 6 share the assumption that intercultural differences in neuroticism may reflect the differences in responding rather than real differences in temperament. Interpretation # 6 suggests that intercultural differences in neuroticism are the results of problematic translations of psychometric personality questionnaires into other languages. From a cognitive perspective, various languages often differ in phrase-structure rules and phrase-structure grammars. These differences may complicate the adequate translations of the Big Five scales into other languages. On the other hand, the neuroticism scale belongs among those scales showing relatively high internal reliability and congruence coefficients across languages (Schmitt et al., 2007; McCrae and Terracciano, 2005).

Another argument is that a culture influences the manner in which its members respond to questions on psychological questionnaires. Interpretation # 4 is based on the assumption that different cultures vary in the response styles of their members and that this cultural influence may be responsible for intercultural differences in neuroticism. Harumi conducted a study that was specialized on cross-cultural comparison in terms of response biases (Harumi, 2011). Several types of response biases were investigated in samples from the United States, Mexico, the Philippines, Australia, Japan and Malaysia. This study confirmed the previous assumption about the existence of intercultural differences in acquiescence bias. Mexico and the Philippines showed a very high acquiescence response bias in relation to other cultures. On the other hand, Japan showed the least acquiescence response bias in relation to other cultures.

The study of Harumi compared only a limited number of cultures, and it does not cover all cultures included in contemporary large cross-cultural studies (Harumi, 2011). However, it brought very significant results, also revealing another kind of response bias that may possibly influence the results of psychological personality assessments. This kind of bias is called the "extreme response style." The extreme response style refers to the tendency to endorse items on the extreme ends of a multiple category response scale, such as "strongly agree/disagree." The study of Harumi revealed significant differences in the extreme response style between the above-mentioned cultures (Harumi, 2011). The extreme response bias was generally highest in Mexico, intermediate in the United States, Japan and Australia, and lowest in the Philippines and Malaysia. This kind of response bias has not been previously discussed in the field of intercultural differences in mean levels of neuroticism, and it should be taken into consideration by future cross-cultural studies.

Intercultural differences in response styles are often described with the word "bias." The word "bias" implies a methodological limitation of the research design – let's say "the results may be biased." This kind of influence of culture on research procedure is understood as something negative, i.e., something that distorts the effort of researchers to get reliable results and compare different cultures with one another. If we try to withdraw from the position of a researcher who wants to get reliable results, another view is then allowed to emerge. The culturally endorsed response style may be understood not as a bias, but as a part of the particular culture, for example, as a component of its cognitive structure or structure of behavior. From this view, culturally specific aspects of response styles should be explored first before proceeding further to cross-cultural comparisons of mean levels in neuroticism or other temperamental traits. Taking the effects of acquiescence response bias and the extreme response style into consideration may be helpful for questioning in cultures where the questionnaire was not originally developed. The yielded results may be adjusted based on the level of acquiescence response bias and the level of extreme response style. This kind of adjustment would enable the mean levels for personality traits to be balanced with the basic levels from the culture where the questionnaire was originally developed. The results after these kinds of adjustments may lead to more calibrated mean levels of personality traits for possible cross-cultural comparisons.

Finally, Interpretation # 2 highlights the role of mainstream religion on the worldwide distribution of neuroticism. Members of Catholic and Confucian cultures were high in neuroticism and, on the other hand, members of Protestant and Muslim cultures reported lower levels of neuroticism in the study of Allik and McCrae (2004). Similarly, mostly Protestant participants from the United States were lower in neuroticism than Catholic participants from Europe in the meta-analysis done by Saroglou (2010). Saroglou and Cohen (2013) pointed out that these results reflect the presence of more positive emotionality in personality traits in cultures with dominant Protestant religiosity and less positive emotionality in personality traits in European cultures with a prevailing Catholic religiosity, which is characterized by high unhappiness, dependency, fear of divine judgment and guilt-inducing (Hills, Francis, Argyle, and Jackson, 2004; Saroglou and Munoz-Garcia, 2008). Protestant cultures also showed lower uncertainty avoidance than Catholic cultures (Georgas, Van De Vijver, and Berry, 2004). It must be said that little is still known about the cultural influence of Catholic, Protestant, Muslim and Confucian mainstream religious denomination on temperamental traits, though this represents a developing and fascinating field for future research.

Systematic Patterns of Distribution or Random Coincidence?

The study of Allik and McCrae (2004) indicated that cultures with adjacent positions based on mean scores of neuroticism and extraversion were also geographically close.

Interpretation # 3 posits that geographically close cultures have similar levels of neuroticism in comparison with geographically distant cultures. Mutual influence between geographically close cultures is one of the possible reasons for these similarities. On the other hand, Schmitt et al. (Schmitt et al., 2007) compared the Euclidean similarities of the personality profiles of 56 different cultures, and these results did not show any clear trend between similarity of geographical region and the mean personality profiles of cultures. Some pairs of cultures with high Euclidean similarity also shared the same geographical region, history and ancestry, while other pairs had very similar personality profiles, but it was not likely to expect any geographical, cultural or historical relatedness. The authors concluded that these similarities occurred because of pure coincidence. Similarly, Ladwig et al. (2012) found similarities in the mean personality profiles in geographically distant cultures.

These suggestions bring us back to the beginning of the Discussion subsection and the question of randomness in the worldwide distribution of mean personality profiles. If some cultures had very similar personality profiles regardless of their geographical, cultural or historical relatedness, it is possible to consider these mean levels of traits as being the result of coincidence, more specifically, the coincidence in the time when data for a particular study are gathered. Schmitt et al. (2007) also pointed out that their results did not show a clear trend between similarity of geographical region and the mean personality profiles of the studied cultures. These comparisons did not support Interpretation # 3 suggesting that geographic distance determines similarity in mean personality profiles. Further, it is likely that the mutual intercultural influences are less determined by physical distance in the age of the Internet and globalization.

When seeking the causal explanation for similar personality profiles in cultures without geographical, cultural or historical relatedness, the principle of equifinality may be posited. Pervin (2001) employed the principle of equifinality when exploring the dynamics of personality on the individual level of analysis. The principle of equifinality simply suggests that the same endpoint can be reached through different routes. Keeping the very speculative nature of this parallel in mind, it would be possible to think about the application of the principle of equifinality for the explanation of geographic distribution of mean personality profiles across some cultures. From this view, the similarities in mean personality profiles of two different cultures may be the random results of two independent routes of cultural development. This line of reasoning is highly speculative and should be approached very critically. On the other hand, the principle of equifinality may explain why some pairs from the 56 different cultures in the study of Schmitt et al. (2007) had similar personality profiles without any geographical, cultural or historical relatedness.

Independence of Neuroticism?

Finally, we would like to pay attention to the question of "independence of neuroticism." Neuroticism has been found to be positively correlated with cultural dimensions of masculinity and uncertainty avoidance (Hofstede model, see Hofstede and McCrae, 2004; Allik, and McCrae, 2004), power distance (Hofstede model, Özkan and Lajunen, 2007) and harmony value (Schwartz model, Schwartz, 2006) and negatively correlated with the interpersonal trust dimension from the Inglehart model (Allik and McCrae, 2004). Thus, it is not likely that neuroticism is an independent personality trait that is not related with any other construct measured on the cultural level of analysis.

High levels of neuroticism predicted higher uncertainty avoidance and masculinity, resulting in more rules adopted to avoid tensions and conflicts. Hofstede and McCrae (Hofstede and McCrae, 2004) suggested that neurotic people are irritable and prone to tensions in general, making social interactions difficult and interpersonal conflicts more probable, especially if new decisions are to be made. From this point of view it is likely that they will avoid new decisions, thus creating high uncertainty avoidance (ibid).

The question is whether culture predicts neuroticism or vice versa? This substantial question cannot be fully answered given the data and methods available at this moment. Simple correlations between neuroticism and uncertainty avoidance or neuroticism and masculinity did not allow us to exclude the influence of possible third variables. Neither of the simple correlations answers the question about causality. Do high levels of neuroticism cause high masculinity and uncertainty avoidance or is it the opposite? Do cultural dimensions predict neuroticism, or are they the effect of neuroticism in a given population? These questions represent incentives for future research in this field.

Further, there are also problems in constructing variables that are used for comparing different cultures. Cultural dimensions were created in order to compare a large number of nations or groups, and the scores for each country were computed on the basis of averaging the answers of relevant questions on questionnaires. The application of these mean scores for cross-cultural comparisons is questionable. For example, Hofstede et al. (2010) suggested that some dimensions need to be divided in two if considered on the individual level. Further, some dimensions may also have more explanatory power for some groups of people than for the others. For example, the differences in masculinity were more pronounced for men than for women and for the younger generation comparing with the older generation. For this reason, Hofstede warned against application of his cultural dimensions on the individual level of analysis (Hofstede et al., 2010). On the other hand, other researchers have claimed that the ecological fallacy in using macro data for deriving micro implications typical for these type of studies can be avoided under some circumstances (for a discussion, see Grenness, 2012).

CONCLUSION

This chapter maps the current approaches for interpreting intercultural differences in neuroticism. Despite previous cross-cultural studies employing different ideas to explain different or similar national mean levels of neuroticism, none of these studies has yet to provide readers with a systematic overview of these interpretations. Our current study outlines the main streams of ideas that have emerged in past cross-cultural research. The present interpretative overview enables the whole spectrum of interpretative approaches to be seen and has important implications for both theory and empirical research in this field.

We put together six different interpretations of the patterns of distribution of neuroticism across different populations (see the section Why Do Cultures Differ in Levels of Neuroticism?) and also discuss the interrelations of neuroticism with cultural dimensions. Further, three main paradigmatic questions were indicated based on previous cross-cultural research on the distribution of neuroticism across different cultural groups. We call them questions of a) heritability of neuroticism, b) randomness, i.e., if worldwide distribution of neuroticism is systematic or random, and c) independence of neuroticism in terms of independence of measurement of neuroticism with the measurement of cultural dimensions.

There are several limitations of the present study that should be noted here. First, only interpretations for intercultural differences in neuroticism have been introduced and summarized here. Neuroticism is just one of the temperamental traits of the Big Five model, and omitting other traits reduces the complexity of the phenomena. Second, the individual interpretations for intercultural differences in neuroticism were not evaluated from the position of their explanatory power, i.e., what interpretation better fits the data available. We decided not to do this, because current research findings are limited and more research is needed to bring further empirical evidence, for example, from cultures that have not been included in previous cross-cultural surveys. We presented all the interpretations as possible explanations and our effort was not to strictly reject or discriminate some of them. We adopt the pluralistic interpretative approach and leave the decision to each reader regarding how he or she shall utilize the incentives provided here.

An important avenue for future research is to study possible moderating effects of cultures on the psychological processes involving neuroticism and other possible variables. Given that cultures, defined above as the value structures or mentalities of populations, can be viewed as an environment in which psychological processes work, it would be interesting to explore how these processes function in different cultures. It would be challenging to study the influence of cultures on other indicators and variables in countries with significantly different levels of neuroticism.

While cultural dimensions are supposed to characterize cultures as a whole on the macro level, the values of neuroticism are more likely to present a certain profile of the culture not only on the level of mean scores, but also on the levels of other distributional characteristics, such as variance and other statistical aggregates. It would be important not only to study the relationships between the average characteristics of cultural dimensions and neuroticism but also to investigate how the within-the-country-differences of these indicators influence each other, i.e., for example, whether countries with more uniform personality profiles in the population show lower degrees of neuroticism compared with countries having more differentiated personality profiles.

Acknowledgments

This publication was supported by the Ministry of Education, Youth and Sports - Institutional Support for Long-term Development of Research Organizations - Charles University, Faculty of Humanities (Charles Univ, Fac Human 2015).

References

Allik, J. (2005). Personality dimensions across cultures. *Journal of Personality Disorders*, 19(3), 212-232.

Allik, J., and McCrae, R. R. (2004). Toward a geography of personality traits patterns of profiles across 36 cultures. *Journal of Cross-Cultural Psychology*, 35(1), 13-28.

Baldwin, J. R., Faulkner S. L., Hecht, M. L., and Sheryl, L. L. (2006). *Redefining culture: Perspectives across the disciplines*. New York: Routledge.

Benet-Martínez, V., and John, O. P. (1998). Los cinco grandes across cultures and ethnic groups: Multitrait multimethod analysis of the Big Five in Spanish and English. *Journal of Personality and Social Psychology*, 75(3), 729-750.

Benet-Martínez, V., and Oishi, S. (2008). Culture and personality. In: O. P. John, R. W. Robins, and L. A. Pervin (Eds.), *Handbook of personality: Theory and research* (pp. 542-567). New York: Guilford Press.

Church, A. T., Alvarez, J. M., Mai, N. T., French, B. F., Katigbak, M. S., and Ortiz, F. A. (2011). Are cross-cultural comparisons of personality profiles meaningful? Differential item and facet functioning in the Revised NEO Personality Inventory. *Journal of Personality and Social Psychology*, 101(5), 1068-1088.

Church, A. T., Katigbak, M. S., Del Prado, A. M., Ortiz, F. A., Mastor, K. A., Harumi, Y., ... and Cabrera, H. F. (2006). Implicit theories and self-perceptions of traitedness across cultures: Toward integration of cultural and trait psychology perspectives. *Journal of Cross-Cultural Psychology*, 37(6), 694-716.

Church, R. R., and Terracciano, A. (2005). Universal features of personality traits from the observer's perspective: Data from 50 cultures. *Journal of Personality and Social Psychology*, 88(3), 547-561.

Costa, P. T., Jr., and McCrae, R. R. (1992). *Revised NEO Personality Inventory (NEO PI–R) and NEO Five–Factor Inventory (NEO–FFI) professional manual*. Odessa, FL: Psychological Assessment Resources.

Eysenck, H. J., and Eysenck, S. B. G. (1975). *Manual of the Eysenck Personality Questionnaire*. London: Hodder and Stoughton.

Georgas, J., Van De Vijver, F. J., and Berry, J. W. (2004). The ecocultural framework, ecosocial indices, and psychological variables in cross-cultural research. *Journal of Cross-Cultural Psychology*, 35(1), 74-96.

Grenness, T. (2012). Hofstede revisited: Is making the ecological fallacy when using Hofstede's instrument on individual behaviour really unavoidable? *International Journal of Business and Management*, 7(7), 75-84.

Harumi, C. A. (2011). *Cross-cultural differences in response styles*. Doctoral dissertation, Washington State University.

Higgins J. P. T., and Green S. (2011) Cochrane handbook for systematic reviews of interventions 5.1.0 [updated March 2011]. *The Cochrane Collaboration*. Retrieved from http://handbook.cochrane.org/.

Hills, P., Francis, L. J., Argyle, M., and Jackson, C. J. (2004). Primary personality trait correlates of religious practice and orientation. *Personality and Individual Differences*, 36(1), 61-73.

Hofstede G., Hofstede G. J., and Minkov M. (2010). *Cultures and organizations: Software of the mind. Intercultural cooperation and its importance for survival*. New York: McGraw Hill.

Hofstede, G., and McCrae, R. R. (2004). Personality and culture revisited: Linking traits and dimensions of culture. *Cross-Cultural Research*, 38(1), 52-88.

Inglehart, R., and Welzel, C. (2005). *Modernization, cultural change, and democracy: The human development sequence*. Cambrige: Cambridge University Press.

Inkeles, A., and Levinson, D. J. (1969). National character: The study of modal personality and sociocultural systems. In: G. Lindzey and E. Aronson (Eds.), *The handbook of social psychology IV* (pp. 418-506). New York: McGraw-Hill (Original work published in 1954).

John, O., Naumann, L., and Soto, C. (2008). Paradigm shift to the integrative Big Five Trait Taxonomy. In: O. P. John, R. W. Robins, and L. A. Pervin (Eds.), *Handbook of personality: Theory and research* (3rd ed., pp. 114-158). New York, NY: Guilford Press.

Kuška M., Trnka R., Tavel P., Constantino M.J., Angus L., and Moertl K. (2015). The role of cultural beliefs and expectations in the treatment process: Clients' reflections following individual psychotherapy. *Sexual and Relationship Therapy*. doi: 10.1080/14681994.2014.1001354.

Ladwig T. J., Richter N. F., Ringle C. M., and Heitger N. (2012). *Cultural hybrid personalities? Clustering nations according to the Big Five personality traits* [Research Papers Series - Hamburg University of Technology, No. 9]. Retrieved from http://papers.ssrn.com/sol3/papers.cfm?abstract_id=2179435.

McCrae, R. R. (2001). Trait psychology and culture: Exploring intercultural comparisons. *Journal of Personality*, 69(6), 819-846.

McCrae, R. R. (2004). Human nature and culture: A trait perspective. *Journal of Research in Personality*, 38(1), 3-14.

McCrae R. R., and Costa P. T., Jr. (1997). Personality trait structure as a human universal. *American Psychologist*, 52(5), 509-516.

McCrae, R. R., and Costa, P. T. (2003). *Personality in adulthood: A five-factor theory perspective*. New York: Guilford Press.

McCrae, R. R., and Terracciano, A. (2005). Universal features of personality traits from the observer‘s perspective: Data from 50 cultures. *Journal of personality and social psychology*, 88(3), 547-561.

McCrae, R. R., Terracciano, A., De Fruyt, F., De Bolle, M., Gelfand, M. J., and Costa Jr, P. T. (2010). The validity and structure of culture-level personality scores: Data from ratings of young adolescents. *Journal of Personality*, 78(3), 815-838.

Migliore, L. A. (2011). Relation between big five personality traits and Hofstede's cultural dimensions: Samples from the US and India. *Cross Cultural Management: An International Journal*, 18(1), 38-54.

Ormel, J., Rosmalen, J., and Farmer, A. (2004). Neuroticism: A non-informative marker of vulnerability to psychopathology. *Social Psychiatry and Psychiatric Epidemiology*, 39(11), 906-912.

Özkan, T., and Lajunen, T. (2007). The role of personality, culture, and economy in unintentional fatalities: An aggregated level analysis. *Personality and Individual Differences*, 43(3), 519-530.

Pervin, L. A. (2001). A dynamic systems approach to personality. *European Psychologists*, 6(3), 172-176.

Saroglou, V. (2010). Religiousness as a cultural adaptation of basic traits: A Five-Factor Model perspective. *Personality and Social Psychology Review*, 14(1), 108-125.

Saroglou, V., and Cohen, A. B. (2013). Cultural and cross-cultural psychology of religion. In: R. F. Paloutzian and C. L. Park (Eds.), *Handbook of the psychology of religion and spirituality* (pp. 330-354). New York: Guilford Press.

Saroglou, V., and Munoz-Garcia, A. (2008). Individual differences in religion and spirituality: An issue of personality traits and/or values. *Journal for the Scientific Study of Religion*, 47(1), 83-101.

Saucier, G., and Ostendorf, F. (1999). Hierarchical subcomponents of the Big Five personality factors: A cross-language replication. *Journal of Personality and Social Psychology*, 76(4), 613-627.

Schmitt, D. P., Allik, J., McCrae, R. R., and Benet-Martínez, V. (2007). The geographic distribution of Big Five personality traits patterns and profiles of human self-description across. *Journal of Cross-Cultural Psychology*, 38(2), 173-212.

Schwartz, S. H. (2006). A theory of cultural value orientations: Explication and applications. *Comparative Sociology*, 5(2), 137-182.

Soto, C. J., John, O. P., Gosling, S. D., Potter, J. (2008). The developmental psychometrics of Big Five self-reports: Acquiescence, factor structure, coherence, and differentiation from ages 10 to 20. *Journal of Personality and Social Psychology*, 94(4), 718-737.

Terracciano, A., Abdel-Khalek, A. M., Adam, N., Adamovova, L., Ahn, C. K., Ahn, H. N., and Meshcheriakov, B. (2005). National character does not reflect mean personality trait levels in 49 cultures. *Science*, 310(5745), 96-100.

Triandis, H. C., and Suh, E. M. (2002). Cultural influences on personality. *Annual Review of Psychology*, 53(1), 133-160.

Trnka, R., Balcar, K., Kuška, M., and Hnilica, K. (2012). Neuroticism and valence of negative emotional concepts. *Social Behavior and Personality*, 40(5), 843-844.

CONCLUSIONS

The present volume aimed to contribute to the study of neuroticism regarding its impact on job performance and health outcomes. The goal was also to widen the reflection individuals have on these issues, offering new theoretical and research perspectives for enhancing the progress both at a theoretical and at an intervention level.

The relations between neuroticism in both job performance and health outcomes were studied since the last century, but these fields of research continue to inspire researchers to enhance the knowledge and relatively applied perspectives.

The first part of this volume collected a series of researches focused on the link between neuroticism, performance and health outcomes in organizational contexts.

The research by Greta Mazzetti, Rita Chiesa, Michela Vignoli and Marco Depolo introduced the role of job satisfaction but particularly of the new variable workaholism in the relation to neuroticism and job performance. Also, the third chapter by Marco Giannini and Yura Loscalzo is focused on the new variable workaholism and on its relation with neuroticism. The authors want to underline a perspective of health risk prevention in organizations for physical and psychological health, as well as for workplace and family wellbeing. The following study by Riccardo Sartori, Arianna Costantini and Andrea Ceschi offered an interesting new perspective regarding the relation between neuroticism (particularly it's opposite, emotional stability) and job performance in a specific sample of trade agents. The results of this study in fact showed as an indirect positive relationship between emotional stability (the opposite of neuroticism) and job performance passing through the effect of the length of service, introducing the importance of considering also this variable relative to the permanence of workers in organizations.

The contribution by Giorgi Gabriele, Javier Fiz Perez and Melissa Morone introduced the study of neuroticism with new variables as organizational emotional intelligence. In particular, the results underlined that personality traits and particularly neuroticism explain organizational emotional intelligence and work-related stress tolerance as drivers behind the effect of work motivation.

The study by Annamaria Di Fabio and Letizia Palazzeschi showed that neuroticism consistently inversely explained a significant percentage of variance both in resilience and life satisfaction in three organizational realities (physicians, nurses, and employees of an insurance company). The results widened the analysis of neuroticism in relation to individual resources and well-being in different organizational contexts.

All the chapters of the first part of the present volume contributed thus to broadening the perspective of the study about the impact of neuroticism on job performance and health outcomes particularly in organizational contexts, offering precious perspectives to continue and improve the research on these issues.

The second part offered readers a wide range of perspectives regarding the study of the characteristics of neuroticism and its possible role in job performance and health outcomes. The contribution by Sowon Hahn and Yumin Chung relative to neuroticism, attention and eye movements enhanced the reflection with the consideration of recent studies regarding physiological correlates of neuroticism. The chapter by Ahmed M. Abdel-Khalek offered a contribution to the analysis of the characteristics of neuroticism in relation to extraversion in different contexts. The chapter by Annamaria Di Fabio and Alessio Gori offered interesting perfectives for the study of neuroticism, introducing in particular the role of a new construct for the 21st century named intrapreneurial self-capital in relation to neuroticism and flourishing as adaptive outcome. The role of neuroticism on career outcomes (career decision-making self-efficacy, career decision, and employability) was underlined in the study by Annamaria Di Fabio and Ornella Bucci, highlighting a preventive perspective.

Finally the last chapter of the book by Radek Trnka and Inna Čábelková underlined the importance to study neuroticism in a cross cultural perspective.

The contributions of the present volume offered a range of reflections and stimuli to continue the research on neuroticism regarding its characteristics, its impact on job performance and health outcomes. The effort of the present book was to try to delineate from the research about this issue, knowing that many challenges are still present that humanity must cope with. So, there are still many perspectives and opportunities for research and interventions to develop in the future.

Annamaria Di Fabio

ABOUT THE EDITOR\CONTRIBUTORS

EDITOR

Title and Name:	**Annamaria Di Fabio, PhD, Associate Professor**
Institutional affiliation:	Department of Education and Psychology (Psychology Section), University of Florence, Italy
Areas of expertise:	Work and organizational psychology, Personality and individual differences, Career and life counseling psychology, Vocational and educational guidance, Positive psychology and prevention, Effectiveness of intervention

CONTRIBUTORS

Title and Name:	**Ahmed M. Abdel-Khalek, PhD, Full professor**
Institutional affiliation:	Department of Psychology, Faculty of Arts, University of Alexandria, Egypt
Areas of expertise:	Personality psychology, Health psychology, Abnormal Psychology

Title and Name:	**Ornella Bucci,** **PhD Student**
Institutional affiliation:	Department of Education and Psychology (Psychology Section), University of Florence, Italy
Areas of expertise:	Work and organizational psychology, Personality and individual differences, Counseling psychology, Vocational and educational guidance, Positive psychology and prevention

Title and Name:	**Inna Čábelková, PhD,** **Full professor**
Institutional affiliation:	Faculty of Humanities, Charles University in Prague, Czech Republic
Areas of expertise:	Cultural differences, economics

Title and Name:	**Andrea Ceschi, PhD,** **Postdoctoral fellow**
Institutional affiliation:	Department of Philosophy, Education, Psychology, University of Verona
Areas of expertise:	Work and organizational psychology

Title and Name:	**Rita Chiesa, PhD,** **Scientific researcher**
Institutional affiliation:	Department of Psychology, Alma Mater Studiorum University of Bologna, Italy
Areas of expertise:	New Careers, Employability, Career Counseling

Title and Name:	**Yumin Chung, PhD,** **Post-Doc**
Institutional affiliation:	Seoul National University, Korea
Areas of expertise:	Cognitive Psychology

Title and Name:	**Arianna Costantini,** **PhD student**
Institutional affiliation:	Department of Philosophy, Education, Psychology, University of Verona, Italy
Areas of expertise:	Work and organizational psychology

Title and Name:	**Marco Depolo,** **Full Professor**
Institutional affiliation:	Department of Psychology, Alma Mater Studiorum University of Bologna, Italy
Areas of expertise:	Well-being at Work; Ageing and Work; Work Training

Title and Name:	**Javier Fiz Perez,** **Full Professor**
Institutional affiliation:	European University of Rome, Italy
Areas of expertise:	Positive psychology, emotional intelligence, work-related stress, PTSD, education

Title and Name:	**Marco Giannini,** **Scientific researcher**
Institutional affiliation:	Department of Health Sciences, University of Florence, Italy
Areas of expertise:	Clinical Psychology

Title and Name:	**Gabriele Giorgi, PhD,** **Scientific researcher**
Institutional affiliation:	European University of Rome, Italy
Areas of expertise:	Workplace bullying, emotional intelligence, work-related stress, PTSD, economic stress

Title and Name:	**Alessio Gori, PhD, Postdoctoral fellow**
Institutional affiliation:	Department of Education and Psychology (Psychology Section), University of Florence, Italy
Areas of expertise:	Clinical Psychology, Personality and individual differences, Work and organizational psychology,

Title and Name:	**Sowon Hahn, Associate Professor**
Institutional affiliation:	Seoul National University, Korea
Areas of expertise:	Cognitive Psychology

Title and Name:	**Yura Loscalzo, PhD student**
Institutional affiliation:	Department of Health Sciences, University of Florence, Italy
Areas of expertise:	Clinical Psychology

Title and Name:	**Greta Mazzetti, PhD, Postdoctoral fellow**
Institutional affiliation:	Department of Education Studies, Alma Mater Studiorum University of Bologna, Italy
Areas of expertise:	Workaholism, Job Stress. Burnout, Work Engagement

Title and Name:	**Melissa Morone, Business@Health Psychologist**
Institutional affiliation:	Business@Health Laboratory, European University of Rome, Italy
Areas of expertise:	emotional intelligence, competencies

Title and Name:	**Palazzeschi Letizia, PhD, Postdoctoral fellow**
Institutional affiliation:	Department of Education and Psychology (Psychology Section), University of Florence, Italy
Areas of expertise:	Work and organizational psychology, Personality and individual differences, Career and life counseling psychology, Vocational and educational guidance, Positive psychology and prevention

Title and Name:	**Riccardo Sartori, PhD, Scientific researcher**
Institutional affiliation:	Department of Philosophy, Education, Psychology, University of Verona, Italy
Areas of expertise:	Work and organizational psychology

Title and Name:	**Radek Trnka, PhD, Post-Doc**
Institutional affiliation:	Faculty of Humanities, Charles University in Prague, Prague College of Psychosocial Studies, Czech Republic
Areas of expertise:	Social psychology, emotions

Title and Name:	**Michela Vignoli, PhD, Postdoctoral fellow**
Institutional affiliation:	Department of Education Studies, Alma Mater Studiorum University of Bologna, Italy
Areas of expertise:	Well-being at Work; Work Training; Absenteeism

INDEX

#

A

B

C

D

E

F

G

J

K

L

M

N

O

P

Q

R

S

T

U

V

W

Y

Z